THE UTOPIAN HUMAN RIGHT TO SCIENCE AND CULTURE

Law, Language and Communication

This series encourages innovative and integrated perspectives within and across the boundaries of law, language and communication, with particular emphasis on issues of communication in specialized socio-legal and professional contexts. It seeks to bring together a range of diverse yet cumulative research traditions related to these fields in order to identify and encourage interdisciplinary research.

The series welcomes proposals – both edited collections as well as single-authored monographs – emphasizing critical approaches to law, language and communication, identifying and discussing issues, proposing solutions to problems, offering analyses in areas such as legal construction, interpretation, translation and de-codification.

The Utopian Human Right to Science and Culture

Toward the Philosophy of Excendence in the Postmodern Society

ANNA MARIA ANDERSEN NAWROT

Center for the Theory and Philosophy of Human Rights, Sweden and Raoul Wallenberg Institute of Human Rights and Humanitarian Law, Sweden

Routledge
Taylor & Francis Group
LONDON AND NEW YORK

First published 2014 by Ashgate Publishing

2 Park Square, Milton Park, Abingdon, Oxfordshire OX14 4RN
52 Vanderbilt Avenue, New York, NY 10017

Routledge is an imprint of the Taylor & Francis Group, an informa business

First issued in paperback 2020

British Library Cataloguing in Publication Data
A catalogue record for this book is available from the British Library

The Library of Congress has cataloged the printed edition as follows:
Nawrot, Anna Maria Andersen.
The utopian human right to science and culture : toward the philosophy of excendence in the postmodern society / by Anna Maria Andersen Nawrot.
pages cm.—(Law, language and communication)
Includes bibliographical references and index.
ISBN 978-1-4724-1832-6 (hardback)
1. Freedom of information—Philosophy. 2. Access to knowledge movement—Philosophy.
3. Science. 4. Culture. 5. Human rights—Philosophy. I. Title.
JC598.N39 2014
323.44–dc23

2013037805

ISBN 978-1-4724-1832-6 (hbk)
ISBN 978-0-367-60081-5 (pbk)

Contents

For my daughters Tea, Toscha, Hanna, Zuzia, my husband Henrik and my parents Danuta and Andrzej

Acknowledgements

This book was created with the help of many people to whom I address words of special gratitude here. However, I utter the most heartfelt and warmest thanks to an outstanding man and an exceptional scientist: Professor and Judge Bartosz Wojciechowski, who continuously inspired me by his scientific inquiries. Without the unparalleled support from Professor Wojciechowski from the Institute of the Philosophy and Theory of Law at the Faculty of Law, Lodz University and the Lodz Centre of the Theory and Philosophy of Human Rights, work on this book would never have been started nor finished.

I am also enormously grateful to Professor and Judge Marek Zirk-Sadowski, Director of the Institute of the Philosophy and Theory of Law at the Faculty of Law, Lodz University in Poland, for all his advice accompanied by such a benevolent judgement. The wonderful atmosphere and scientific tutelage that Professor Zirk-Sadowski delivers to his alumni are one of a kind.

I am also very grateful to Professor Gudmundur Alfredsson, former Director of the Raoul Wallenberg Institute of Human Rights and Humanitarian Law in Lund in Sweden for many years, who is an ideal mentor and a great scientist, constantly supporting the implementation of emerging scientific ideas. I am indebted to Professor Alfredsson for his many years of fascinating discussion, criticism and inspiration. They are, for me, a source of reflection, the significance of which goes far beyond the value of this book.

I also address words of exceptional gratitude to Nina-Louisa Arold Lorenz PhD, former Managing Director of the Master Course of Human Rights and Humanitarian Law at the Faculty of Law, Lund University in Sweden. Her invaluable guidelines and comments have undoubtedly increased the value of my book, and the numerous thoughts were an intriguing intellectual adventure. The important observations of Nina-Louisa Arold Lorenz PhD led me to rethink more deeply about certain issues and contributed significantly to the reasoning contained in this book.

For helping me in finding materials I also thank Lena Olsson and Karl Adam Tiderman from the Library of the Raoul Wallenberg Institute of Human Rights and Humanitarian Law in Lund, Sweden.

I address thanks for collaboration and discussion to Mr. Rolf Ring (Deputy Head of the Raoul Wallenberg Institute of Human Rights and Humanitarian Law in Lund, Sweden), Ms. Gao Hang (Director of the Copyright and Development Division, World Intellectual Property Organization), Karol Nowak, PhD (Managing Director of the Master Course of Human Rights and Humanitarian Law at the Faculty of Law, Lund University, Sweden), Christina Johnsson, PhD (Head of the Academic

Department at the Raoul Wallenberg Institute of Human Rights and Humanitarian Law in Lund, Sweden), Karolina Cern, PhD (Department of Philosophy, Poznan University, Poland), Johanna Sjöwall (former program officer, Raoul Wallenberg Institute of Human Rights and Humanitarian Law in Lund, Sweden), Professor Zdzislaw Brodecki (Faculty of Law and Administration, Gdansk University, Poland), Professor Radim Polcak (Faculty of Law, Masaryk University, Brno, Czech Republic), Professor Ulf Maunsbach, (Faculty of Law, Lund University, Sweden), Doctoral Candidate Peter Gottschalk (Faculty of Law, Lund University, Sweden), Stefan Larsson, PhD (Lund University Internet Institute, Sweden), Timothy Maldoon (publishing officer, Raoul Wallenberg Institute of Human Rights and Humanitarian Law, Lund, Sweden) and Doctoral Candidate Jan Woodlock-Brand (Department for Sociology of Law, Lund University, Sweden).

I address particularly warm thanks to my students specializing in Human Rights and Intellectual Property at the Master Course of Human Rights and Humanitarian Law at the Faculty of Law, Lund University in Sweden. Here, exceptional thanks are owed to my former Master students and at the moment two Doctoral Candidates Lida Ayoubi and Aurelija Lukoseviciene.

I also most sincerely thank my publisher Ashgate Publishing and my publishing reviewers, especially Professor Anne Wagner from the Université du Littoral Côte d'Opale in France and China University of Political Science and Law in Beijing.

And, finally, completion of this work would not have been possible without the scientific and publication scholarships granted to me by the Swedish Institute in Stockholm, and without the very professional and friendly support of the translators Bartosz Rogowski and Anna Klein, who undertook to support me thanks to my friendship with Ewa and Pawel Krupinski – I also take this opportunity to thank them very much.

The book could not have been possible without the comprehensive help of my beloved parents Danuta and Andrzej to whom I address the warmest possible thanks. But, above all, I thank my husband Henrik Andersen, who with such a special love and patience supported me in achieving my academic goals. In some ways my work on this thesis has been his too. My deadlines have also in a sense been his too. Thank you for being there always for me.

And, at the end, I feel gratitude towards Ms. Sofie Magnusson and Professor Per Wickenberg from the Department for Sociology of Law, Lund University, Sweden. I will never stop being impressed by their belief in the Other. Thank you.

Anna and Calle Söderquist from Östra Torn in Lund are the last ones I want to thank since to me they are friends forever.

Without the Utopias of other times, men would still live in caves, miserable and naked. It was Utopians who traced the lines of the first city … Out of generous dreams come beneficial realities. Utopia is the principle of all progress, and the essay into a better future.

Anatole France in Zygmunt Bauman,
Liquid Times: Living in an Age of Uncertainty

A map of the world that does not include Utopia is not worth even glancing at, for it leaves out the one country at which Humanity is always landing. And when Humanity lands there, it looks out, and seeing a better country, sets sail. Progress is realization of Utopias.

Oscar Wilde in Zygmunt Bauman,
Liquid Times: Living in an Age of Uncertainty

Introduction

We are constantly looking for an ideal promise of an ideal law.[1] The aim of my treatise is to find *an ideal* right to science and culture. I suggest that the human right to science and culture constitutes a promising ground for this *ideal* in the era of postmodernity. Like every human right, the right to science and culture is both Myth and Reason, while Myth stands for idea, Reason stands for reality.[2] I seek here to present both the *Myth* and the *Reason* for the human right to science and culture. In my argument an appeal to utopia is a must if the human right to science and culture is to flourish into the postmodern future. Faced with the drama of current postmodernity as well as the challenges of digital technologies, the human right to science and culture needs a revived debate that fully explains its long-marginalized, normative content. This debate has to be accompanied by the systematically performed re-comprehension and further development (not only in certain narrow instances) of the right to science and culture from the ideal and moral perspective.[3] Therefore the crucial condition would be that the human right to science and culture needs to be moved away from governmental and diplomatic triumphalism to the realm of rights that are purely utopian but bring also moral energy that utopian element or impulse.That utopian element consists of past memories of analogue society and the future hopes of the postanalogue,

1 B. Wojciechowski, *Philosophical Approach to the Interculturality of Criminal Law* (Peter Lang. International Academic Publishers, Series: Studies in Philosophy and Social Science, Frankfurt am Main – Berlin – Bern – Bruxelles – New York – Oxford – Wien 2010). See also: B. Wojciechowski, *Interkulturowe prawo karne. Filozoficzne podstawy karania w wielokulturowych spoleczenstwach demokratycznych* [*Intercultural Criminal Law. Philosophical Grounds for Penalization in Democratic Societies*] (Wydawnictwo Adam Marszalek, Torun 2009), pp. 12–13.

2 J. Habermas, *The Concept of Human Dignity and the Realistic Utopia of Human Rights* (Metaphilosophy LLC and Blackwell Publishing Ltd. 2010), p. 478. In his article Jurgen Habermas presents the tension between idea and reality when human rights were translated into positive law.

3 B. Wojciechowski, M. Zirk-Sadowski and M.J. Golecki (eds), *Between Complexity of Law and Lack of Order. Philosophy of Law in the Era of Globalization* (Wydawnictwo Adam Marszalek, Torun-Bejing 2009), p. 9. See also K. Cern and B. Wojciechowski, 'O koniecznych zwiazkach miedzy dyskursem prawnym a moralnym' [About required connections between legal and moral discourse], in: J. Zajadlo (ed.), *Dziedzictwo i przyszlosc. Problemy wspolczesnej niemieckiej filozofii prawa* (Arche, Gdansk 2010), pp. 107–108; E. Nowak and K.M. Cern, *Ethos w zyciu publicznym* [*Ethos in the public life*] (PWN, Warszawa 2008), p. 122.

digital one, promise beyond conventions, promise that connects the Individual and the communal.[4] I furthermore argue that this type of promise opens up a global communication and brings utopia – yet is still realistic and vital.

The right to science and culture seems not to have established its philosophical path yet or, to put it differently, deploying a metaphor taken from the philosophy of Antoni Kępiński,[5] it has not found its 'philosophical settlement' in postmodernity, in which both protection of intellectual property rights and an access to knowledge are subordinated to various 'philosophies', 'ethics' and 'moralities' that reflect only some political and economic 'positions'.[6]

This study works from the assumption that postmodern man[7] has not yet come to terms with himself and focuses mainly on insuring himself against the unknown as brought about by the changes of time.[8] We observe the postmodern man as a passive man without needs. This assumption is related to a postmodern treatment of moral behaviour as a contract in compliance with the principle: I behave in a moral manner as I rely on the Other [Others] to return my moral behaviour. I posit here that a falsification of the sense of morality was effected in postmodernity. Given the background it will be essential in my treatise to respond to a question of what 'philosophical settlement' the human right to science and culture needs to be able to fulfil the requirements of the postmodern times. If we assume that we would like to carry out a merger of postmodern morality with the specific right, we have to consider a number of issues within *Myth* (hence phenomena beyond reason) and *Reason* and then try to connect the both of them.[9] Where the current discussion about the right to science and culture might lead if we propose to include/emphasize the notion of postmodern morality at the same time in that discussion? What are a man and a moral collectivity that represent postmodernity like? How does that which is worthy and that which is social look and what do these concepts promise in the context of the right to science and culture? These, and a greater number of more detailed questions are discussed in the text. I make the presupposition

4 'Individual' means here a human being, a person who possesses certain rights. Individual is written in the work with upper case in order to emphasize the meaning of Individual alongside the notion of Text and Speech.

5 A. Kępiński, *Rytm życia* [*The Rhythm of Life*] (Wydawnictwo Literackie, Krakow 1972), p. 9.

6 Z. Bauman, *Etyka ponowoczesna* [*Postmodern Ethics*] (Wydawnictwo Aletheia, Warszawa 2012), pp. 72–73; see also in English: Z. Bauman, *Postmodern Ethics* (Blackwell, Oxford 1993).

7 The word 'man' in the text is not used in the gender sense but in the wider sense of any human being.

8 E. Levinas, *O Uciekaniu* [*On Escape*] (Wydawnictwo Instytutu Filozofii i Socjologii PAN, Warszawa 2007), p. 8. The essay 'On Escape' marks the beginning of an individual and original line of thinking of Levinas. It was first published in: *Recherches Philosophiques Journal* (1935/1936).

9 J. Habermas, *The Concept of Human Dignity and the Realistic Utopia of Human Rights* (Metaphilosophy LLC and Blackwell Publishing Ltd. 2010), p. 466 *et seq.*

that, if the human right to science and culture succeeds in finding its 'philosophical settlement', all human actions within it, associated with the significance of the role of a man (the Individual and moral community created by him), his communication (the Speech) and interpretation of the law in force (the Text) will have no need to put on a mask or set others limits. The work also advances a tenet that postmodern man fails to distinguish between truth and extremes in the context of the right to science and culture, for example with extremes such as 70 year copyright protection after the death of the author or extreme patent protection over medicines. The lack of a comprehensive philosophical vision regarding the human right to science and culture means that we, as postmodern people, have lost a critical insight along the way, which once enabled us to discern the differences between truth and extremes. I assume here that both within human rights in general and within the right to science and culture, which is the focus here, a hope exists for the creation of such philosophical foundations which will guide postmodern human reality to perceive these differences. I see this hope not in discovering one great philosophy, but more in numerous and various lines and paths of thinking which could lead to an 'open debate about the foundation of one philosophy' and give it a name.

Thus, I set out to respond to the question of whether the *ideal* human right to science and culture exists. The right that protects ownership sufficiently but provides for an access to knowledge; the right which supports free culture and protects the interests of creators, producers at the same time as those in need of medicine; the right which eventually contributes to building and supporting of sustainability of the public domain; the human right that will ensure that society in 50 or 100 years will be the society of well-educated, creative, healthy people, who are responsible both in temporal and spatial terms for the Others and for that which is Other.

Taking the above statements into consideration, I advance in my work a thesis that the human right to science and culture is of a utopian character. I attempt to prove the necessity of the human right to science and culture's existence by developing a philosophical project situated in postmodernity, one which is based on the assumption of 'thinking in terms of excendence'. I concentrate mainly on thinking in terms of excendence with respect to the Individual, the Speech and the Text. My main sources of inspiration constitute the thought of Emmanuel Levinas and Hans-Georg Gadamer, but also to a significant extent the thought of Knud Ejler Løgstrup, Zygmunt Bauman and Jurgen Habermas. The selection of these thinkers is not random, since all of them at some point arrived upon the concept of the Individual, the concept of social and the concept of communication. Of crucial importance is that the mutual interrelations of the thought of these philosophers are accompanied – or even enabled and interwoven – by the philosophical paths of, among others, Leszek Kołakowski and Antoni Kępiński. In the first part related to *Myth* I put forward a structure of thinking according to excendence with respect to the Individual, the Speech and the Text, this recurs throughout the work in various dimensions and contexts. In the second part, entitled *Reason,* I focus on thinking according to paradigms brought about by the postanalogue society as well as on thinking within the metaphor. This leads to the revealing of, as it seems, a long-neglected, normative content of the human right to science and culture. The final justification of the thesis for the utopian character of the human right to science and culture is presented in the third part: *Myth* and *Reason*, and in the Epilogue. This part, *Myth* and *Reason*, allows an introduction to a far-sighted morality, dignity and solidarity along with Gadamerian *verbum interius* situating them in a postmodern context.[10] The Epilogue constitutes my response to the questions posed by Emmanuel Levinas on happiness, dignity and that which is social. The questions come from a pioneering essay published in 1935 by Levinas entitled 'On Escape'.[11] In the Epilogue I am extending the responses to Levinas questions with an element of utopia. They are as follows: What is the ideal of happiness that excendence could promise? What is the ideal of human dignity that excendence could promise? How does that which is social arise through excendence? How does that which is utopian arise through excendence? In addition, the book includes a short appendix. This comprises my personal project related to an interesting line of thinking in the context of the journey from the *Myth* (in this context metaphor and morality) to *Reason*.

The philosophical approach taken here presupposes a concept of the Individual parting with a 'model of a self-sufficient man'. The Individual, whom I call the excendent Individual (i.e. an Individual practising excendence) is characterized by a strong need to escape. This need leads the Individual to the very essence of philosophy. I also emphasize that the practice of excendence itself by the Individual enables him to go beyond *being* a new path.[12]

The excendent Individual is characterized by thinking toward unilateralism and not reciprocity. Owing to this fact, the Individual who practises excendence is also the Individual who de-falsifies the sense of morality, since he omits to treat moral behaviour as a contract in compliance with the principle: 'I behave in a moral manner as I rely on the Other [Others] to return my moral behaviour'. The Individual is, therefore, not afraid of taking unconditional responsibility for the Other and his radical demand. Consequently, regardless of the fact if the Other is for the Individual, the Individual is always for the Other. In other words, the Individual will act as if he was the only Individual willing to assume and perform a particular duty. It is of no importance to the Individual if the Other will return it. The excendent Individual created for the purposes of this work overcomes his own self-sufficiency and the self-sufficiency of *being* simultaneously. He understands that he is a man whose task is to 'be ahead of oneself', improve oneself and be in

---

10 H.-G. Gadamer, 'Granice Języka' [The Limits of Language] in: *Język i rozumienie* [*Language and Understanding*] (Fundacja Aletheia, Warszawa 2003), p. 38. See also H.-G. Gadamer, *Prawda i Metoda* [*Truth and Method*]. *Zarys hermeneutyki filozoficznej* [*An Outline of Philosophical Hermeneutics*] (Wydawnictwo Inter Esse, Krakow 1993), p. 359.

11 E. Levinas, 'O Uciekaniu' [On Escape] ... , p. 39.

12 E. Levinas, 'O Uciekaniu' [On Escape] ... , p. 39.

constant motion in which the past joins the present and the future. The Individual knows that it is not true that what is most important to a man is his *being*. The Individual perceives something more, something beyond. The *something more* is *anxiety* for Others.[13] It is precisely *anxiety* which has a significant power to move the thought of *being* to the background. The anxiety is a conviction of the responsibility of the excendent Individual. The anxiety is, thus, before *being*. In other words, the responsibility for the Other is given more prominence than *being*.

It is of paramount importance for the whole study's justification of the argument for the utopian character of the human right to science and culture that the Individual establishes relations with the Other. Due to such relations with the Other, the Individual gains something which has not been in him before – something unique and odd. The excendent Individual establishes a relation with the Other. What is important for the thesis is that the Other cannot be embraced, fathomed out, comprehended and calls on the Individual and questions his egoism. It can be other man, God or yet other Other. Thus, the Other is completely, absolutely Other.

Nonetheless, it is only after the three perspectives of Levinas, Løgstrup and Bauman are presented collectively, along with moral attitudes derived from the thoughts of Ingarden, Bauman and Kołakowski that a holistic depiction of the Individual, in the context of postmodern dilemmas, can be made. These 'attitudes' become a part of the Levinasian question of metaphysics of whether by *being* here and now we have justified our existence. The following attitudes are suggested in the work: a) *moral attitude* of Ingarden where the Individual feels a noble need which lies in his nature as a man. He combines in this way the past with the present and the future. In these circumstances the Individual develops, changes, transforms and improves; b) *Baumanian moral attitude where* an individual belonging to a moral community cannot be replaced with other Individuals. In this sense he is unique and exceptional; 'we' is not a sum total of various 'I' but a sum of unique 'I'; the Individual has a power with which we can separate ourselves as a given moral community from common indifference[14] toward developing a postmodern solidarity;[15] c) *Moral attitude according to Kołakowski where* an individual is merciful. This serves as an example of such a *quality* which, in Kołakowski's view, cannot be derived from justice.[16] Thus, mercy (which I refer to as the care

13 B. Skarga, 'Wstęp do' [Introduction to]: E. Levinas, *Całość i nieskończoność Esej o zewnętrznośc* [*Totality and Infinity. An Essay on Exteriority*] (Wydawnictwo Naukowe PWN, Warszawa 2012), pp. 15–16.

14 L. Kołakowski, *Mini wyklady o maxi sprawach* [*Mini-lectures on maxi-issues*] (Wydawnictwo Znak, Krakow 2006), p. 42.

15 Z. Bauman, 'Wywiad z Baumanem' [An interview with Bauman] which is a transcript of conversations held in Leeds, England between 15–17 July. Published in: *1 Odra* (1995), pp. 19–29.

16 L. Kołakowski, *Mini wykłady o maxi sprawach* [*Mini-lectures on maxi-issues*] ... , p. 266.

that is missing in postmodern people) and not justice is to be taken into account by the excendent Individual in his relation to the Other.

I will justify the thesis of a utopian character of the human right to science and culture by situating thinking in terms of excendence with respect to the Speech as well. For this purpose I make a presumption, again inspired by the philosophy of Levinas, that a relation with the Other is the Speech. It is the Speech that conditions thought, but the Speech not conceived in its physical materialness but as a contact. Such a Speech gives rise to meanings. Of key importance for the thesis become: the role of expression in the process of language creation, an intimate connection between expression and the desire for communication with the Other, spontaneous crystallization in a conversation of word meanings and senses of all objects. By coming from outside, the Speech transforms the consciousness of the excendent Individual. Due to the Speech conceived in this way, the Individual already thinks in other ways, maybe he thinks more completely. This work argues that it is only such a Speech, marked by a commitment in this way, which becomes the Speech compelling the Individual to a conversation. What is also of tremendous consequence for the whole study is the building up of the justification for the thesis of the utopian character of the human right to science and culture by putting forward the construct of 'active utopia' as a utopia capable of Levinasian 'awakening' or Baumanian 'sobering up' of a moral action of the Individual.[17] For the purposes of the work, the utopia will be referred to as an excendently active utopia focused on looking both 'ahead of' and 'beyond' the being. Keeping the above-mentioned assertions in mind, an argument is advanced that the excendent Individual is predestined in a utopian manner. The excendent Individual locates his world of unrealized values (that is his Utopia) in the Speech. The moral self of the excendent Individual is aroused. The expression of the Face conveys a heroic order, the first teaching that the Individual has to listen to. 'Active utopia' is sought precisely in this transformation. The very miracle (an effort) of 'awakening' is treated as giving rise to the 'possibility of morality' or as the 'hope of morality'.

I adopt an extremely important Levinasian stance that utopia initiates this very morality. Morality would not exist without an element of utopia. What is crucial to justification of the thesis of a utopian character to the/a human right to science and culture is that the miracle of moral awakening, which the transcendent Individual undergoes here, makes the Individual discover that he is not 'for himself' or 'alone with Others' but that he is 'for Others'.[18] 'Active utopia' is thus epitomized in the intention to take unconditional responsibility for the Other without expecting payment, that is with a complete exclusion of reciprocity. Thereby I advance the thesis that this is a decisive moment in the Speech. The excendently active Utopia motivates to moral action, it becomes a moral impulse orientated towards the future.

17 Z. Bauman, *Etyka ponowoczesna* [*Postmodern Ethics*] (Wydawnictwo Aletheia, Warszawa 2012), pp. 115–116.

18 *Ibidem*, p. 116.

This discussion leads to a question of what a paradigm of a dialogue marked with excendence is to look like? I call this paradigm an 'excendent dialogue'. In order to create a proposal of such a paradigm, I devise a fictitious encounter between two prominent thinkers of the last century – Emmanuel Levinas and Knud E. Løgstrup.[19] The prophetic word not only calls into question the freedom of the Individual, not only calls him, through the Other, to responsibility, it is not only a word which makes the Individual part with everything he owns (and what makes him withdraw). The prophetic word seems to be a basis of every dialogue. The prophetic word here testifies to the presence of humanity as a whole, of the community as a whole. Thus, the fact that fraternity between people emerges and a community emerges, is dependent on my responsibility to the Face that looks at me and is absolutely foreign.[20]

In this way a subsequent tenet is introduced in the work that the responsibility of the Individual to the Face is shaped by society, by humanity.[21] Thus, it seems that the propheticity of a dialogue itself (prophetic word) will lead to solidarity between people. The society will be viewed as a fraternal community which *will* be up to the standards of simplicity (proximity in the proper meaning) within which the Face manifests itself and is accepted. The society will therefore be such *as* the excendent Individual. Such an image of solidarity relates to Baumanian solidarity as a continuation of postmodernity. It seems that the radicality of a dialogue itself is presented in the book as leading toward shaping of a dialogue in which what is spoken fails to originate in an abstract environment but in a world in which one has to take care and demand the care from oneself.[22]

This leads to a significant conclusion in the work that propheticity viewed in conjunction with radicality – as a 'notional hybrid' denoting an excendent dialogue – will model the dialogue toward gaining a moral practice. This will constitute an unusual moral practice, as one based on, in Baumanian terms, 'impractical foundations'. It will perceive unattainable standards in its horizon 'and it can never console itself by the fact that it has fully met specific standards'.[23] Thereby, I postulate in this book that, in the present postmodernity, the Face will

---

19 Knud E. Løgstrup (1905–1981) was an outstanding Danish theologian and philosopher. His greatest works include: *The Ethical Demand*, *Metaphysics* and *Beyond the Ethical Demand*. He is considered as one of the four great 'theologians from Aarhus'. Løgstrup was an ethical intuitionist who was critical of rule-based ethics of the type advocated by Immanuel Kant. In other words, he disliked ethical systems which try to determine basic moral laws. Morality is not about rules, but about the so-called 'sovereign expressions of life'. Løgstrup takes the opposite point of view to Kant, who believed that moral laws are the only truly moral basis for action and that natural desires can never be moral.

20 E. Levinas, *Całość i nieskończoność. Esej o zewnętrzności* [*Totality and Infinity. An Essay on Exteriority*] (Wydawnictwo Naukowe PWN, Warszawa 2012), p. 253.

21 *Ibidem*, p. 254.

22 *Ibidem*, p. 257.

23 Z. Bauman, *Etyka ponowoczesna* [*Postmodern Ethics*] … , p. 124.

also be the one who asks for mercy (derived from Kołakowski) but also demands solidarity (derived from the thought of Bauman). Furthermore, what unites a request and a demand is expressed in the philosophy of good hope of Kępiński. And such will be a dialogue. In postmodernity it will be solidarity more than justice that will rely on the restoring of the possibility of expression, in which a person forsaking relations of reciprocity is manifest as unique and exceptional.

Moreover, the language of an excendent dialogue is translated into the language of metaphor and called a 'dialogue of saints' because of the fact that its aim is not a continuous meeting or satisfying everyday reality or normality, but going beyond everyday reality and normality as well as outgrowing them. It constitutes a dialogue orientated to something better than being, to something which literally has no essence on its own. A dialogue orientated not to 'being with', but to 'being for' and 'that which outgrows and goes beyond normality sets the horizon of that which is normal'.[24] As a result, in this book the excendent Individual is contrasted with a construct of the adiaphoric Individual inspired by 'Baumanian adiaphorisation'.[25] The adiaphoric Individual presented here is the one who escapes from moral responsibility. The escape is epitomized by adiaphorization. Consequently, I stress in the work that, in the postmodern society, issues that used to be moral are redefined as mere technical problems. Greater and greater fields of human behaviour are completely excluded from any moral discussion and contemporary life generally tends to cut off effects from causes and treat life as a set of episodes (the so-called inconsequentiality assumption).[26] This results in the sustaining of the Baumanian tenet that adiaphorization is mainly an effect of a division of life processes into separate episodes; whereas the cruelty of an episode is that one never knows for sure if a particular encounter was truly only an episode. Its echoes may return. In addition, I develop Bauman's thesis by supplementing it with the philosophy of Kępiński and I rely on the assumption that a lack of an excendent dialogue will result in adiaphorization of human behaviours in the postmodern society, where people can no longer perceive their own humanity in a man and refrain from passing judgements in moral issues.

The justification in my book of a utopian character of the human right to science and culture will be subsequently enriched with a presentation of thinking in terms of excendence also with respect to the Text. For this purpose I make a presupposition inspired by the philosophy of Gadamer that the word (similar as in the case of Levinasian Individual and Speech) is not self-sufficient. Thus far the Individual and the Speech have been at the centre of discussion on thought surrounding excendence. At this stage the attention will focus on the Convention in the written form (i.e. the Text, word). At issue is a Convention which is more often than not followed blindly (uncritically) by contemporary Levinasian self-sufficient man (i.e. the adiaphoric Individual). The Convention will be illustrated

24 *Ibidem*, p. 124.
25 *Ibidem*, p. 124 *et seq.*
26 *Ibidem*, p. 124 *et seq.*

in this part of the work with a specific example of norms directly related to the human right to science and culture. The discussion will revolve around the Text by means of which the Convention is generally expressed.

What follows in the treatise is a fundamental question of how the Text should be interpreted to prevent adiaphoric behaviour in postmodern society (or at least to reduce it). To put it differently, how to read the Text and how to interpret it, how to analyse it to prevent escape from moral responsibility in social life, to put an end to cutting off effects from causes and treating life as a set of Baumanian episodes? It is precisely the Augustian idea that was an inspiration for Gadamer and which enables me to go beyond an understanding of language typical of Greek ontology and characterized by nominalistic and technical understanding.[27] I refer here to liberation from a *stricte* ontological understanding of the Text. This thought posits that a 'particular something' is present in the word and yet it refers to what is Other.[28] Thus the word is not a reflection of something certain, of something related to self-possession, 'we-do-not-self-possess' the word. The word is no mirror image of understanding the certain but a reflection of understanding something uncertain and imperfect. Consequently, while interpreting we seek a particular word-spirit.[29] This leads to a pre-eminent tenet for the thesis: that the word is not self-sufficient; the word itself is not a self-sufficiency, just as a man and the Speech which accompanies a man are not self-sufficient.

For this part of the work, of significance seems to be the question of what an interpreter of the non-self-sufficient word utilizes when it is to be interpreted. I argue that an interpreter of the Text applies a particularly unclear knowledge, 'something unspecified in our minds' to help thoughts in their expression. The 'something unspecified in our minds' is not completely formed; it fails to originate from a clear vision, but is rather derived from infinite formation.[30] Augustine refers here to the word of God and the presence of God. What could a postmodern man, a petit bourgeois, refer to while reading the Text to eliminate or minimalize adiaphoric behaviours? In other words, how to interpret in order to invite morality? It becomes significant in the context that, in Gadamerian hermeneutic interpretation, a fusion of horizons takes place – of the past horizon and of our contemporary horizon, which is not motionless but is in constant motion, it is

---

27 J. Grondin, *Wprowadzenie do hermeneutyki filozoficznej* [*An Introduction to Philosophical Hermeneutics*]. *Myśl Filozoficzna* [*Philosophical Thought*] (Wydawnictwo WAM, Krakow 2007), p. 47. Professor Jean Grondin writes also in German and is also translated into Polish. He is a professor of philosophy who also teaches in Ottawa and Montreal. The title of the original that has been translated into Polish is: J.Grondin, Einfuhrung in die philosophische Hermeneutic, 2001 by Wissenschaftliche Buchgesellschaft, Darmstadt.

28 J. Grondin, *Wprowadzenie do hermeneutyki filozoficznej* [*An Introduction to Philosophical Hermeneutics*]. *Myśl Filozoficzna* [*Philosophical Thought*] (Wydawnictwo WAM, Krakow 2007), p. 47.

29 *Ibidem*, p. 50.

30 *Ibidem*, p. 51.

continuously formed, *inter alia* by being with tradition and by interpreting its Texts. By confronting our presuppositions with the message from the Text, we can confirm or reject them, thereby broadening our horizons, our understanding of ourselves and of the world. A hermeneutic interpretation, thanks to its characteristic feature of openness, turns out to be a path to broadening our self-awareness. Such an interpretation is considered in the work as a creative activity and enriching the Individual in every respect.

Accordingly, I assume – for the purposes of this study – that the Individual aims at an understanding of 'recovering notions from the historical past' so that the notions could find their own place in our contemporary thinking and understanding of a particular issue. And this is viewed in the work as the essence of a Gadamerian fusion of horizons, because the reconstruction of the question to which the Text is a response becomes our own questioning. As a consequence, what authority will say will have a status of 'other truth'. The truth may seem difficult for us to accept, 'incomprehensible due to its otherness'. But the Truth has a potential of opening before us (saying before us) a perspective of going beyond the current horizon of understanding. The Individual proposed here has to be able to hear in the Text a linguistic response to questions of times in which he lives, that is our postmodern times. Before the times which are contemporary to the adiaphoric Individual, a conversation started. Understanding will be its continuation. Understanding, as suggested here and now by the adiaphoric Individual, will be a continuation of a conversation from the past, from tradition. I will therefore understand the Text if I continue a conversation about the text which has started long before me. The Individual thus encounters a new sense. It is presumed in this work that, thanks to these encounters, the Individual assumes in this way and modifies in himself some aspects of the sense conveyed to him by tradition and modernity. Now the Text will be able to speak only through questions which the adiaphoric Individual asked the text today. As a result, in the dialogue suggested by Gadamer, there are 'no' utterances but questions and responses which give rise to new questions again – and such a stance is adopted here.

The justification of the thesis of a utopian character of the human right to science and culture will be subsequently enriched with a proposed utopian character of *verbum interius*. It will be supplemented with an assertion that the Text, like the Individual and the Speech, is not self-sufficient, and the non-self-sufficiency is supported precisely by a utopian element. Gadamerian words which we use simply because they come to mind cannot exhaust what we have 'in our souls', i.e. the conversation which we are.[31] I emphasize in the work at the same time that we have to relate the Text to our world, to our unique postmodern

31 H.-G. Gadamer, 'Granice Języka' [The Limits of Language] in: *Język i rozumienie* [*Language and Understanding*] (Fundacja Aletheia, Warszawa 2003), p. 38. See also H.-G. Gadamer, *Prawda i Metoda* [*Truth and Method*]. *Zarys hermeneutyki filozoficznej* [*An Outline of Philosophical Hermeneutics*] (Wydawnictwo Inter Esse, Krakow 1993), p. 359.

modernity, for the Text to speak to us. In other words, we have to relate it to our world and to our historical horizon. We have to refrain from our own bias and prejudice and assume an attitude open to the message of the Text. Being open entails being able to confront our own presuppositions with presuppositions contained in the Text. I stress that it is only by assuming such an attitude that we can understand that a product of a culture from the past is not an object at all, but a relation linking the reality of history with the reality of an interpreter. In Gadamerian hermeneutic interpretation, a fusion of horizons takes place – of the past horizon and of our contemporary horizon, which is not motionless but is in constant motion, it is continuously formed *inter alia* by being with tradition and by interpreting its Texts. By confronting our presuppositions with the message from the Text, we can confirm or reject them, thereby broadening our horizons, our understanding of ourselves and of the world. A hermeneutic interpretation, thanks to its characteristic feature of openness, turns out to be a path to broadening our postmodern self-awareness.

As the discussion proceeds to *Reason*, of consequence to the treatise becomes accounting for the works of Hornborg. He claims that economic growth is not about increasing a total sum of order but on expropriation and redistribution of the order.[32] This theory leads to an analysis of the following paradigms in the treatise: the well-being, the reflectivity, the knowledge commons, the pooling, the Open Source and the rule of balancing. This part of the study sets out to present these paradigms as 'representative *sensu largo*' of a 'total sum of order of the postanalogue society' in the postmodern era, which seeks opportunities to redistribute the order. Then, through applying the metaphor of the Cathedral as a more structural approach on the one hand and the Bazaar as a creative, more chaotic approach on the other hand, the work highlights that Commons might be located beyond these two metaphors. This means for the human right to science and culture that it conceptually needs to embrace both: Myth and Reason.

The aim here is to warn that Myth (hence phenomena beyond reason) as part of creativity should not be overlooked when legally defining rights. It argues for a philosophical human rights approach. Philosophical approaches, like those of Levinas, Gadamer, Løgstrup, Bauman and Habermas open up the legal dimension to a social one. Such a social sharing dimension needs to be added to traditional approaches to our legal understanding of intellectual property rights and to the human right to science and culture – with its crucial interpretations of the UN Committee on Economic, Social and Cultural Rights. Especially, when trying to regulate creativity, a higher acceptance of the non-reasoned elements needs to be taken into account in law. The aim of the examples presented here is to show the interconnectedness of legal and other dimensions. The underpinning claim is that we need a renaissance of ideas for the future of the human right to science and culture.

This renaissance comes together with *Myth*, *Reason* and Epilogue. From this perspective it is essential to account for the fact that, in the postmodern era, we

32 Z. Bauman, *Etyka ponowoczesna* [*Postmodern Ethics*] … , pp. 329, 331.

have lost this important sense of balance. We have lost a critical insight which allowed us to discern the differences between truth and extremes. As Lessig aptly argues, a fundamentalism of ownership rights dominates in our culture. For this purpose the work strongly emphasizes that our responsibility is a kind of a 'short-distance' premodern responsibility, a responsibility mature only from a temporally – and spatially-limited perspective (or, to put it differently, Levinasian bourgeois 'localness'). Of significance for the work thus becomes an assertion that, as a contemporary society, we have lost an important morality to a morality of a feudal character. The morality that we have lost (or which, I would rather believe, remains dormant) is called a 'far-sighted morality' in the thought of Jonas and Bauman.

Thus, the justification of the thesis of a utopian character of the human right to science and culture will be subsequently enriched with the proposed Baumanian construct of a 'far-sighted morality' in the treatise. This is accompanied by an assertion that we, as contemporary people, are inheritors of a kind of morality which each of us received (that is which each Individual or which we as a moral community received) as a legacy of premodern times. And it is the only morality that we have at our disposal. The thesis postulates that the postmodern Individual simply has no other and knows no other morality. By belonging to a moral community, we have no other and know no other morality either. The morality is characterized by its functionality of an only short-distance character. That is why the morality acts at a limited short distance.[33] The work posits that a 'short-distance responsibility' is then of no use in the postanalogue times, when most important actions (above all related to paradigms of the postanalogue society) have distant effects (access to knowledge – a well-educated and autonomous society; access to medicines – a healthy and participating society and so on). As a consequence, we generally feel no responsibility for events distant in time or in space, even if they are connected with who we are and what we do.

Thereby, it is a crucial statement in the treatise that the ethical scope of our actions has increased in an unprecedented manner when we think of a specific postanalogue 'I' or a postanalogue moral community. We regard our reason as self-sufficient and, consequently, we have become 'moral impotents'. This also comes as a result of the fact that the moral basis which existed (for instance the faith in God constituted such a basis of a moral education) has almost entirely vanished in the process of an intensive modernization. Moreover, the work discusses not only the lack of any foundations for morality in the postanalogue society living in the postmodern era, but it strongly emphasizes the lack of the very material which could be potentially used to build such foundations. This raises important questions of how to create a far-sighted morality so that we become reasoning and succeeding in our matters Eldreds[34] here and now, a morality responsible

33 *Ibidem*, p. 336.

34 An expression used as a metaphor which refers to the court case presented while elaborating on one of the paradigms in the part dealing with *Reason*.

for future generations who, thanks to a wider access to knowledge in the era of digital technologies, are creative and responsive and do not die slowly? How to arouse the Baumanian solidarity discussed in this thesis, which is a promise of postmodernity's continuation? It is only the concept of 'need', introduced in this treatise and derived from Levinasian philosophy, and the notion of responsibility of an 'active utopia' character inspired by the thought of Løgstrup and Bauman that have, jointly, a preliminary potential to delineate future directions for the presence of a 'far-sighted morality' in the postanalogue society, in the society of self-sufficient Individuals, their Speech and Text.

Another crucial question arises in the work of how to translate the intuitive need of a 'far-sighted morality' into a language of material social interests and therefore real political powers in the case of the right to science and culture? In other words, how to enter a universal level into one's argumentation from a local level? The study seeks the answer to the question of how to introduce the *Myth* of the human right to science and culture and link it with the law and trends. In other words, how do we link it with the *Reason* that belongs to the human right to science and culture and how do we make use of the argument of utopia in this context?

Of the utmost importance for the whole treatise is the justification of the thesis of a utopian character of the human right to science and culture, which will be enriched with an assumption made in the treatise that thinking in terms of excendence should find both its universal and practical continuation in Habermas's thought. This opens up the possibility of referring to the right of science and culture to be a specification of human dignity – dignity as the moral source from which human rights to science and culture derives its meaning. According to Habermas, what explains the explosive political force of concrete utopia is the origin of human rights in the moral notion of human dignity.[35] From this point of view it is vital to account for the fact that the idea of human dignity is the conceptual connection that links on one side the *Myth* – which is the morality of equal respect for all of the people and on the other side the *Reason* – which is the law. All of the happenings in between have a potential to give rise to a political order based on human rights.[36] The treatise stresses that this type of reconciliation of morality and law under the umbrella of dignity will hopefully release the tension between idea and reality in the postanalogue society in the postmodern era, if carefully applied. Thereby, the possibility of the act of specification shows that applied dignity in this sense is a dynamic concept that can always start from a different beginning(s) and act in 'different becoming(s)'.[37] This means that I can start my life from the new beginning in the same way as you can. The beginning

35 J. Habermas, *The Concept of Human Dignity and the Realistic Utopia of Human Rights …* , p. 466.

36 *Ibidem*, p. 466.

37 C. Dupre, 'Unlocking Human Dignity: Towards a Theory for the 21st Century', 2 *European Human Rights Law Review* (2009), p. 8.

is aporetic in character and changes depending on the kind of request of the Other (the diversity and aporetics of beginnings) and then evaluates itself in the process and starts from a new beginning over and over again. In this way, applied dignity has a potential to reverse what we/I thought was/is irreversible; The role of the act of specification would be to construct a new beginnings(s).[38]

In this context it becomes significant to pay attention to the right to access the knowledge in books, medicines or accessible formats for the visually impaired on behalf of preserving the quality of our education and our progress as humanity might serve as a functional application of this logic – in terms of our humankind. It is based on the idea that the more people who share useful knowledge, the greater is the common good. It is a request on behalf of humankind. We can also imagine a request from the human being (on the individual level like the Author) or human group level (like the group of Commons, state or postanalogue society). Every specification of dignity will seem unique. However, one can assume that the notion of reversibility accompanied by the process of reflexivity is predominant. This can be merged with the idea of the reflective society at stake. Additionally, it is postulated that what is very vocal about the Habermasian idea is that his very focus is on the demand. It is argued here that this might actually make it more functional on the societal, global, or, if one wishes, universal level. This invites us to think about 'rights not in terms of having been acquired once and for all by our generation, but in terms of rights that we are borrowing from future generations and that will be our legacy to them'.[39] The treatise takes into consideration the thoughts of Kołakowski and Bauman and attempts to place them in the context of the above discussion, the postmodern era and the postanalogue society. As a result of this analysis, it turns out that what 'the spirit of the world' expects from the Individual is not primarily justice, in whatever sense we would like to describe, present or understand it.[40] Kołakowski's thought is supplemented in the treatise with Bauman's opinion that what is more crucial today (and goes beyond tolerance which is a mere introduction to postmodernity) is solidarity. Moreover, it is solidarity which most staunchly acknowledges the dialogism of a situation in the postmodern era. When dialogism becomes a feature of postmodernity, tolerance gives way to solidarity; and solidarity itself can be considered as a continuation of postmodernity.[41] In this respect it is argued in the treatise that the most present activity for the postanalogue society (as a social world) is the idea of 'communicative solidarity' and not 'communicative justice' – as in the era of modernity.

38 *Ibidem*, p. 10.

39 *Ibidem*, p. 10.

40 L. Kołakowski, *Mini wykłady o maxi sprawach* [*Mini-lectures on maxi-issues*] … , p. 266.

41 Z. Bauman, 'Wywiad z Baumanem' [An interview with Bauman] which is a transcript of conversations held in Leeds, England between 15 and 17 July. Published in: *1 Odra* (1995), pp. 19–29.

It is suggested in the treatise that the Individual will be able to transform the Text into language if he does not view language as a limitation or an impediment – we have an obligation to pursue *verbum interius*. Language is not a copy of meaning or an outer border. Gadamer conceives of language as a medium in which understanding is affected. Following the Gadamerian path, the Individual can go beyond language, can leave the space of writing, the space and constraints of the Text. One can imagine such a reading of the Text with understanding in postmodernity in which notions would speak in the authentic voice of a conversation again – there is no issue which we could not agree upon.

The work advances a premise that endowing *verbum interius* with a utopian character will bring hope for such a political discourse, in which one can at last be supported by the word liberated from the constraints of the Text. After all, the 'particular something' which refers to what is Other is present in the word.[42]

I attempt to prove that it is feasible to talk of a utopian human right to science and culture tracing its foundation precisely in thinking in terms of excendence. That would mean: with respect to the role of a man (the Individual and moral community created by him), with respect to his communication (the Speech) and finally with respect to the interpretation of the law in force (the Text). It will be, then, neither the Individual (or a community to which he belongs), nor the Speech, and the Text will have no need to put on a mask or set others limits. Thereby, not the Individual, nor the Text, nor the Speech will ever be self-sufficient in postmodernity. And if interlocutors think they can be self-sufficient, there is no hope for a utopian impulse in the human right to science and culture. The hope of postmodernity is therefore related to Levinasian and Gadamerian 'non-self-sufficiency' of the Individual, the Speech and the Text, which refer to what is Other and even utopian. Obviously, this entails situating the excendent Individual predestined in a utopian manner in the foreground in the postmodern era. The goal is an attempt at proving that such an excendent Individual is likely to cure us from – putting it in Tischnerian terms – our narrow-mindedness and against this new minimalism that relaxes the claim of human rights by cutting them off from their essential moral thrust, namely the protection of the equal dignity of every human being, as Habermas claims.[43]

42 J. Grondin, *Wprowadzenie do hermeneutyki filozoficznej* [*An Introduction to Philosophical Hermeneutics*]. *Myśl Filozoficzna* [*Philosophical Thought*] (Wydawnictwo WAM, Krakow 2007), p. 47.

43 J. Habermas, *The Concept of Human Dignity and the Realistic Utopia of Human Rights* … , p. 478.

PART I
The Myth

The point is to begin with being a new path, even at a risk of a redefining of certain notions which for common sense and in accordance with wisdom of nations seem to be most self-evident.

Emmanuel Levinas, *O Uciekaniu* [*On Escape*]

Chapter 1
Excendence Stance on Thinking: The Individual

On a Man Without a Need

If one is somewhat absorbed in Roman Ingarden's *Little Book About Man*, one can assume that a basic set of values exists, established by people who strive to live by them in a manner characteristic of a particular time (and they even feel called to living by these values). The values are difficult to pinpoint. And presumably the values as a whole change within strictly defined boundaries depending on a particular kind of man and on a historical epoch. Ingarden advances a thesis that of the most importance to man is the feeling of a special need (and even a necessity) to engage with values or live by them (fulfilling values) provided that it is feasible in a particular epoch.[1]

A man is thus deeply unhappy if he is devoid of a direct and intuitive engagement with values. In other words, he cannot live his life to the full without the joy of this engagement. By such values Ingarden means not 'life' values but values absolute in their immanent character, whose fulfilment depends on man's creative power, namely moral values. Nonetheless, a man fails to find such values simply in Nature, in the material world. First he has to create actual conditions for their existence and manifestation in the world. Owing to a special ability to foresee their character, a man creates a new world on the foundations of the real world by transforming certain things and triggering certain processes, a world in which these values are manifest. The content of this world significantly exceeds the world of Nature while simultaneously dressing it with various particular qualities, assigning certain things and issues of peculiar significance and certain momentousness which are unlike the things, beings and issues of Nature and to which they are not entitled. Such a world of man creates a certain atmosphere necessary to give his life a new meaning and a new, fuller importance whereby his every deed and his overall role in the world is transformed. Otherwise a man could not accept his own existence. As Ingarden states: 'Faced with this new reality, a man forgets to a certain extent about his true, primitive nature … . He feels happiness when he is aware of the presence of values created by himself or by his relatives'.[2]

---

1 R. Ingarden, *Książeczka o człowieku* [*Little Book About Man*] (Wydawnictwo Literackie, Krakow 2003), p. 23.

2 *Ibidem*, p. 24.

The world of man in which these values manifest themselves is a reality peculiarly human, more permanent and long-lasting than the life of a man. It becomes to each of us a kind of a legacy 'which we find in our world as a gift of predecessors and as a rebirth of past historical epochs and a meeting with people who are long dead.' … 'And we strive not only to keep the treasure of values received from previous epochs, but also to enrich and transform it by our creative acts and our new works'[3] – thus reaching to the future. Therefore, in human nature lies the possession of a noble need. Consequently a man will attain full satisfaction if he has succeeded in creating values particular to his personality. In this way he joins the past with the present and the future – a man draws on, creates and enriches himself and others. Being influenced by his own 'works' which he created and with which he remains in intuitive closeness, he comes back to life by himself. This happens against his will, as a result of an effort of a man in the service of a realization which may be called 'intuitive realization' in its full sense.

A man who possesses such an enormous spiritual power contributes his best powers to creating the reality of man as such. However, he has to take into account the situation in which there will come a time when his spiritual power weakens or entirely vanishes. This phenomenon will cause a fading away or a complete disappearance of something which Ingarden refers to as the 'Human Reality layer in the world'.[4] To his own amazement, a man will begin to discover the original character of Nature – an element in the surrounding world and even in himself and will feel abandoned in a strange and horrible world. A man will experience loneliness despite the fact that he will be connected with the being. He will not be connected with something other, with something noble, with something greater than himself. Ingarden posits that human nature involves a continuous effort of exceeding limits of animalism present in a man and outgrowing it with humanity. Without the mission and the effort of outgrowing oneself 'a man descended again and with no hope, in his pure animalism which constitutes his death'.[5] It is therefore of importance in the understanding of man to focus on those aspects crucial to his humanity.[6] Then he may find his path to the others and the other easier, if he omits to ask about the beings but stops at such a request and demand to which he has to respond and in which he has faith; and then he will not be 'a man without a need' and 'something' or 'someone' will be 'somewhere' of future importance to human hope.

3 *Ibidem*, p. 24.

4 *Ibidem*, p. 25.

5 *Ibidem*, p. 25.

6 See also Z. Brodecki 'Art the Comparison', in: Z. Brodecki, M. Konopacka and A. Brodecka-Chamera, *Komparatystyka kultur prawnych* [*Art de comparison of the legal cultures*] (Wydawnictwo Wolters Kluwer, Warszawa 2010), pp. 64–66.

Against 'Philosophy without Responsibility' – on Non-existence of the Truth *Sensu Stricto*

If we intend to comprehend the mystery of human morality, the path does not lead by making rational, unquestionable, 'stiff presumptions', Bauman says.[7] Morality never is and cannot be 'stiff', while in modernity's dream morality was to be made stiff. What has become of morality in our times of postmodernity (taking into account Bauman's assertion that postmodernity has become a chance for modernity)? What is the dream of postmodernity?[8] In an attempt to respond to the question one can follow two paths: first, the one delineated by the philosopher Leszek Kołakowski and subsequently the one suggested by the sociologist Zygmunt Bauman.

The potential of intolerance is in each of us. This may be the case because the need to impose one's view of the world on others is usually extremely pronounced. The Individual wants others to believe in what he believes in. Then the Individual enjoys spiritual safety and does not have to consider his own faith or beliefs or confront them with others. Following the path delineated by Kołakowski in his lecture entitled *Tolerancja* [Tolerance] we speak of tolerance with reference to human attitudes which constitute our own behaviour, morality and actions.[9] The Individual will thus be tolerant (in the primitive sense) if he fails to be aggressive or fails to persecute (refrains from persecution or condemnation of) something he clearly dislikes or disapproves of. The word tolerance is used in a quite similar manner in medicine and technology, i.e. medicines are harmful by definition, but we talk about a tolerance to a medicine if our body tolerates the medicine to a certain extent. In other words, our bodies tolerate it with no serious effects. The above-mentioned reasoning points out that 'tolerance' was used as an opinion or a stance.

However, another form of tolerance also exists, a tolerance very frequently used in the sense of indifference, or no stance or opinion (and sometimes even no approval of all we happen to know about people and beliefs).[10] Kołakowski claims that this demand of tolerance forms a part of our contemporary times in

7 Z. Bauman, 'Wywiad z Baumanem' [An interview with Bauman] which is a transcript of conversations held in Leeds, England between 15–17 July. *1 Odra* (1995), pp. 19–29.

8 Z. Bauman, *Liquid Modernity* (Polity Press, Cambridge 2012), pp. 2–15.

9 L. Kołakowski, *Mini wykłady o maxi sprawach* [*Mini-lectures on maxi-issues*] (Wydawnictwo Znak, Krakow 2006), p. 40.

10 See also text about solidaric relations that go beyond the so-called 'passive tolerance', in: B. Wojciechowski, *Interkulturowe Prawo Karne: Filozoficzne Podstawy Karania w Wielokulturowych Spoleczenstwach Demokratycznych* [*Intercultural Criminal Law: Philosophical Grounds for Penalization in Democratic Societies*] (Wydawnictwo Adam Marszalek, Torun 2009), pp. 252–253. See also in this context cited by B. Wojciechowski: A. Honneth, *Kampf um Anerkennung. Zur moralischen Grammatik sozialer Kämpfe* (Frankfurt am Main 1994), p. 209.

which literally nothing is of significance to us. This philosophy is referred to by the outstanding Polish scholar as 'philosophy without responsibility', one with no beliefs. As a result of this philosophy, the Individual learns that truth *sensu stricto* is non-existent and one can even despise it which, according to Kołakowski, destroys our civilization to no lesser a degree than the fanaticism of truth.[11] We are becoming a society of an indifferent majority (and, what follows, a civilization accepting fanatics) and a society in which everything can be perceived as a play or even a jest.

It seems important to respond here to the question of how tolerance (not the tolerance in the sense of indifference just mentioned) should be protected in postmodernity? Following Kołakowski's reasoning, one should assume that tolerance is protected to a lesser extent by law and to a greater extent by consolidation of tolerant morality. In this way the very potential of tolerance is in each Individual. The point is that intolerance is not removed by such morality in which ' … nobody believes in anything, nobody makes any point so long as life is fun', Kołakowski states.[12] Thus, in the context, how significant are these developed special qualities to our morality in postmodernity? These qualities are vital for the power which enables us as a moral community to separate ourselves from the common indifference.[13]

The second path of thinking originates in Bauman's *Modernity and Ambivalence* in which he considers tolerance as a chance of postmodernity, and solidarity as a chance of tolerance.[14] The commonest version of tolerance in Bauman's view can be expressed in this way: 'your customs are weird, I would never accept them, but you are a weirdo or can be a savage so these customs are suitable for you'.[15] Such tolerance, as the philosopher asserts, is marked with disdain and fails to consolidate equality but *de facto* consolidates superiority of the Other over the Individual. The Individual is even 'magnanimous' and 'understanding' towards an Otherness. This entails that the Individual judges; the Individual passes a judgement and refrains from criticizing or penalizing the Other even though he could do so.[16] That being the case, one cannot conclude with observations on tolerance. Tolerance by itself does not rule out oppression in the sense of humiliation, insult to one's own dignity or perpetuation of a stiff hierarchy. In Bauman's opinion, what is crucial and goes

11 *Ibidem*, pp. 41–42.

12 *Ibidem*, p. 42. See also J. Zajadlo (ed.), *Leksykon wspolczesnej teorii i filozofii prawa* [*Lexicon on the contemporary theory and philosophy of law*] (Wydawnictwo C.H. Beck, Warszawa 2007), pp. 247–250.

13 See also Z. Bauman, *Liquid Modernity…* , pp. 2–15.

14 Z. Bauman, *Modernity and Ambivalence* (Cornell University Press, Ithaca, NY 1991), p. 153.

15 Z. Bauman, 'Wywiad z Baumanem' [An interview with Bauman] … , pp. 19–29.

16 *Ibidem*, pp. 19–29.

beyond tolerance is solidarity.[17] It is solidarity (and not tolerance) which most staunchly acknowledges dialogism of situation. Bauman claims that: ' … here two assertions interact with each other, both have something valuable and we can learn a lot from each other'.[18]

Taking into consideration the above-mentioned claims, it seems justified to suggest several comments to summarize the assertions initiated with a question about dreams of the postmodernity era, its morality and chances for the future:

1. Tolerance is a preliminary potential of postmodernity.
2. Tolerance is protected by tolerant morality more than by law.
3. When dialogism becomes a feature of postmodernity, tolerance gives way to solidarity.
4. Solidarity can be considered as a continuation of postmodernity.

Who is Our Neighbour?

In a very short but telling chapter entitled *Who is Our Neighbour?*, of a great work by Amartya Sen entitled *The Idea of Justice*, the author discusses our contemporary dilemmas concerning the definition of the Neighbour and beyond.[19] Sen makes a preliminary assumption that the Neighbour is above all someone who cares for an Individual.[20] In order to explain more clearly what constitutes the essence of being the Neighbour, Sen recounts the story of 'the good Samaritan' in the Gospel of Luke.[21] Sen writes:

> Jesus is arguing with a local lawyer about his limited conception of those to whom we owe some duty (only our physical neighbours). Jesus tells the lawyer the story of the wounded man lying on one side of the street who was helped eventually by the good Samaritan, an event that was preceded by the refusal of a priest and a Levite to do anything for him. Indeed, instead of helping, the priest and the Levite just crossed and walked on the other side of the street, without facing the wounded man. Jesus does not, on this occasion, directly discuss the duty to help others – all others – in need, neighbours or not, but rather raises a classificatory question regarding the definition of one's neighbour. He asks the

17 In this context see also an extremely powerful passage on the duty of human respect (while the lack of respect is against human dignity) in: B. Wojciechowski, *Interkulturowe Prawo Karne …* , pp. 244–246.

18 *Ibidem*, pp. 19–29.

19 A. Sen, *The Idea of Justice* (Allen Lane *an imprint of* Penguin Books, London 2009). The quoted chapter is included in pp. 170–173 of the work by Amartya Sen.

20 *Ibidem*, p. 171.

21 One can also refer on this subject to Jeremy Waldron's analysis in 'Who is My Neighbour? Humanity and Proximity', 86 *The Monist* (July 2003) as Sen recommends.

> lawyer with whom he is arguing: 'Who was the wounded man's neighbour?' And that was, of course, Jesus' point exactly. The duty to neighbours is not confined only to those who live next door. In order to understand the force of Jesus' argument, we have to remember that Samaritans did not only live some distance away, but also were typically disliked or despised by the Israelites. The Samaritan is linked to the wounded Israelite through the event itself: he found the stricken man, saw the need to help, provided that help and was now in a relationship with the injured person. It does not matter whether the Samaritan was moved by charity, or by a 'sense of justice', or by some deeper 'sense of fairness in treating others as equals'. Once he finds himself in this situation, he is in a new 'neighbourhood'.[22]

As Sen points out, the Neighbour is someone who has the autonomy to project through his considerate attitude towards the Individual, the whole neighbourhood at stake (even if the Neighbour was not part of that neighbourhood from the start); the neighbourhood that is constructed by our relations; in Sen's view the Neighbour is someone who above all cares for a particular Individual.

What I find relevant to this thesis is that the relation is reversed and the attention focused on the Neighbour as the Other, that is someone who is above all taken care of by the Individual and to whose call the Individual responds. Consequently, the Neighbour will be perceived as a subject (object) of the Individual's care and beyond. Despite the reversed relation of care the story of 'the good Samaritan' in the Gospel of Luke remains valid so that it is analysed by Sen consequences inspired initially by just a Gospel in fact – however less pretentious, humbler and simpler … .[23]

The Individual in Terms of Løgstrup's Philosophy ('the Løgstrupian I' Concept)

The concept of the Individual according to Løgstrup is actually a structure designed to create at the outset an atmosphere saturated with morality as a reference point for this entire book. Løgstrup's philosophy, despite in a sense being marked with religiousness, also serves as a good model for analyses of a more secular character (as in the model of Levinas applied in the subsequent part of this book). Such analysis will always be doomed to saturation with escape to the Other. For Løgstrup the religious proclamation of Jesus of Nazareth 'must answer to something in our own existence',[24] provided of course that we want a proclamation to have any relevance for us. But even if we do not want that there is still something to think

22 A. Sen, *The Idea of Justice…* , pp. 171–172.

23 *Ibidem*, p. 172.

24 Interestingly enough, it will constitute a digression in the thesis (and one possibly should not devote too much attention to digressions in such theses). Amartya Sen was

about and that is the concept of the proclamation from the Neighbour of ours – and that would take away its primary religious context at stake. That would put the Individual in front of the Neighbour.

Thus, if we focus on the real understanding of a proclamation it will give us the answers to decisive features of our existence. It refers to an understanding suggested by Løgstrup, an understanding in the personal and objective sense. This type of thinking would disclose to the Individual his own existence. Løgstrup raises the following questions: what does the Individual mean for a situation in which the essential thing in his life is being with or against each other? And how can that be stated in strictly human terms?[25] On the one hand, the Neighbour becomes dependent on the Individual – on what he does and says. The Individual solely can do or say something in relation to the Neighbour. None other can replace him in his doing and saying which are so specific in their uniqueness. The reasoning of Løgstrup results from his theological background ('the one thing in our existence which the proclamation of Jesus touches upon more than any other is the individual's relation to the Neighbour'). On the other hand, the demand from the Neighbour is silent, radical, one-sided. The same type of demand is contained in the proclamation of Jesus.[26] Løgstrup states that:

> If my relation to the other person is the place where my relation to God is determined, then it must at the same time be the place where that person's existence is so totally at stake that to fail him is to fail him irreparably. In other words, what I withhold from him in one situation he will not be able to recoup in another situation, either from me or from anyone else. If human beings were so independent of one another that the words and deeds of one were only a dispensable luxury in the life of another and my failure in relation to the life of the neighbour could easily be made up later, then God's relation to me would not be as intimately tied up with my relation to the neighbour as the proclamation of Jesus declares it to be. In short, the intimate connection in which Jesus places

---

inspired to write the *Who is Our Neighbour?* chapter not directly by the Bible but by the Gospel. Sen writes:

> When recollecting this story from the Gospels and its remarkable reach and effectiveness, I remember being reminded of what Ludwig Wittgenstein said about the Gospels, in contrast with the more formidable Epistles of St Paul: 'In the Gospels – as it seems to me – everything is less pretentious, humbler, simpler. There you find huts; in Paul a church. There all men are equal and God himself is a man; in Paul there is already something of a hierarchy; honours and official positions'.

25 K.E. Løgstrup, *The Ethical Demand. Introduction by Hans Fink and Alasdair MacIntyre* (University of Notre Dame Press, Notre Dame and London 1997), p. 1. See also K. Løgstrup, *Beyond the Ethical Demand* (University of Notre Dame Press, Notre Dame 2007).

26 S. Andersen and K. Niekerk (eds), *Concern for the Other: Perspectives on the Ethics of K.E. Løgstrup* (Notre Dame, University of Notre Dame Press 2007), pp. 52–80.

> our relation to God and our relation to the neighbour presupposes that we are, as Luther expressed it, 'daily bread' in the life of another. And this presupposition for the intimate connection in the proclamation of Jesus between the two great commandments in the law can indeed be described in strictly human terms.[27]

The proclamation that comes from the Neighbour is addressed directly to 'the Løgstrupian I'. In order to be human (that means to understand the demand contained in the proclamation of the Neighbour) the Individual shall proceed from the standpoint of its own existence. However, that existence is full of contradictions and conflicts.[28] Contradictions and conflicts tearing at a man are related to a contemporary, postmodern treatment of moral behaviour as a contract in compliance with the principle: 'I behave in a moral manner as I rely on the Other [Others] to return my moral behaviour'. This constitutes a falsification of the sense of morality. It happens because 'justification' of the duty to be moral states that 'it is worth your while to be good as then the others will be good to you'.[29] This may be the reason why Løgstrup, to improve the above situation, introduced in his philosophy the notion of radical demand, which is radical since it is not defined specifically enough. Løgstrup thus creates the Individual who is refused full satisfaction from a well fulfilled duty.[30] In this way I come to de-falsification of morality according to Løgstrup. In Bauman's opinion:

> Løgstrup asserts that the notion of Christian ethics is pointless, since, as he claims, if Jesus had told us exactly what entails being moral, he would have annihilated human morality. When one 'says precisely, from A to Z, do such-and-such and all will be well, no-one and especially not you yourself will have any objections, then morality will be destroyed. This is the case as morality entails living in uncertainty. Only if one sacrifices life for the other man, as did, for instance, Maksymilian Kolbe, one can be assured – yes, I have done all what I should! Until this moment, until this point, you are not sure.[31]

'The Løgstrupian I' concept will follow the path in the direction of being the Individual human if his moral actions are marked with uncertainty. One could ask a question here: what does this 'path to uncertainty' look like? What does Løgstrup use to build uncertainty (predestining it even to the meaning of morality)? To analyse this issue I return to Løgstrup and his ways of describing the nature of trust and radical demand. To do so two groups of paradigms are suggested. The

27 K.E. Løgstrup, *The Ethical Demand. Introduction by Hans Fink and Alasdair MacIntyre* (University of Notre Dame Press, Notre Dame and London 1997), pp. 2–3.

28 *Ibidem*, p. 3.

29 *Ibidem*, p. 5.

30 See also S. Andersen and K Niekerk (eds), *Concern for the Other: Perspectives on the Ethics of K.E. Løgstrup* (Notre Dame, University of Notre Dame Press 2007), pp. 52–80.

31 Z. Bauman, *Wywiad z Baumanem …* , pp. 19–29.

first group constitutes 'metaphorical paradigms of trust', the second group form 'paradigms of radical demand'.

The first group was given the attribute of 'metaphorical' owing to the fact that they originate from the following metaphor according to Løgstrup: 'have something in one's hand' or even 'holding another person's life in one's hand' (that endows this metaphor with a certain emotional power).[32]

1. The Neighbour shall surrender oneself (in that trust) to the Individual.
2. The Neighbour need not confide in the Individual.
3. Both the Neighbour and the Individual are in the situation where everything hangs in balance.
4. The Individual determines the outcome of the situation; ('everything which happens or does not happen is traced back to him or her; it is the consequence of what he or she does or fails to do'[33]).
5. The Neighbour, through the self-exposure, risks the chance of being rejected (in this case the trust was not accepted).
6. The Neighbour keeps his or her independence no matter if demand is rejected or accepted.[34]

Løgstrup asserts: 'Out of this basic dependence and direct power arises the demand that we take of that in the other person's life which is dependent upon us and which we have in our power. However, the same demand forbids that we ever attempt, even for his or her own sake, to rob him or her of his or her independence. Responsibility for the other person never consists in our assuming the responsibility which is his or hers'.[35]

The second group constitutes Løgstrup's 'paradigms of radical demand':[36]

1. The demand is of the silent character since nothing is said about how this carrying for the Neighbour is to be done.
2. The demand brings about moral and cognitive effort on the part of the 'I' since the 'I' assumes responsibility which I refer to, after Bauman, as responsibility seen as 'active utopia' (utopia based on moral behaviour!)[37], which can also be called 'responsibility in pursuit' (or responsibility of pursuing nature) and therefore the one which, in its deep care, desires to

32 *Ibidem*, pp. 19–29.

33 *Ibidem*, pp. 19–29.

34 K.E. Løgstrup, *The Ethical Demand …* , pp. 16–17, 28.

35 *Ibidem*, p. 28.

36 *Ibidem*, p. 22.

37 Z. Bauman, *Etyka ponowoczesna …* , p. 116. See also text in English: Z. Bauman, *Postmodern Ethics*, MA (Basil Blackwell, Cambridge 1993). See also on utopia in the age of uncertainty Z. Bauman, *Liquid Times: Living in an Age of Uncertainty* (Polity Press, Cambridge 2007), pp. 94–110.

> design what the demand requires for the future. I would like to emphasize: what the demand requires according to the Individual unique in his responsibility (unique as a result of his relation to the Neighbour).

Løgstrup writes: 'It is the essence of the demand that with such insight, imagination and understanding as he or she possesses a person must figure out for him or herself what the demand requires'.[38]

Bearing in mind both 'metaphorical paradigms of trust' and 'paradigms of radical demand' advanced for the purposes of this text, it may be regarded as crucial to uncertainty structure to suggest joint treatment of 'independence of the Neighbour' (paradigm 6) and the paradigm on 'responsibility of active utopia nature' (paradigm 2). In this way one can make an assumption that responsibility and uncertainty (which in a sense is modelled by responsibility) are marked with utopian thought. It seems that it may be sought here and developed from this point. Consequently, 'Løgstrupian I' moral behaviour is intimately connected with what can be called departure from self-sufficiency of a contemporary, postmodern man. This contradicts self-sufficiency which stops us from taking a path marked by the Individual according to Løgstrup's philosophy. As contemporary, postmodern and self-sufficient people, taking unconditional responsibility for the Neighbour and his radical, silent demand is something we fear most.[39]

Self-Sufficiency Category of Man in the Philosophy of Levinas

The depiction of the Individual in his self-sufficiency is one of the basic determinants of the spirit of the bourgeois and its philosophy. In Levinasian terms it constitutes self-sufficiency of a petit bourgeois. The self-sufficiency in itself sustains courageous dreams of a turbulent and entrepreneurial capitalism and directs the pious worship of the bourgeois of effort and discovery. Nevertheless the effort and discovery aim not so much at reconciliation of man with himself, but at protecting him against the unknown brought about by the course of events and time.[40] A man-bourgeois is someone who seeks security, who wants to conceal this antagonism under the mask of 'inner peace', an antagonism which each day pits him against the world. The bourgeois does not confide his inner dilemma.

38 K.E. Løgstrup, *The Ethical Demand …* , p. 22.

39 S. Andersen and K. Niekerk (eds), *Concern for the Other …* , pp. 52–80. See also J.-Ch Põder, *Evidenz des Ethischen. Die Fundamentalethik Knud E. Løgstrups* (Tübingen, Mohr Siebeck 2011), pp. 21–49.

40 E. Levinas, *O Uciekaniu* [*On Escape*] (Wydawnictwo Instytutu Filozofii i Socjologii PAN, Warszawa 2007), p. 8. The essay entitled *On Escape* was first published in 1935 and marked the beginning of Levinas's own, original (brilliant) way of thinking. It was published first in the journal *Recherches Philosophiques* (1935/1936). See also original text in French: E. Levinas, *De l'evasion* (Editions Fata Morgana 1982).

His attitude is characterized by his worrying about reality and the future. This results from the fact that both categories threaten to destabilize the unquestionable balance of the present. The bourgeois is, after all, an unquestionable holder of the balance. He defends himself from unpredictability. And his characteristic feature is conservatism.[41] He lives in a 'static', 'unshakeable' manner, he does not want to worry, to fear for anything or anyone – and even if he is afraid – it is a fear in a previously calculated manner. He reasons how much he has to give from himself and how much to leave for himself and if it is worth it. Will I lose something if I have to 'give' something from myself, or maybe I will gain something (in the sense of being, things and issues of Nature), which will cover my loss?

Things are always present. This category of self-sufficiency stems from the image of *being* derived from things. Lack of scruples of a bourgeois is a shameful result of the peace of his conscience. As depicted by Levinas, a bourgeois is a moderate materialist who prefers the certainty of tomorrow to the pleasures of today. He would like to receive insurance against unknown quantities which the future adds to problems he has already resolved and to the solutions with which he lives. His possessions become a capital sustaining business or an insurance against risk. The future tamed in this way begins to merge as a whole with the past.[42] Accordingly, Levinasian bourgeois identity is an expression of self-sufficiency, of the fact of being an absolute and definitive character which no-one, as it seems, would be able to question. Western philosophy has never developed beyond these findings and, even in periods of fighting ontologism, it fought for better *being*, for a harmony between us and the world or for improvement of our own *being*, Levinas argues.[43] Its ideal of peace and balance assumes self-sufficiency of *being*. And nowadays this is the case with us, postmodern people, 'dormant' in our petit bourgeoisie.

Justice as an Unexpected Reality

From the point of view of the Baumanian 'postmodernity dream' one could suggest making at the outset an attempt at healing the category of self-sufficiency from the 'dormancy', at least to some extent. The proposal to do so can be put forward by drawing on Kołakowski's lecture entitled *Sprawiedliwość* [Justice].[44] Kołakowski considers the notion of justice as reality in this work and advances a valuable argument for this book.

In order to provide an adequate explanation thereof, one should go back with Kołakowski to the times of Aristotle's *Nicomachean Ethics* in which justice

41 *Ibidem*, p. 8.

42 *Ibidem*, pp. 8–9.

43 *Ibidem*, pp. 9–13.

44 L. Kołakowski, *Mini wykłady o maxi sprawach* [*Mini-lectures on maxi-issues*] … , pp. 260–266.

is frequently viewed simply as a general name for moral good. Thus, being a respectable and just man was synonymous with behaving in compliance with a moral code and was a synonym of just actions. As Kołakowski posits in his lecture, in such an all-embracing meaning the idea of justice is still of little use since moral codes tend to vary (supplementing my own examples with instances of Kołakowski:

> here is a call to pardon and there there is a requirement for revenge; here is access to knowledge and there there is restriction of ownership resembling feudalism; here one is allowed to murder political opponents and there one is forbidden; here one receives free medicine for HIV and there one has to purchase it).[45]

Since we have no precise knowledge of what, how much and to whom is owed (or 'how little' is owed) we cannot make full use of the ancient principle: to give each his due. If, in the end, we are to divide it, then in compliance with which justice? Kołakowski asks. Distributive (concerning distribution of goods) or maybe redistributive (where goods constitute anti-goods, namely punishments and no access)? Justice cannot also be defined so that each good would be exchanged for its equivalent. Kołakowski states that the idea of justice cannot demand from the Individual an equal treatment of all people, without favouring in any way his relatives, friends or loved ones.

If I did that – Kołakowski argues – I would be a monster. I am free, with respect to my feelings, to grant different people privileges [assuming that everyone is free to do this] unless it refers to such relations in which the law, with its duty of impartiality, imposes some obligations. And so we consider it inappropriate for a lay judge or a judge to participate in a case in which his brother is a defendant … We assume therefore [and I think rightly so] that each person is suspected of granting, when he can, unjust privileges to people he favours.[46]

This remarkable Polish philosopher claims in the end that there is no metaphysics of justice or pathos of Antigone.[47] Yet the world insists with the full force of the bureaucracy involved in politics and economy for the Individual to be above all just and that it is justice which forms the foundations of everything and so, presumably, of that which the world demands from the Individual.

What is it, then, that the world demands from the Individual?[48] What else can the world demand from a self-sufficient bourgeois, from a self-sufficient Individual? What more can the world want in postmodernity? Or is there

45 *Ibidem*, p. 261.

46 *Ibidem*, pp. 262–266.

47 *Ibidem*, p. 265.

48 See also with regard to justice as a planetary issue and liquid modern life and its fears: Z. Bauman, *Liquid Times* … , pp. 5–26.

something that the Individual may offer to the world?[49] It turns out that what 'the spirit of the world', according to Kołakowski, expects from the Individual is not justice as foundation in postmodern reality, in whatever sense we would like to describe, present or understand it. In Kołakowski's opinion, what we need most as contemporary people are 'such values which could not be derived from justice'.[50] As Kołakowski asserts:

> But what the spirit of the world truly expects from us is not justice at all but kindness to neighbours, friendship and mercy, in other words such values which cannot be derived from justice. In this regard, as the doctrine of Christianity teaches us, we become like God. Since God, as they usually say, does not treat us with justice in mind but he acts on love without any rules. As no-one, the doctrine preaches, can have such merits to earn eternal redemption in a just manner; it suffices to say this for it to regarded as common knowledge. Extreme trends of Christianity of Augustinian provenance even asserted that, if God ruled in accordance with justice, we all would be in hell with no exception as we all deserve eternal condemnation. Even if we are not advocates of such extreme statements, it stands to reason that eternal redemption cannot be a just payment for our even greater but still finite merits. Thus God is not just but merciful. Let us also be like this, paying no heed to justice, as here is good advice.[51]

Excendence of Levinas as a Category of Thinking and a Promise of a Moral Attitude in Postmodernity

As Levinas points out in his pioneering and brilliant *On Escape*: 'A creative process is never completed with an approving acceptance of its work'.[52] In this way he notices the limitations of the philosophy of being. Moreover, he condemns it and contrasts it with the category of escape. Levinasian escape characterizes the fact that our fundamental aim is getting out, leaving, going beyond and, to be more precise, the very process of going beyond (beyond patterns of thought). This

---

49 See also human solidarity perceived as 'other side of justice' (J. Habermas). See also in this context cited by B. Wojciechowski in *Interkulturowe prawo karne* … , p. 272: J. Habermas, 'Justice and Solidarity: On the Discussion Concerning Stage 6', in: T.E. Wren (ed.), *The Moral Domain: Essays in the Ongoing Discussion between Philosophy and Social Science* (The MIT Press, Cambridge, MA 1990), pp. 224–251.

50 L. Kołakowski, *Mini wykłady o maxi sprawach* [*Mini-lectures on maxi-issues*] … , p. 266.

51 *Ibidem*, p. 266.

52 E. Levinas, *O Uciekaniu* [*On Escape*] (Wydawnictwo Instytutu Filozofii i Socjologii PAN, Warszawa 2007), p. 12.

experience can be described by the term *evasion*, taken from contemporary literary criticism, which means slipping away, breaking free, separating oneself, escaping.[53]

This category of thinking, as Levinas emphasizes, should be clearly differentiated from renewal or creation. A unique Levinasian motif constitutes here a unique motif of a proposal to leave *being* and pursue an escape. This structure characterizes a need of something which cannot be described in terms other than by a neologism: the need of excendence [from the French *excendance*] – as a need to escape. In the need to escape, *being* does not seem to be a mere obstacle which has to be overcome by free thought. *Being* fails to be a stiff structure either, a structure which by the threat of routine forces us to make the effort of originality.[54] The need to escape to us personifies a place rather like a prison, from which one has to break out. However everyday or epoch-making, becoming constitutes no opposite of being at all. This remarkable philosopher of the twentieth century considers it as a particular being ahead of oneself [*au devant de soi*] characterized by being in a continuous motion. The momentum itself is thus creative and overwhelming.[55]

The need of excendence leads us to the essence of philosophy.[56] As Migasiński emphasizes, the experience of the need to escape allows us to put forward the problem of *being* anew and to discover a disease of a civilization in the attachment to the problem, a civilization which cannot break free from an overwhelming power of factitude.[57] It is the need that forces us to pose the following questions according to Levinas: Is excendence possible in our postmodern civilization and how would it happen? What characterizes an ideal of happiness, of human dignity and of what is social which excendence could promise?[58] An attempt at responding to these questions will be made in the Epilogue at the end of this book, although responses to them constitute a primary motif present in the whole text and thus may be unveiled in different parts of it.

An analysis of the structure seems indispensable at this point. A crucial assumption, according to Levinas, is that the need is not exclusively a shortage. In the structure of the need there exists something Other than the shortage, much more than the shortage itself. Levinasian need turns us towards something Other than ourselves. It constitutes an insufficiency of our being in the world. The need conceptualized in this way presses us to seek shelter in something other than

53 J. Migasinski, 'Posłowie' [Afterword] in: E. Levinas, *O Uciekaniu* [*On Escape*] (Wydawnictwo Instytutu Filozofii i Socjologii PAN, Warszawa 2007), p. 12.

54 E. Levinas, *O Uciekaniu* [*On Escape*] … , pp. 12–13.

55 M.B. Smith, *Toward the Outside. Concepts and Themes in Emmanuel Levinas* (Duquesne University Press 2005), pp. 11–20.

56 A. Peperzak, *To The Other: An Introduction to the Philosophy of Emmanuel Levinas* (Purde University Press, West Lafayette Indiana 1993), see Foreword and pp. 39–40 on truth, totality, infinity and being.

57 J. Migasinski, 'Posłowie' [Afterword] in: E. Levinas, *O Uciekaniu* [*On Escape*] (Wydawnictwo Instytutu Filozofii i Socjologii PAN, Warszawa 2007), pp. 41–47.

58 E. Levinas, *O Uciekaniu* [*On Escape*] … , pp. 14–15.

the shelter. It is not right that within it (within the psychology of the need) one interprets too quickly the insufficiency of the need as the insufficiency of being, Levinas claims. In consequence, one assumes a certain kind of flawed metaphysics in which the need is characterized *a priori* as emptiness in the world, where what is obvious is identical to the wholeness.[59] Levinas argues that this identification poses a threat to each thought which could not distinguish between the existant and the existence and which attributes to one of them what would make sense solely with reference to the other.[60]

Another assumption significant to the structural analysis of the need is the notion of its urgency. The need becomes urgent only when it becomes suffering. Levinas points here to feeling bad as a particular type of suffering. An original metaphor of feeling bad is utilized to point out that the need is of a dynamic rather than a static character. The need reveals itself as a refusal to be in a particular state, as an effort to leave an unbearable (unacceptable) situation. A particular character of the situation involves an unspecified aim of this leaving. Levinas describes this as a positive characterization. The willingness to leave is not complemented by the knowledge of where to go. Therefore, it is ignorance that defines the essence of this drive. There exist needs in which there is a lack of awareness of a defined object which could satisfy it. The needs remain in the stage of feeling bad, which is overcome by a state closer to liberation rather than to satisfaction. However, this is not always the case. It is usually something which influences us from outside, that opens for us the knowledge of objects which could satisfy our need. It is worth stressing that it stimulates pondering on the value of such objects.[61] Even if awareness is not developed considerably, it still remains an awareness of the object. It creates a protection over our being by stating what is beyond us and what is outside. Bearing in mind the above-mentioned assertions, Levinas draws attention to a problem which remains to be resolved. He poses the question whether the fundamental aim of the need is being properly acknowledged, whether satisfaction of the need is precisely responsible for the anxiety of feeling bad.[62] The Levinasian need to escape from being is an anonymous burden that may stem from various sources. It might have been at that time that Levinas had an imprecise vision which crystallized into words at subsequent stages of his thinking, that beyond being in human life resides good.[63] As Levinas writes: 'We discern in the phenomenon of feeling bad a certain demand … which can be superior: a kind of dead burden deep in our being, a burden which no satisfaction can relieve us from'.[64]

The suffering of the need to escape does not point at the shortage which should be quickly compensated. In this light it does not entail our being finite beings

59 M.B. Smith, *Toward the Outside* … , p. 11.

60 E. Levinas, *O Uciekaniu* [*On Escape*] … , pp. 18–19.

61 *Ibidem*, p. 19.

62 *Ibidem*, p. 19.

63 J. Migasinski, 'Posłowie' [Afterword] in: E. Levinas … , pp. 41–47.

64 E. Levinas, *O Uciekaniu* [*On Escape*] … , p. 20.

(a being which fails to satisfy his needs dies). In Levinas's view, these undisputed claims derive from external sources. This is the case since the need (within itself) does not involve the aim. The need relies on what is present. The need remains thus and is characteristic of what manifests at the outset of a potential future. Levinas strongly emphasizes, however, that mere satisfaction of the need does not remove the need at all.[65] Needs constantly regenerate themselves. Satisfaction fails to alleviate the need. The need is thus of a perpetual and dynamic character, limitless in the future.[66]

Following this thinking, Levinas attempts to justify the thesis that the need expresses the presence of our being rather than its insufficiency. The need is connected with the refusal to be in a particular state (Levinas compares this state to the situation in which we feel nauseous) and the effort to escape it is in a way completed. As Levinas continues, one is here and one can do nothing about it, add nothing to the fact that we have been completely uncovered, that everything has come to an end (this is the experience of pure being mentioned at the outset of Levinas's analysis). What constitutes a Levinasian feature of an ultimate situation is the fact that 'one-can-do-nothing-about-it'. The pointlessness of any action shows that it is high time to leave it. Levinas stresses that the experience of pure being is simultaneously an experience of internal antagonism and escape which suggests itself. Levinasian need is not aimed at a total complementation of a finite being – at satisfaction – but at liberation and escape. Levinasian being is imperfect as a being and not because it is finite.[67] Being is thus imperfect as it is filled with the need to escape from itself.[68]

Bearing in mind the Levinasian structure analysis of the need, it seems appropriate to make an assumption that 'inadequacy of satisfaction towards the need' becomes a pivotal category, bringing us closer to the response concerned with the ideal of happiness and of human dignity. As Levinas himself states, the issue of every man gains its importance owing to this inadequacy.[69] An exemplary Individual feels the need to escape. The need is the insufficiency of his being in the world. The need of the Individual is not a shortage for him. What there is constitutes 'something-which-is-insufficient'. This is the reason why the Individual escapes. The very experience of insufficiency by the Individual is explicit and overwhelming. The Individual has no knowledge of where to go in order to name the insufficiency. The Individual has no knowledge on the issue. What the Individual emphasizes is the insufficiency. The need expresses the presence of our being, Levinas asserts. The need of the Individual expresses the presence of 'something-which-is-insufficient'. He realizes 'something-which-is-insufficient'. The Individual becomes present via this activity and this observation.

65 *Ibidem*, p. 20.
66 M.B. Smith, *Toward the Outside* … , p. 11.
67 *Ibidem*, pp. 20–33.
68 J. Migasinski, 'Posłowie' [Afterword] in: E. Levinas … , pp. 45–46.
69 E. Levinas, *O Uciekaniu* [*On Escape*] … , p. 20.

The Individual *is* therefore the Individual who 'needs' to escape. He begins his calling in 'insufficiency-of-something'. His calling is, therefore, thoroughly original and unique. In the same way Levinasian inadequacy of each Individual becomes original.[70]

Taking into consideration Levinasian excendence as a category of thinking, one could suggest perceiving such excendence in postmodernity as a moral attitude, which could be complemented by introducing one of the above-mentioned thoughts of Ingarden, Kołakowski and Bauman. Firstly, Ingarden's 'Human Reality layer in the world' assigns, via a moral attitude to certain things or issues, a particular meaning and momentousness which is unlike them as things or issues of Nature and to which they are not entitled. Owing to this fact, the Individual is not a man without a need; he feels significant as he is chosen and unique in his mission.[71] The Individual feels a noble need which lies within his nature as a man. The Individual will attain full satisfaction if he succeeds in creating values characterized by his otherwise excendent personality. He joins, in this way, the past with the present and the future. In these circumstances a man develops, changes, transforms and improves. Secondly, excendence may be viewed in postmodernity as a Baumanian moral attitude on which depends the particular power with which we can separate ourselves as a particular moral community from the common indifference[72] towards developing postmodern solidarity.[73] Excendence will be, in a way, responsible for this power and its functionality. Thirdly, excendence may constitute a moral attitude characterized by mercy in Kołakowski's view. It serves as an example of such a moral attitude which cannot be derived, in Kołakowski's opinion, from justice.[74] Thus mercy (which I will not fail to call the 'missing care of contemporary postmodern people'), and not justice, is to be taken into account by the Individual in his relation to the Neighbour.

In Løgstrup's view the radical demand causes moral and cognitive effort on the part of the Individual because he takes a unique responsibility for an 'active utopia' character as a searching responsibility and thus such that in its deep care desires to design what is required of it by the demand. Taking this into consideration it is useful to introduce mercy in the form of 'missing care of postmodern people' to the notion of searching responsibility. This does not entail that the Individual is to replace justice with 'care', and that the notion of justice disappears from this book. Nothing could be further from the truth. It only entails that: 'we pay no heed to justice' (not too much heed), as Kołakowski argues, particularly in the case of

70 M.B. Smith, *Toward the Outside* … , pp. 11–16.

71 R. Ingarden, *Książeczka o człowieku* [*Little Book About Man*] … , pp. 23–24.

72 L. Kołakowski, *Mini wykłady o maxi sprawach* [*Mini-lectures on maxi-issues*] … , p. 42.

73 Z. Bauman, 'Wywiad z Baumanem' [An interview with Bauman] … , pp. 19–29.

74 L. Kołakowski, *Mini wykłady o maxi sprawach* [*Mini-lectures on maxi-issues*] … , p. 266.

the question of what the spirit of the world expects from the Individual, bearing in mind excendent thinking.[75]

Baumanian Moral Attitude in Asymmetry and Thinking Towards Unilateralism

Let us proceed to the category of moral attitude in postmodernity. In Bauman's terms there exist tenets which raise no doubt when they are taken at face value. Nevertheless, when one intends to inspect them they are no longer self-evident, on the contrary they raise serious doubt. This is the case with a tenet that morality can be solely 'collective'. We find it easy to merge single (various 'I', various 'Individuals') moral selves into an all-embracing 'we'. In this way the moral 'I' is reduced to the singular of the ethical 'we'. As a consequence of our behaviour the ethical 'we' consists of a number of Individuals replaceable with a number of 'she' or 'he'. Thus moral judgement expressed in the first person will retain its moral value if expressed in the second and third person. What follows is that all Individuals grouped under 'we' can replace one another and become a sum, a derivative of digits, a derivative of counting, the plain Plural of 'I'. Morality will thus be perceived as collective, for example, as a result of authoritative legislation or as an unintentional but equally enormous influence of a 'position', a policy or an economy.[76]

If one intends to follow the Baumanian thought and apply ideas of supraindividual totality to the field of morality, one should view it in a more dynamic and less aggregate way. This entails that our supraindividual totality confronted with morality should form a totality consisting of: 'orders made, received and performed by moral subjects for the reason that *each of these subjects is irreplaceable and* relations between them are asymmetrical'.[77] Each of these subjects is unique. Importantly, we assume a moral attitude before we enter into a relation and not during its realization. Definitional features of Baumanian moral attitude include such a moral attitude which *happens before* a relation is entered into and, as a result, is of a unilateral and not reciprocal character, a unilateral character that is irreversible.[78]

In Bauman's words:

> The 'we' signifying collectivity of a moral character is not the Plural of 'I' but denotes an intricate structure combining elements unequal to one another. In a moral relation I and the Other cannot replace each other and thus we cannot 'be

75 *Ibidem*, p. 266.

76 Z. Bauman, *Etyka ponowoczesna* [*Postmodern Ethics*] (Wydawnictwo Aletheia, Warszawa 2012), pp. 72–73.

77 *Ibidem*, p. 74.

78 *Ibidem*, p. 74.

> added to each other' to have aggregate 'we'. All 'duties' and 'rules' conceivable in a moral relation are addressed exclusively to me, bind exclusively me, form me and exclusively me as the only, unique 'I'. And responsibility addressed to me and borne by me, is of a morally unique character. However, it may lose this character immediately if, in an attempt to reverse the situation, I shoulder it on the Other.[79]

Consequently, regardless of the fact of whether the Other is always for me, I am always for the Other. In other words, I will act as if I were the only Individual willing to assume and perform a particular duty. It is of no importance to me if the Other will return it. I do not think in the categories of reciprocity but in the categories of unilateralism. I assume and perform a particular duty without analysing if others with respect to yet others behave likewise.[80]

And, thus, symmetry and reciprocity are disposed of at this point and are replaced by source asymmetry[81] and unilateralism (recurrently criticized in the philosophy of Levinas).[82] It is, however, this asymmetry and unilateralism which allow the moral attitude of the Individual as the 'I' belonging to moral collectivity to become unique and irreversible. In conclusion, it is not universality but uniqueness and irreversibility of my responsibility which constitute the cornerstone of the moral attitude.[83]

Individuals of an Excendence Practitioner and Moral Collectivity

Petit bourgeois of contemporary times endowed with the category of self-sufficiency will easily allow single moral selves (various 'I', various 'Individuals') to merge into the all-embracing 'we'. But a man practising excendence (for the purposes of this book I suggest creating the construct of the excendent Individual) believing in particular 'being ahead of oneself' becomes an entirely irreplaceable

79 *Ibidem*, p. 77.

80 E. Levinas, *Humanism of the Other* (Fata Morgana, University of Illinois 2006). See Introduction by A. Cohen.

81 See also about the need for a philosophical perspective in an asymmetric world: E. Gerle, *Features of Contemporary Globalization and Ethical Challenges they Pose to Universal Ethics. Globalization with Many Faces* in: Bexell, G. and D.-E. Andersson (eds), *Universal Ethics. Perspectives and Proposals from Scandinavian Scholars* (Martinus Nijhoff Publishers, Kluwer Law International, The Hague/London/New York 2002), pp. 176–178.

82 D. Kreft, 'Dialog podstawa więzi międzyludzkiej w filozofii Bubera i Bartha' [Dialogue as a foundation of an interpersonal bond in the philosophy of Buber and Barth] in: S. Kruszyńska, K. Bembennek and I. Krupecka (eds), *Dialog. Idea i Doświadczenie* [Dialogue. Idea and Experience] (Wydawnictwo Uniwersytetu Gdanskiego, Gdansk 2011), p. 56.

83 Z. Bauman, *Etyka ponowoczesna* [*Postmodern Ethics*] … , p. 79.

subject. A man practising excendence – the Individual – in this way faces his internal dilemma and takes anxiety for something significant and indispensable. Such a man accepts unpredictability. He is anxious. The excendent Individual overcomes the self-sufficiency of himself and, by doing so, overcomes the self-sufficiency of *being*. He concurrently understands that he is a man whose demand is to be ahead of himself, to be in a continuous motion in which he combines the past, the present and the future.

The excendent Individual can therefore reconcile with himself. Consequently, he fails to focus solely on being insured against the unknown brought about by time and the course of events. Such a man believes that momentum is overwhelming and creative. His motion becomes unique. My 'I' as an excendent 'I' possesses greater responsibility than all the other 'I'.[84] The Individual practising excendence does not expect reciprocity and demands from himself more than from Others.[85] He does not expect the motion from Others. It is the Individual which is to be ahead of himself, it is to improve himself in this way. The Others are likely to do the same. Or possibly they do not. But the excendent Individual fails to seek norms which enable precise examination if his responsibility matches his particular moral attitude. It is of critical importance that 'I' practising excendence seeks balance. He accepts the asymmetry of his behaviour as the asymmetry is creative, unique, other, his own, maybe greater and fuller than the one shown in any norms or 'positions', whether political or economic. Consequently, it seems appropriate to suggest at this point that, if all excendent Individuals practise excendence in this way, then moral collectivity in Baumanian terms (as opposed to contractual partnership) can be realized in our postmodern times.

Joint Filling of Time and Levinas's Other Beyond 'I-dentical'

The practise of excendence itself allows *being* to follow a new path, even at the risk of redefinition of certain notions, which, as Levinas writes, for common sense and wisdom of nations seem to be most self-evident.[86] It seems that the 'redefinition' mentioned by Levinas is intimately connected with moral foundations previously derived from the thought of Ingarden, Bauman and Kołakowski.

At this stage it would be advisable to suggest proceeding with observations in an attempt to respond to the following question: How (in what manner) is excendence proposed by Levinas to happen? It is not true that most significant to a man would be his *being*. Levinas believes that there has to be something

84 E. Levinas, *Etyka i nieskończony* [*Ethics and Infinity*]. *Rozmowy z Philippe'em Nemo* [*Interviews with Philippe Nemo*] (Wydawnictwo Panstwowej Akademii Teologicznej, Krakow 1991), p. 56.

85 E. Levinas, *Humanism of the Other* (Fata Morgana, University of Illinois 2006). See Introduction by A. Cohen.

86 E. Levinas, *O Uciekaniu* [*On Escape*] ... , p. 39.

considerably more important and more characteristic behind the question of *being*. This eludes the definition of ontology. Levinas argues that there is more to the effort of philosophy. In his opinion this *something more* (and which Heidegger failed to discern and develop) is the anxiety for the Others.[87] This very anxiety possesses a characteristic power to move thoughts of *being* to the background. The anxiety involves conviction of responsibility prominent in various theoretical approaches but always going beyond *being*, that is the desire for infinity.

What, however, holds promise of transferring thoughts into a different dimension is Plato's giving precedence to the idea of good over the idea of being, Descartes' assertion that without the idea of infinity a man would never be able to comprehend his temporal limitation and Kantian questions of what I should do and what I can expect. These questions demonstrate a rational hope of being in another way. Being is the desire for good. The hope does not make us immortal, though it destroys human time. The hope unveils something characteristic, namely: the possibility of joint filling of time.[88] What follows excendence happens by joint filling of time. The joint filling of time is based on a continuous anxiety of the Individual for the Other and consistently for a contact (a contact in the form of the Speech, which will be elaborated on in the subsequent parts of this book) of the Individual with what is Other.

It seems that moral collectivity will be realized fully if particular Individuals notice two components: metaphysical and ethical. Metaphysical, because such is the relation of a human being to infinity, the desire for infinity does not leave us destroying all attempts of totalization, enclosing oneself in a totality.[89] Ethical, as this book discusses the relation to the Other, an asymmetrical relation since the Other is concurrently the master and the suffering for whom one is responsible, as Skarga analyses.[90] Such relation provides conditions for the idea of infinity. Such relation should be distinguished from the symmetry of a dialogue where the relation I–You is equivalent, this is a relation of partnership with no room for the idea of infinity.[91]

Importantly, the Other is not someone who participates in the common totality. The Other is not someone who participates in what is known to the Individual (what 'I' knows). The Other is beyond 'I-dentical', beyond this horizon within which 'I' lives and creates. The Other cannot be embraced, fathomed out,

---

87 B. Skarga, Wstęp do [Foreword to]: E. Levinas, *Całość i nieskończoność* [*Totality and Infinity*]. *Esej o zewnętrzności* [*An Essay on Exteriority*] (Wydawnictwo Naukowe PWN, Warszawa 2012), pp. 15–16.

88 *Ibidem*, p. 16.

89 A. Peperzak, *To The Other: An Introduction to the Philosophy of Emmanuel Levinas* (Purde University Press, West Lafayette Indiana 1993), see Foreword and pp. 39–40 on truth, totality, infinity and being.

90 B. Skarga, Wstęp do [Foreword to]: E. Levinas … , pp. 19–20.

91 *Ibidem*, p. 21.

comprehended.[92] The Other calls on us and questions our egoism. It can be other man, God or yet other Other. The Other is completely, absolutely Other.[93] The Other is transcendent with respect to my world. But when the Other calls, I am bound by this call.[94] What is unique and what Skarga strongly emphasizes in his analysis, is that neither the Other nor I find themselves on the same plane. The Other utters as if from the heights, orders to go over oneself. Levinas believes that such heights constitute disposing of selfishness and self-complacency. Such heights involve an understanding of responsibility and the fact that no-one is able to relieve the Individual from the responsibility.[95] We encounter the Other in the epiphany of the Face. The term the Face is of significant character at this point. Levinas argues that the Face is not power, it is an authority. Authorities very frequently have no power. The Face is an opposite in itself, it is no mask. Levinas utilizes the term of the Face because he intends to liberate himself and us from the habit of considering the Other as a being regardless of the fact of it being an other man, or a perfect, divine being. This is of no consequence.[96] The Other is someone beyond being. 'L'Autre' in the neuter – the Other – refers not to the absolute Otherness of other man, but to the Otherness of the world (which is relative) or otherness in general, not defined yet as relative or absolute.[97] Depending on the context this is either a broader or narrower notion than the notion of personal Otherness or an opposite notion.[98] Being is not important in the ethical relation (this is an ethical relation between the Face of the Other–the Individual). I cannot, therefore, attribute the Face with such or such qualities. I cannot get to know it or describe it in this way. The Face is naked and as a naked Face it speaks to me. The Face fails to appear as a qualitative datum which forms a synthesis of images of the others encountered in specific experiences (as one can experience the presence of another man but not see his face). The Face inspires, provides food for thought. However it is not thinking of something or someone. It is a particular thinking: thinking for, thus the thinking which is not knowledge but surrender. The surrender calls into question me, that is the Individual himself. The Face raises responsibility in the Individual.[99]

In such a joint filling of time the collective morality becomes an achievement of a number of moral Individuals. But the excendent Individual is based on a moral

92 E. Levinas, *Humanism of the Other* (Fata Morgana, University of Illinois 2006). See Introduction by A. Cohen. See also E. Levinas, *Time and the Other* (Duguesue University Press 1990), pp. 18–32.

93 A. Peperzak, *To The Other* ... , pp. 39–45.

94 E. Levinas, *Humanism of the Other* (Fata Morgana, University of Illinois 2006). See Introduction by A. Cohen.

95 J. Derrida, *Adieu to Emmanuel Levinas (Meridian: Crossing Aesthetics)* (Stanford University Press, Stanford 1999), pp. 4–30.

96 B. Skarga, Wstęp do [Foreword to]: E. Levinas ... , pp. 20–21.

97 E. Levinas, *Humanism of the Other* (Fata Morgana, University of Illinois 2006). See Introduction by A. Cohen.

98 B. Skarga, Wstęp do [Foreword to]: E. Levinas ... , p. 38.

99 *Ibidem*, p. 21.

impulse frequently defined as something elusive, subjective and even capricious. One could thus pose the question: How can something so subjective serve as foundations? For a number of 'I' can behave in a moral manner on a regular basis. Does there exist a more substantial ground for this than a mere moral impulse? Such a question is a society's lack of trust in a subjective, own potential of self, the potential of a subjective, lonely 'I'. The morality of the Individual has no foundations. Morality itself is present here before freedom. The Individual is not interested in being as such. The Individual acting in compliance with a heroic order from the Other wants to be something better than being itself.[100]

As has been mentioned, excendence happens via joint filling of time. The joint filling of time is based on the continuous anxiety of the Individual for the Other and consistently for his contact with the Other. It may be this questioning of all entity which is the essence of joint filling of time. Such filling of time disturbs the peace of the spirit of being. The joint filling of time by the Individual morally excendent is fulfilled in what Bauman calls 'being condescending towards' *being* and even 'being condescending in disdain' for *being*. The Individual becomes himself (becomes himself in moral terms) when he prefers 'being for' to be marked with reciprocity 'being with'. Consequently, the Individual behaves as if *being* which stems from ontology had *nothing* significant and clear to say.[101] Tischner even states that 'I' becomes important at this stage. He even applies the notion: 'the scope of importance' of a specific 'I'.[102] Interestingly enough, the importance of the Individual becomes, what in Tischner's words, combines specificity with universality. Even when 'I' gains more and more importance it is still a unique 'I'. Tischner utilizes the metaphor of a work of art which does not cease to be specific as each work of art does not, although many admire it. The Individual is, according to Tischner, axiological in a radical sense of the word and as such is an addressee of the question and a provider of the response.[103]

The Other gives a particular heroic order to the Individual and the Individual acts as a recipient of the order.[104] This is an order overcoming human weakness and natural being enclosed in a world of one's own. Thus it is an order overcoming

---

100 A. Peperzak, *To The Other …* , see Foreword.

101 Z. Bauman, *Etyka ponowoczesna* [*Postmodern Ethics*] … , p. 110.

102 J. Tischner, *Filozofia Dramatu* [*Philosophy of Drama*] (Wydawnictwo Znak, Krakow 2012), p. 106. As Tischner writes:

> When I say I – I am a value for myself. When I hear someone telling me You – I know that I am 'important' to him and then he also becomes important to me. When I say He – I know that someone is important to me, but I am not important to him … . When I say We – I know that we are important to one another: I to you and you to me. When I say You – I know that you are important to me, as I am to you. When I say they – I know that I am not important to them, although they are important to me.

103 *Ibidem*, p. 106.

104 See also E. Levinas, *Unforseen History* (University of Illinois Press 2004). See Introduction by A. Cohen.

separation. When the Individual subordinates everything which is Other to his own world, he includes otherness in 'I-dentical'; when otherness is self-enclosed we call it the notion of separation.[105] As Levinas writes: 'The point is to replace the idea of totality which unites the philosophy of ontology, that is conceived of multiplicity, with the idea of separation based on synthesis'.[106] The separation becomes a precondition of entering into contact with the Other. It is in separation that the desire arises to enter into contact with the Other. This is then the desire to take a heroic order. The separation can even be reduced to egoism. Egoism itself is not for Levinas one of man's qualities casting a shadow over his life. This 'ontological event' of significant importance, a tearing apart of the totality which he created for himself, may only take place in egoism, where man remains alone in his loneliness a desire for the Other arises. This is a metaphysical desire.[107] However, focusing on oneself should not close receptivity to what is outside, so that in a separated being existed an openness to accept emerging Other. As Skarga rightly points out, an encounter with the Other in no negation of separation. It comes here to questioning neither the value of reason, nor knowledge, nor rational social constructs. Levinas discerned in them something which is secondary, which depends in genesis and form on social ethical contacts, unique and that could not be captured in the form of a general and all-embracing law.[108]

The project of Levinas should be treated as 'an attempt at a restructuring of metaphysics for which a fundamental experience fails to be an intentional cognitive act aimed at being or *being*, but is rather an act of separation and an intimately related to it desire of another and, through him, of infinity, thus a moral act'.[109] The Individual receives the order of heroic ethics overcoming his separation, but not necessarily negating it. In collective morality, to which I would like to return at this point, a particular 'I' would be unique recipients of a unique heroic order. Consequently, moral collectivity conceived in this way is supplemented with a Levinasian question of metaphysics of whether in being here and now we have justified our existence.[110] In other words, if we have justified our existence and, if in relation to this, we can be, we can exist 'in opposition', we can be 'in other way', can we, for instance, be without doing 'something' (for example: do not keep 'something' only to yourself) but suffering 'something' for others? In this way great Kantian questions about what I should do and what I can expect as a man are interwoven in these observations.

There is no objective 'I'. What it constitutes is: a thoroughly subjective 'I'. Subjective 'I' wants to live for the Other. The philosophy of infinity is to defend

105 B. Skarga, Wstęp do [Foreword to]: E. Levinas … , p. 21.

106 E. Levinas, *Całość i nieskończoność* [*Totality and Infinity*]. *Esej o zewnętrzności* [An Essay on Exteriority] (Wydawnictwo Naukowe PWN, Warszawa 2012), p. 352.

107 A. Peperzak, *To The Other* … , pp. 39–40 on truth, totality, infinity and being.

108 B. Skarga, Wstęp do [Foreword to]: E. Levinas … , pp. 26–29.

109 *Ibidem*, pp. 29–30.

110 J. Derrida, 'Adieu to Emmanuel Levinas …' , pp. 4–30.

this precious subjectivity. It defends it not because of its egoism, of its rebellious attitude to totality but because of the desire for infinity existing in it and inalienable, which comes from a source more than any reasoning thought does.[111] This refers to uncovering the sense of intersubjective relations and creating community which will be discussed in subsequent parts and in the Epilogue to this thesis.[112] Let us return, in the conclusion of this chapter, to the 'redefinition' mentioned by Levinas and its relations to moral attitudes previously derived from the thought of Ingarden, Bauman and Kołakowski. It seems that these 'moral attitudes' are to some extent incorporated in Levinasian question of metaphysics of whether by 'being' here and now we have justified our existence. In this way the question becomes otherwise a part of moral collectivity.

111 B. Skarga, Wstęp do [Foreword to]: E. Levinas … , p. 14.

112 *Ibidem*, pp. 14–15.

Chapter 2
Thinking from the Perspective of Excendence: Speech

Levinasian Speech and the Primary Order of Moral Collectivity

Levinasian relation to the Other is Speech. It is Speech that conditions thought, but Speech not conceived in its physical materialness but as a contact. Such Speech gives rise to meanings. Of key importance become: the role of expression in the process of language creation, an intimate connection between expression and the desire for communication with the Other and spontaneous crystallization in conversation of word meanings and senses of all objects and as a result of intelligibility. Speech becomes, in this case, the condition for thinking and functioning of a rational thought. Speech finds me, it comes to me from another man. Subsequently, Speech finds its place in my consciousness, it becomes loud there. Most importantly, owing to the fact that it resonates in my consciousness, it calls into question my consciousness. Speech is therefore an irreducible event. Speech thus fails to take place inside my consciousness.[1] By coming from outside, Speech changes the consciousness of the Individual. Due to Speech conceived in this way, the Individual already thinks in another way, maybe he thinks more completely.

Speech is a live expression, ethical openness to the Other, a response to a call. Speech 'is the presence of the Face'. As significantly and consistently emphasized by Skarga in his interpretations of Levinas, a sign is, for Levinas, a mute and blocked language. An emerging meaning is an extraordinary event, an illumination. A particular dialectic exists between *dire* and *dit* (here: the distinction between live speech which is always open [*dire*] and what was spoken, recorded in its form, recognized and in a sense dead [*dit*]; this is an explicit Bergsonian motif). *Dire* tears *dit* apart as an act of creation, but simultaneously subordinates itself to it; it is absorbed by it in order to take the form of a definition or an opinion. Thus, on an ethical plane which is constantly pivotal here, *dire* is an impulse towards the other. *Dire* is a diachrony towards *dit*, it is always in the past, the first. *Dit* is a set of moral rules and therefore a moral order. If, however, the order rejects its ethical foundations, then it may accept various forms of social being, including fascism and totalitarianism, since it cannot evaluate or distinguish between them.[2] Consequently, we live in a language and the language shapes us. Of importance in

1 E. Levinas, *Całość i nieskończoność* [*Totality and Infinity*] … , p. 241.
2 B. Skarga, *Wstęp do* [*Foreword to*]: E. Levinas … , pp. 22–23.

Speech is what is original and individual, as only then do we have the guarantee of authenticity in contact and directness of a reciprocal presentation. The Speech of Levinas is a breaking with what is agreed upon, with what there is, a detaching from patterns of thought. The Speech of Levinas in this way puts each moral collectivity in order. It seems that one can make a suggestion that Speech within this meaning may constitute a primary order of a moral collectivity.

Between Expression and Responsibility of the Philosophy of Levinas

Each excendent Individual in a moral collectivity speaks. It is worth asking: What constitutes the ethical essence of such speech or, in other words, the function of speech in a moral collectivity? It seems that one can begin responding to the question with an assumption that a characteristic feature of such moral collectivity will be a relation between expression and responsibility inspired by the thought of Levinas. An expression introduced to the world by the metaphor of a face fails to unfold the weakness of the Individual's authority but undermines the very ability of the authority as such. The Face talks to the Individual and invites him to the relation, which has nothing in common with authority or the desire for authority.[3] The expression fails to give us the inwardness of the Other.[4] In the expression manifests being. It calls the Individual in such a manner that the Individual cannot ignore the call. Through manifestation of being in the expression, an act of intensification of good in the Individual takes place and not a limitation of his freedom.[5] Following Levinas further, one can refer to the notion of happening of expression, which involves the appearance of the Face that establishes for the Individual a beginning of understanding and becomes itself the 'beginning in its own right' – it becomes a principle which orders in an unconditional way.[6]

The principle has a function of an order here. Levinasian expression fails to be a ready-made formula made up of numerous segments. The Individual receives no parts in expression, parts which are temporarily at a distance from totality. What the Individual obtains via expression is what precedes, what is prior to all acts of coordination of parts noticeable to an outside observer.[7] Expression is here a particular function of the word, where the word goes beyond the level of usual activity, the word renounces the function of an act or a representation, but its primary function, its centre, constitutes expression. The word thus goes beyond the level of usual activity as in the depths of the word is an omnipresent expression.[8] One cannot walk away from the Face, one cannot leave it. It is the Face that is

3 E. Levinas, *Całość i nieskończoność* [*Totality and Infinity*] … , p. 232.
4 *Ibidem*, p. 238.
5 *Ibidem*, pp. 235–236.
6 A. Peperzak, *To The Other* … , pp. 39–40 on truth, totality, infinity and being.
7 E. Levinas, *Całość i nieskończoność* [*Totality and Infinity*] … , p. 237.
8 *Ibidem*, pp. 237–238.

Speech to the Individual. The first word is commitment and no inwardness permits avoiding the commitment. The excendent Individual can neither walk away from the Face, nor leave it. It is only such Speech, marked by commitment in this way, which becomes Speech compelling the Individual to conversation. This is how the responsibility of the Individual looks with respect to the Face.[9]

Words are important in the encounter, they can convey values; thanks to which good manifests itself and it exists in each encounter. The relation which connects me with the Other is a relation of 'teaching' and 'ruling'. A precondition of such encounter occurrence is for someone to talk to me. The encounter occurs in the language.[10] Levinas writes on the encounter in the following terms: 'There is a speech which obligates a conversation, which is the beginning of a discourse longed for by rationalism, which is a "force" persuading even "those who do not listen" and which therefore lays foundations for genuine universalism of the reason'.[11] Due to such relation with the Other, the Individual gains something which has not been in him before – something unique and odd.[12] Consequently, what is of importance to Speech itself, is that the Other is not outrageous to the Individual, but is something which Levinas calls the first teaching, the first rational preaching or even a condition of all teaching.[13] As Levinas states: 'To think it is to have the idea of Infinity, to think it is to be taught. Rational thinking refers to teaching'.[14] The Individual's demand is to think rationally. And rational thinking refers to teaching, to the first lesson. Only by being 'equipped' in this manner, does the Individual start a conversation. The very conversation, however, is, according to Levinas, a prose which inspires speakers, they are carried away by it – it is breaking and starting, tearing the rhythm apart and so on.[15]

It seems that what occurs between expression and responsibility determines to a great extent the essence of Speech. This 'in between' functions not only as Levinasian relation, but also as a space. The space will turn into a conversation. The conversation will thus become a continuation of the first lesson, the first teaching. The continuation is a responsibility of the excendent Individual. His responsibility is in this regard exclusive and unique and such should be a conversation. In this

9 J. Derrida, 'Adieu to Emmanuel Levinas ...', pp. 4–27.

10 A. Kubiak, *Emmanuel Levinas – prologomena do instrukcji obslugi* [*Emmanuel Levinas – Prologue to a User Manual*] (Polska Siec Filozoficzna, 2001) www.psf.org.plpublication.php?pid=196, last visited August 2012. See also: B. Karpińska-Musiał, 'Czy można przezwycieżyć sokratejską aporię w postmodernistycznej wizji dialogu kulturowego?' [Can Socratean aporia be overcome in the postmodern vision of a cultural dialogue?] in: S. Kruszyńska, K. Bembennek, I. Krupecka (eds), *Dialog. Idea i Doświadczenie* [*Dialogue. Idea and Experience*] (Wydawnictwo Uniwersytetu Gdanskiego, Gdansk 2011), pp. 50–51.

11 E. Levinas, *Całość i nieskończoność* [*Totality and Infinity*] ..., p. 236.

12 *Ibidem*, p. 240.

13 *Ibidem*, pp. 239–240.

14 *Ibidem*, p. 240.

15 *Ibidem*, p. 239.

way a conversation of a unique character commences. Uniqueness and a brilliant non-repeatability of such a conversation lie in the fact that the excendent Individual by itself gives the conversation a rhythm and is responsible for this rhythm in the spirit of the first teaching. The excendent Individual becomes responsible for such a continuation of the word. This raises a question: how can one depict such continuation best?

Socratean Aporecity and Identity of Autonomous Subject

Socrates maintained that the form of communication between the Individual and any Other is always aporetic, i.e. impassable. In this way he expressed an assertion that a speaker who 'knows that he knows nothing' before starting a dialogue, always finishes the dialogic relation being enriched in some way. On finishing the communication he simply knows more, irrespective of the fact if conclusions or a specific portion of knowledge or achieved consensus is at issue. That is not to say that he was not wise before the relation. He was the one who knew that 'he knows nothing'. Thus, as Karpińska-Musiał rightly points out, Socrates might have been thinking not so much of reaching an agreement, as a classical motif of a dialogue, but rather of a shift in perspective. Since the aim of a dialogue is not a victory or an advantage but building a relation with another man and a shift in a point of view as a point of thinking.[16] Tischner states that, thanks to an intentional openness, a world of things is manifest; thanks to dialogic openness the Other emerges in front of 'I'.[17] For Buber, for example, a dialogue with another man is above all the very situation of encounter, meeting face-to-face with another person as a person: 'A conversation requires no voice, not even a gesture, speaking may resign from everything which is perceived with senses and still remain speaking'.[18] A contemporary man has divided his life into two spheres: a sphere of intuition and a sphere of feelings, of private life. However, in reality in both spheres one needs the relation I–You.[19]

16 B. Karpińska-Musiał, 'Czy można przezwyciężyć sokratejską aporię w postmodernistycznej wizji dialogu kulturowego?' [Can Socratean aporia be overcome in the postmodern vision of a cultural dialogue?], in: S. Kruszyńska et al., *Dialog* [*Dialogue*] … , pp. 50–51.

17 J. Tischner, *Filozofia Dramatu* [*Philosophy of Drama*] … , pp. 8–9.

18 J. Doktor, Wstęp [Foreword] in: M. Buber, *Ja i Ty, Wybór pism filozoficznych* [*I and You: a Selection of Philosophical Writings*], selected and translated by J. Doktor who wrote the Foreword (Warsaw 1992) p. 27 as cited in: K. Rosner, 'Dialog jako temat filozofii wspołczesnej: Buber, Gadamer, Habermas' [Dialogue as a Subject of Modern Philosophy: Buber, Gadamer, Habermas] in: S. Kruszyńska et al., *Dialog* [*Dialogue*] … , p. 19.

19 K. Rosner, 'Dialog jako temat filozofii wspołczesnej: Buber, Gadamer, Habermas' [Dialogue as a Subject of Modern Philosophy: Buber, Gadamer, Habermas] in: S. Kruszyńska et al., *Dialog* [*Dialogue*] … , p. 19.

Relation with the Face involves immediately taking responsibility for the Face in the 'ethical' manner. The Individual is therefore expected to be inactive, passively open and to anticipate no reciprocity. Sensitivity, discussed by Levinas, signifies, apart from openness to the Other, passivity more passive than the passivity of experience. It is a patient passivity, it is a passivity of not anticipating payment, it is a passivity waiting for the orders of the Other. Its sense entails a non-disturbance of listening to the Other and a fulfilment of a mission in relation to him. Following the course of Karpińska-Musiał's analysis it can be noticed that it is precisely in the mission that the identity of a free, autonomous subject is realized.[20] Thus, it is in the mission of passivity that an identity of an excendent, autonomous Individual is realized. I concur with the opinion of Levinas in the assumption of separation of subjects entering into relations, their disconnection, autonomy stretched to the pain of egoism so that, by being aware of oneself with 'ethical' peace, the subjects look at the Other's face and his communicative behaviour. Only then will we treat the hardships of reaching an agreement with peace and hope. It seems that a concurrent need for autonomy to know and a need for knowledge to become autonomous testify to the uniqueness of a mission of the Individual.

However, Levinas claims that a subject has always been endowed with anxiety which will mark him forever. As Korzeniowski writes: 'He [subject] is disturbed by the Other from the outset and has never had time to rest from the anxiety. The more he is unsettled, the less he feels safe, the more he is capable of serving others'.[21] Nonetheless, Levinas says that it is the sensitivity of a subject which causes the anxiety, and anxiety at the same time is a condition of attaining autonomy (equal to rising against the system that is Totality). Anxiety has to exist, since it proves that a man is composed of a soul and body – and Levinas omits to neglect this dualism. Passivity is thus needed here as a patience to discover the essence of the Other. The Individual is, therefore, with respect to the Other nothing other than a maximum of feasible and passive in his kind of participation.[22] The monologous existence of himself fails to go beyond the boundaries of his own self, of his 'I'.[23]

Passivity in Levinasian terms may also be conceived as an 'outward' motion and Levinas himself regards it as patience. He conceives of passivity (or patience) as coming to terms with the fact that a return to 'I-dentical' (thus to me

20 B. Karpińska-Musiał, 'Czy można przezwyciężyć sokratejską aporię w postmodernistycznej wizji dialogu kulturowego?' [Can Socratean aporia be overcome in the postmodern vision of a cultural dialogue?], in: S. Kruszyńska et al., *Dialog* [*Dialogue*] … , p. 48.

21 B. Korzeniewski, 'Levinasa podróż po krainie wrażliwości' [A Journey of Levinas through the Land of Sensitivity] in: P. Orlik (ed.), *Rozdroża i ścieżki wrażliwości* [*Crossroads and Paths of Sensitivity*] (Poznan 2000), p. 6. See also: B. Karpińska-Musiał, *Czy można przezwyciężyć sokratejską aporię w postmodernistycznej wizji dialogu kulturowego?* [*Can Socratean aporia be overcome in the postmodern vision of a cultural dialogue?*] … , p. 50.

22 J. Tischner, *Filozofia Dramatu* [*Philosophy of Drama*] … , p. 19.

23 *Ibidem*, p. 19.

in an unchanged form) will never occur. As Karpińska-Musiał states: 'Passivity conceived in this manner is indispensable for avoidance of a characteristic of western philosophy and criticised by Levinas "discovering and comprehending by appropriation, by reducing all that is other to the identity of a subject who discovers"'.[24] Nevertheless, that is not to say that we have no way out and we are drowning in aporia. This only entails that we show respect and understand the motives of verbal and non-verbal actions and practice our symbolism and a symbolism of the Other.

Levinas, though, risks bringing the subject 'to lose identity', which is why he is criticised as an advocate of asymmetry in a dialogue which, however, does not entail hegemony or subordination. It is more likely to denote free, rational concession. Autonomy of the Individual is based here on sensitivity and transcendence. The Individual thus fails to expect gratitude, enjoys his non-integrability and continuous opposition to Totality. It may denote Totality as a unification of norms, an agreement based on consensus, universalism or, as in the case of this book, a predominant and continuous extension of the intellectual property protection in postmodern society. Generally speaking, according to the analysis of Kymlicka knowing correct principles matter less for a person who wants to be moral (the ethics of care). What matters is having the right disposition. That might be for instance 'the disposition to perceive people's needs accurately, and to come up with imaginative ways of meeting them'.[25] The excendent Individual taking no care of Others will not be able to behave in a moral manner. He cannot be called the excendent 'I'. Consequently, no morality exists without the capacity to be considerate of Other. Nothing can be carried out by a cold and unfeeling moral 'I'.

The Individual is still an autonomous subject, lonely but happy in his autonomy and disposition. The Individual does not want to integrate but he also cannot do so, as he can 'appropriate' no-one and so no-one will appropriate him. Levinas's model seems to support the fact that the Individual will not reach, and does not want to reach, an agreement in the sense of adoption of someone's point of view. That is why one should not even pursue agreement. One should stop at the level of aporia which is, moreover, enhanced by an axiological barrier, the system of values.[26] Karpińska-Musiał writes as follows: 'Thus an awareness of disagreement levels

---

24 B. Karpińska-Musiał, 'Czy można przezwyciężyć sokratejską aporię w postmodernistycznej wizji dialogu kulturowego?' [Can Socratean aporia be overcome in the postmodern vision of a cultural dialogue?] in: S. Kruszyńskaet al., *Dialog.* [*Dialogue*] … , p. 52.

25 W. Kymlicka, *Contemporary Political Philosophy. An Introduction* (Clarendon Press, Oxford 1990), p. 265. W. Kymlicka, based on her analysis of Joan Tronto, underlines that the ethic of care 'involves a shift of the essential moral questions away from the question, What are the best principles? To the question, How will individuals best be equipped to act morally?'

26 B. Karpińska-Musiał, 'Czy można przezwyciężyć sokratejską aporię w postmodernistycznej wizji dialogu kulturowego?' [Can Socratean aporia be overcome in the postmodern vision of a cultural dialogue?] in: *Dialog* [*Dialog*] … , p. 54.

emerging in each new interaction is – paradoxically – the best common ground for agreement. It allows keeping one's own face, to look directly at the Other's face thanks to an understanding of his intention or – if not – an understanding of why the intention has been misinterpreted. To put it differently: agreement does not have to be understanding. It rather involves understanding why understanding fails to take place'.[27] By stopping at the level of aporia, the Individual is not the Individual of an 'appropriatory' character, but on the contrary, he is committed to listen to and to listen intently to what is preached as the first teaching.

The Condition of Listening Intently to Levinasian Speech – within the Philosophy of Tested Hope of Kępiński

The excendent Individual belonging to moral collectivity is, therefore, listening intently to Speech. But the Individual was maturing in some way before being able to achieve such a maximal and unique level of listening intently. In other words, it may be assumed that something more had to occur earlier. A 'pre-state' had to occur for the Individual, which enabled such focus and acceptance of the first teaching. The sooner the Individual seems able to take the first lesson the fuller, the more settled he will be, the more in his place he will be in his Ingardenian 'Human Reality layer in the world'. Elaborating on this thought, one can derive inspiration from the 'philosophy of tested hope' advanced by Antoni Kępiński[28] and from unique analyses of his philosophy conducted by the Polish philosopher Józef Tischner.[29]

Preliminary observations on this issue may be based on the tenet that each Individual seeks – according to Kępiński – his 'place of settlement', i.e. a particular 'circle of familiarity'. If the Individual creates conditions for such an atmosphere by himself, he will feel safe and will have no need to put on a mask or set others limitations. The Individual will be open, patient, letting be. The rational Individual, consequently, will be fully ready to take the first lesson from the Other. It seems that taking the lesson will not be possible or will be made considerably more difficult if discovery is constrained within previously set limits. Kępiński advocates, as one of the component parts of such 'pre-state of settlement', refraining from

27 *Ibidem*, p. 54.

28 Antoni Kępiński was a Polish physician, thinker and a renowned psychiatrist from Kraków who died in 1973. He was head of the Department of Psychiatry of Medical College in Kraków. Kępiński is the author of numerous, original scientific papers, which were unfortunately published as a book only in Polish. 'Rytm życia' (The Rhythm of Life) (1972), 'Psychopatologia nerwic' (Psychopathology of Neuroses) (1972) and 'Schizofrenia' (Schizophrenia) (1972). In them the author summarised his over 20 years of experience as a psychotherapist, when he was bedridden for almost two years due to an incurable disease.

29 J. Tischner, *Myślenie według wartości* [*Thinking in Values*] (Wydawnictwo Znak, Krakow 2011), pp. 434–453.

passing moral judgements. Kępiński writes as follows: 'Each man presented with a new situation or with a new man tends to evaluate the circumstances quickly from the perspective of a "good", "bad" alternative ...'. As we were taught by the experiences of the last war and post-war years, situations we encounter presently are too complex to evaluate in a schematic way of: 'good – bad'. Facing a patient's conflicts – frequently of an ethical nature – we often feel a 'moral itching' to give an opinion in the form of 'good – bad'. However, we never have the right to do this as, firstly, a patient comes to us for help and not for judgement and, secondly, we never know a patient well enough to be able to give a just opinion.[30]

Kępiński claimed that of key importance is the ability to refrain from judging, but also, and accompanying it with equal force, the desire to see in the Other his humanity. The currently dominant 'technical' approach to man which notices to a lesser and lesser extent human traits in him, while focusing more and more on attributes related to the proper functioning of a technical, political and economic machine, may be one of the greatest dangers of a postmodern civilization. The above intuitions of Kępiński are supported by the cognitive directive. It is usually expressed as follows: 'To know, one has to let it be'. Nonetheless, Kępiński thinks of something more, that of accepting freedom in another person. The emphasis on freedom emerged in Kępiński's thought, i.e. from observations made during examinations of former prisoners of concentration camps from World War II. Inspired by Kępiński, moral attitude of the excendent Individual will be characterized by refraining from judgements on moral issues and by the Individual pursuing an acceptance of, above all, the humanity in a man and of his freedom. It seems that, owing to creation of such conditions, the Individual will be able to evaluate himself and will be freed from various fears. From this point his own realization begins.

The excendent Individual thus appears as a free entity who recognizes his place of settlement. Thanks to this, he can be a non-appropriatory 'I'. It happens so, as this kind of an axiological atmosphere – as Tischner reminds us – originates from a general intuition of a man's humanity, his dignity and, above all, from an unclear and yet impossible to conceal premonition of where the 'place of settlement' of a man lies.[31] It is worth emphasising that the Individual, according to Kępiński, feels able to be free. Furthermore, he brings with himself a particular hope for the future. The main discovery, which hope intends to protect, is that the humanity of

30 A. Kępiński, *Rytm życia* [*The Rhythm of Life*] ... , pp. 186–187. Prof. Zdzisław Jan Ryn entitled one of his books: *Antoni Kępiński – samarytanin naszych czasów* [*Antoni Kępiński – A Samaritan of our Times*]. The expression 'Samaritan' refers us to Christianity. Prof. Ryn states:

> The moral attitude of Kępiński, pervasive in his work and practised in his life, derives from Christian ethics in which love of the neighbour and pursuit of perfection are overriding norms. For this reason, Kępiński is considered as a quiet, modest, patient and merciful man – particularly with respect to the ill.

31 J. Tischner, *Myślenie według wartości* [*Thinking in Values*] ... , p. 452.

a man manifests itself and remains in direct relation to an inner freedom which he feels able to experience. This may be the most significant truth included in the philosophy of a tested hope of Kępiński. This philosophy has its roots in Polish humanistic tradition, in a Polish way of thinking about man and in a practice with man, as well as in the experiences of Polish hope which history failed to save in ultimate situations. Consequently, the excendent Individual is moral in a manner unsuitable for universalization, i.e. owing to the discovery of one's own 'place of settlement'. The morality of such an Individual does not have to justify itself by referring to something other than itself. Morality may cease being itself when the Individual feels a need, or is even forced to explain, what morality persuaded him to do. It seems that we may attribute a quality of reciprocity to morality and we cannot attribute to it a quality of universality. Reciprocity may be postponed, it may be immediate, it may be generalized or it may be specific. Morality is different. Bauman even writes that morality is irrational, in the sense that it is not subject to calculation, and it cannot be depicted as an activity subordinated to norms to which one can attribute or from which one can gain a status of universality.[32] So, if the excendent Individual 'is with the Others' or 'is with the Other', then such *being* is regulated by codifiable norms. And here reciprocity functions well. But with respect to 'being *for* the Other' (or *for* the Others) such regulation is not possible. Bauman, inspired by Durkheim, refers to morality as a state of a continuous and irreparable anomy. 'Being moral is identical to being dependent on one's own freedom', Bauman writes.[33]

A moral calling is, by definition, personal and the morality of the excendent Individual could be called 'non-universalised morality'. Initially, it is a lonely morality which only at a later stage can be transformed into a community. Bauman writes as follows:

> ... if a moral act is conceived in solitude, then at its end a community emerges – as a 'moral collectivity', a collective although not collectively planned achievement of moral subjects, each of whom reaches beyond his own solitude in an impulse of self-sacrifice, which is both the essence and expression of 'being for'. We are not moral entities because of society [we owe it only to the fact that we are ethical creatures, that we subordinate ourselves to ethical law] – we live in a society, we *are* a society thanks to the fact that we are moral entities. At the heart of the society lies the solitude of a moral person. By the time society, its legislators and philosophers get around to creating ethical laws, there are already entities who were given the honour of being moral with no restrictions and without the luxury of codified good.[34]

32 Z. Bauman, *Etyka ponowoczesna* [*Postmodern Ethics*] ... , pp. 87, 93.

33 *Ibidem*, pp. 93–94.

34 *Ibidem*, p. 94.

It should be concluded in the closing remarks on the thought that refraining from moral judgements and a desire to see in the Other his humanity are principal conditions of postmodern listening intently of the excendent Individual to Levinasian Speech – obviously if we want to relate it to the philosophy of a tested hope by Kępiński.

Undeprecated Utopia

Present utopias which stand a chance in our postmodern society are, in Roman Tokarczyk's view, utopias combining the sense of rebellion against the existing status quo with a real, no less common desire to take suitable measures to eliminate the status quo and replace it with the world of hope in which people could interpret their humanity.[35] The more utopian are concepts during their creation, the more importance their authors attribute to the chances of their realization – of future realism. Utopian thought embraces all social concepts suspended in an unspecified time or directed to an also unspecified future, with no chances of realization then and there where they originate – contrary to realistic thought.[36] However, from the stance of realism, judging the utopian thought leads sometimes to poorly justified deprecation of the thought. The deprecation derives from a misconception of the practical value of such unrealistic discussion.[37]

However, if we locate the purposes of utopia in a moral sphere, then a proposal of Nicolai Hartmann will prove interesting, which treats the existence of axiological intuition, in which it places a world of values which have not been put into practice. Hartmann defined a utopian discourse as an assertion on values to be realized.[38] From the sociological perspective, the realism of utopia as a form of representations, involves their existence, fulfilling functions that exert influence on the whole social life (not only on its political components).[39] As Tokarczyk argues:

> Utopias become more *real* and *actual* when they become part of the expectations of a particular epoch or of a social group, particularly when they begin to serve

35 R. Tokarczyk, *Współczesne doktryny polityczne* [*Contemporary Political Doctrines*] (Wolters Kluwer Polska, Warszawa 2006), p. 43. See also: R. Tokarczyk, *Polska myśl utopijna. Trzy eseje z dziejów* [*Polish Utopian Thought – Three Photos Among Essays*] (Wydawnictwo UMCS, Lublin 1995).

36 W. Tatarkiewicz, *O Szczęściu* [*On Happiness*] (Państwowe Wydawnictwo Naukowe, Warszawa 1979), pp. 447–471.

37 cf. R. Tokarczyk, *Współczesne doktryny polityczne* [*Contemporary Political Doctrines*] (Wolters Kluwer Polska, Warszawa 2006), p. 39. See also: I. Pankow, *Filozofia utopii* [*The Philosophy of Utopia*] (Państwowe Wydawnictwo Naukowe, Warszawa 1990).

38 F. Kraenzel, 'Nicolai Hartmann's Doctrine of Ideal Values: An Examination', 18 *Journal of Value Inquiry* (1984), pp. 299–306.

39 R. Tokarczyk, *Współczesne doktryny polityczne* [*Contemporary Political Doctrines*] … , p. 41.

> roles of guiding principles which direct and motivate social hopes and release collective energy ... utopias has become at present more real than ever before ... our epoch is an epoch of utopia in action.[40]

Utopias focus on the future and in the moment of their creation they have no knowledge of their practical effectiveness, which is the degree and scope of their realism. After some time their realism can be established. Tokarczyk comes to the following conclusion with reference to the state of a modern utopia:

> Nowadays, in the times of a predominance of a realistic, pragmatic and calculated liberalism it is difficult to be a utopist, however, precisely because of that, being a utopist becomes even more important and significant. Capitalists claim that their utopia has eventually triumphed and that the fall of communist hopes has entitled them to do with our world as they please. For this reason, we even hear, here and there, of a death and the end of utopia. I strongly believe, though, that just as a monopoly of liberalism is apparent, the thesis proclaiming a crisis of utopia is false as well. There is no end of utopia and there cannot be an end of utopia.[41] Utopianism is still alive ... . It is crucial to changes, development and social progress and, in consequence, it can never end ... .[42]

Utopia, thus, cannot be deprecated if its principal aim is depicting paths of living on the earth today, which future generations would like to take tomorrow.[43]

Excendently Active Utopia in the Speech According to Levinas

One might suggest after Bauman that although 'semantically, escape is the very opposite of utopia, but psychologically it is, under present circumstances, its sole available substitute: one might say its new, udated ... refashioned to the measure of our deregulated, individualized society of consumers'.[44] Therefore one can no longer seriously hope to make the world a better place to live in unless one escapes. Taking into account assertions from Tokarczyk's analysis, a point of departure for a future discussion may be considering utopia as the 'fundamental ethical principle of an inner magnanimity'.[45] Moreover, a subsequent assumption will state that the excendent Individual is predestined to utopia. To put it differently,

40 *Ibidem*, pp. 41–42.

41 Z. Bauman, *Liquid Times ...* , pp. 94–110.

42 R. Tokarczyk, *Współczesne doktryny polityczne* [*Contemporary Political Doctrines*] ... , pp. 49–50.

43 *Ibidem*, p. 50.

44 Z. Bauman, *Liquid Times ...* , p. 104.

45 R. Tokarczyk, *Współczesne doktryny polityczne* [*Contemporary Political Doctrines*] ... , p. 49.

utopia will be dealt with on the plane of unrealized values and a practice of the excendent Individual. This will be supplemented with an essential tenet that the excendent Individual locates his world of unrealized values (that is his utopia) in the Speech. Consequently, it is a utopia of a unique character, stemming from the excendent Individual (bearing in mind that what happens between expression and responsibility always constitutes an ethical essence of speech).

Thus, a utopia introduced in this discussion will be a utopia of an existential character [*existential utopia*].[46] Such a utopia was proposed in an inventive way in Marder and Vieira's essay where authors suggest replacing 'the empty form of utopian hope with the figure of existence; and that recovers the material underside of utopian projections, even if it spells out their limitations'.[47] As Marder and Vieira state:

> Existencial utopia is, precisely, this *energeia*, a putting of possibilities to work, without postulating an underlying essence and without any guarantees for a successful outcome; it is the energy and capacity for a fresh start that still remains after everything has been actualized. Unlike a utopia beholden to essentialism [that is, an *essential utopia*], the one wedded to the concerns of existence does not foretell a happy resolution of the human drama at the end of history, when all potentialities have fully blossomed, given that it subscribes to a view of the human as a crossroads of volatile possibilities.[48]

However, a primary aim of this part of the discussion is to bring the suggested construct of utopia closer to Baumanian assumptions of 'active utopia' as a utopia capable of an 'awakening' of moral action.[49] For the purposes of this book, the utopia will be referred to as the excendently active utopia, a utopia focused on looking both 'ahead of' and 'beyond' being. Taking into consideration the above assumptions, I suggest that the excendent Individual is predestined in a utopian manner and his utopia is active in an excendent direction. Utopia conceived in this

---

46 See also R.M. Bader, 'The Framework for Utopia', in: R.M. Bader and J. Meadowcroft (eds), *Nozick's Anarchy, State and Utopia* (Cambridge University Press, Cambridge 2011), pp. 255–284. Introduces the concept of minimal state based on Nozick's analysis and concludes as follows on page 284:

> … the minimal state does not specify a particular utopia that is to be achieved, but is instead a framework within which all possible non-coercive utopian conceptions can be realized. It is a system that allows people to create the communities they wish, to live their lives as they desire and to pursue their utopian dreams.

47 M. Marder and P. Vieira, 'Existential Utopia: Of the World, the Possible, the Finite', in: P. Vieira and M. Marder (eds), *Existential Utopia. New Perspectives on Utopian Thought* (Continuum International Publishing Group, New York, London, 2012), pp. 35–36.

48 *Ibidem*, pp. 41–42.

49 Z. Bauman, *Etyka ponowoczesna* [*Postmodern Ethics*] … , pp. 115–116. See also Z. Bauman, *Liquid Times* … , p. 104.

way involves an escape to something other than being as well as a responsibility of an escape to something other than being. It is of importance that the escape may be combined with a desire to see humanity, as defined in Kępiński's philosophy, in the Other.

To clarify the above discussion, it is worth emphasising that one can discern some system of interrelations, which in Levinasian terms may be called prose. The excendent Individual escapes to something Other than being, simultaneously undergoing transformation into the moral self thanks to the expression of the Face. The moral self of the excendent Individual is aroused. The expression of the Face conveys a heroic order, the first teaching that the Individual has to listen to. The Individual is aporetic in every respect (an important moment of the Speech). It is in this transformation that one pursues something which may be called *active utopia*. That is not to say that one discovers oneself as a self 'other than before', but that one discovers the Other as the Face in the expression of the Face. The very miracle (an effort) of awakening (Levinasian awakening!) initiates all morality, without being an ethical event itself. The miracle itself gives rise to a possibility. It can be described as the 'possibility of morality' or as the 'hope of morality'. The miracle of moral awakening which the transcendent Individual undergoes here makes the Individual discover that he is *not for himself* but that he is *for others*. Bauman even refers here to a moral sobering up.[50] *Active utopia* is thus epitomized in the intention to take unconditional responsibility for the Other, without expecting payment, that is with a complete exclusion of reciprocity. One seems justified to suggest at this point that this is a decisive moment in the Speech. The excendently active Utopia motivates to moral action, it becomes a moral impulse orientated towards the future.

The moral attitude of the excendent Individual constitutes a chance. The moral attitude conceived as taking responsibility for one's own responsibility constitutes a chance but, furthermore, it is above all a hope for the future. The chance (a chance included in a moral situation) may obviously be lost or may be seized. It seems that the moral attitude in the sense of taking responsibility for the Responsibility is, in this case, not only a chance but, what is more, a hope. Such hope for the future (a chance included in the moral situation) may, unlike chance, be sustained all the time (obviously it can also eventually be lost).

The consequences of losing the chance are tantamount to losing a chance to have any moral self as well. This is also the case with hope. There will, therefore, be no self if there is not 'being for'. Thus, 'being for' becomes a *sine qua non* condition of the excendent Individual's moral self existence. Consequently, Levinasian 'awakening' or Baumanian 'sobering up' to 'being for the Other' is concurrently the awakening of the self;[51] or breaking out of the self from 'not being'. The point here is to raise a particular anxiety in the excendent Individual, an anxiety that will stimulate a desire for taking an unconditional responsibility

50 Z. Bauman, *Etyka ponowoczesna* [*Postmodern Ethics*] ... , p. 116.

51 *Ibidem*, p. 117.

for the Other, without expecting payment. I take responsibility for the Other as a response to a heroic order. The order is of a particular character, because it is non-noisy, unspoken and revealed in the Face. The demand is unspoken, inaudible but heroic and thus – as Bauman describes it – 'totally different from all too noisy norms and claims of law'.[52] The order is unspoken but revealed, so it cannot be subject to judgement. Nonetheless, it is precisely this character that makes the order unquestionable, indestructible and unconditional. It is the foundations on which the moral self of the excendent Individual can be based. It is the foundations which foretell the moral anxiety but, thanks to the attitude of the excendent Individual who is predestined in a utopian manner, it may be considered that it is the foundations foretelling a rich in values hope for a contemporary petit bourgeois of postmodernity. The moral anxiety releases in the Individual the unique utopian impulse to take responsibility.

Excendent Dialogue in the Philosophy of Levinas and Løgstrup

As a result of the above discussion a question arises of how a paradigm of a dialogue marked with excendence can look, which I call the 'excendent dialogue'. Levinas argues in his telling 'dimensions of speech':

> A face to face character of a conversation omits, therefore, to link a subject with an object and is something other than thematization that is, by definition, adequate, since exteriority eludes comprehension. … A thematised object does remain in himself, but his essence determines the fact that I know him and a surplus which his being in himself is with respect to my knowledge, is gradually absorbed by the knowledge. … Since a being who talks to me and to whom I respond or whom I ask, fails to reveal himself before me, fails *to give himself* in such a manner for me to take him and make his revealing of himself mine [*assumer*]; make him comply with my interiority so that I can take him as if he came from myself. This is how looking acts, but this is absolutely impossible in a conversation.[53]

In order to create a proposal of such paradigm, I devise a fictitious encounter of two prominent thinkers of the century – Emmanuel Levinas[54] and Knud E. Løgstrup. The common ground for the encounter of Levinas with Løgstrup will constitute the following two notional hybrids:

52 *Ibidem*, p. 122.

53 E. Levinas, *Całość i nieskończoność* [*Totality and Infinity*] … , p. 355.

54 See also statement by M. Kozak, 'Dlaczego Levinas nie jest filozofem dialogu' [Why Levinas is not a philosopher of a dialogue] in: S. Kruszyńska et al., *Dialog* [*Dialogue*] … , pp. 33–34.

1. Propheticality and radicality.
2. The certainty of a surplus and a reduction of convention.

Propheticality is a notion utilized by Levinas in 'Totality and Infinity' in the part entitled 'the Other and the Other'. A point of departure constitutes here an expression which fails to unfold its inner, previously enclosed world, fails to discover a new land which could be comprehended and appropriated. Expression 'calls me above what is given and what speech makes universal for us'.[55] Levinas emphasizes that it is only the revelation of the Face which introduces 'I' to a relation with a being. Levinas states: 'everything which happens here "between us" concerns everyone; the Face that looks at me reveals itself in a full blaze of public order, even if it tries to break out of it by seeking a tacit agreement with the speaker in pursuit of a private and secretive relation'.[56]

Accordingly, Levinasian speech as a presence of the Face does not invite a tacit agreement with a chosen being, a relation 'I – you' which is sufficient for itself and forgets about the whole world. An agreement becomes in a way 'loud', as Levinasian Face in its destitution shows the excendent Individual nakedness of the stranger (the poor). The strangeness and poverty call the power possessed by the Individual. A stranger, a poor, needy man appears here as an equal. Levinas writes as follows:

> *You* appears before *we*. Being *we* does not involve jostling in the crowd or gathering around a shared task. The presence of the Face – the infinity of the Other – is a destitution, a presence of the third [that is the humanity as a whole that looks at us] and is an order which orders me to order.[57]

And thus, as Levinas points out, a relation with other man, a conversation is preaching, reprimanding, a prophetic speech. It not only calls into question the freedom of the Individual, not only calls him, through the Other, to responsibility; it is not only a word which makes the Individual part with everything he owns (and what makes him withdraw). The prophetic word seems to be a basis of every dialogue. The word is also no disquisition on moral issues. The prophetic word corresponds significantly to the epiphany of the Face and accordingly, is intimately connected with it. The prophetic word is an unspoken word. The word may be viewed as 'an irreducible moment of a conversation related in being to the epiphany of the Face and proving the presence of the third, the humanity as a whole in the eyes which look at me'.[58]

The prophetic word thus testifies to the presence of humanity as a whole, of the community as a whole. Thus, the fact that fraternity between people emerges and a

55 E. Levinas, *Całość i nieskończoność* [*Totality and Infinity*] … , p. 252.
56 *Ibidem*, p. 25.
57 *Ibidem*, p. 253.
58 *Ibidem*, p. 253.

community emerges is dependent on my responsibility to the Face that looks at me and is absolutely foreign. One should add that the epiphany of the Face embraces both these moments. The responsibility of the Individual to the Face is shaped by society, by humanity.[59] Thus, it seems that propheticality of dialogue itself (prophetic word) will lead to solidarity between people. Society will be viewed as a fraternal community, which will be up to the standards of simplicity (proximity in the proper sense) with which the Face manifests itself and is accepted.[60] Society will therefore be such, as the manner in which the excendent Individual will experience the Face. Such an image of solidarity relates to Baumanian solidarity as a continuation of postmodernity.

Radicality is a notion highlighted by Løgstrup in his work entitled *The Ethical Demand*.[61] Løgstrup relates the notion of radicality to the demand. If this notion is applied to the 'Individual–Other' relation, it will become apparent that Løgstrupian demand is radical precisely because it is unspoken. Løgstrup claims that of critical importance is the fact that a person, for whom I care, has no right to demand anything from me. This constitutes radicality of the Other's demand with respect to the Individual. The Individual, therefore, *de facto* has no right to demand anything from the Other.[62] Accordingly, it is the Other and only the Other who can trace, who can 'find out', as Løgstrup writes, what is best for another man. Løgstrup claims that:

> … the demand makes the person to whom it is addressed the 'Individual' *sensu stricto*.[63] It is a finding out which stems from care, protection and anxiety. It is a finding out orientated to 'being for'. The demand is not based on the strength of an authority (although the Other is 'only' an authority), but on defencelessness. The demand resonated before it was spoken; and resonates even if it was never to be

59 *Ibidem*, p. 254.

60 *Ibidem*, p. 255. Levinas argues that:

> Human fraternity has two aspects: on the one hand, it assumes individuality … ; the particularity of individuals entails the fact that each of them relates to himself (individuals who would be linked in a community of a kind would not be separated from one another sufficiently); on the other hand, it assumes a community of father, as if a community of a kind brought them closer to one another to an insufficient extent. Society has to be a fraternal community to be up to standards of simplicity – proximity in the proper sense – with which the Face manifests itself and is accepted. The idea of human consanguinity, the human race that derives from an acceptance of the Face of the Other in the dimension of the heights, of responsibility for oneself and for the Other constitutes monotheism.

61 K.E. Løgstrup, *The Ethical Demand* (Fortress Press, Philadelphia 1971) (the original was published in 1956).

62 *Ibidem*, pp. 46–47.

63 *Ibidem*, pp. 46–47.

> spoken, if it was to remain silent forever.[64] The radical demand is, consequently, a barely audible or a basically mute demand. The demand is non-noisy. Only the Individual can hear it. It is addressed only to the Individual. As a result, the Individual has to make his own, individual interpretation of a message – thus, an independent and free interpretation. It seems that the radicality of a dialogue itself will lead to shaping of a dialogue in which what is spoken fails to originate in an abstract environment, but in a world in which one has to take care and demand the care from oneself.[65]

While propheticality viewed in conjunction with radicality – as a 'notional hybrid' denoting an excendent dialogue – will shape the dialogue to gain a moral practice. This will constitute an unusual moral practice, as one based on, in Baumanian terms, 'impractical foundations'. It will perceive unattainable standards in its horizon 'and it can never console itself by the fact that it has fully met specific standards'. No conviction of one's integrity of conduct, dissatisfaction and suspicion of one's achievements is the most trustworthy stronghold of morality.[66]

It is worth proceeding now to the notion of 'certainty of a surplus' by Levinas which he asserted in *Totality and Infinity* entitled 'Will and Reason'. An analysis of the Levanisian notion of an 'impersonal reason' seems to be of significance here. Levinas notices with concern that we live in a world where there is no 'real plurality'. This results in speakers giving up their own uniqueness. Speakers do not want one another but that which is universal.[67] Consequently, the Reason becomes impersonal and non-unique. Such reason is present in persons constituting society. Thus, as Levinas emphasizes, a language created by an impersonal reason (fulfilling its discursive essence) becomes a universal discourse, realizes a universality of the state. At the final stage plurality dissolves and a conversation ceases due to the lack of speakers.[68]

At this point a question arises: how to prevent this? How to retain a uniqueness of a person (and not his 'universality')? In other words, how to retain plurality in being? Following in Levinas's footsteps, it should be stated that he prepared a quite precise response to the question. This is a response expressed by Levinas in the form of an objection. If we unfold his objection from prose surrounding his writings (otherwise proving his prominence and uniqueness) we will come up with the following result:

1. I object to distinguishing will from intellect and will from reason. It is unjustified the more so if we state, nonetheless, that a good will is a will which, in taking decisions, acts exclusively with respect to universality.

64 Z. Bauman, *Etyka ponowoczesna* [*Postmodern Ethics*] … , p. 121.
65 cf. E. Levinas, *Całość i nieskończoność* [*Totality and Infinity*] … , p. 257.
66 Z. Bauman, *Etyka ponowoczesna* [*Postmodern Ethics*] … , p. 124.
67 E. Levinas, *Całość i nieskończoność* [*Totality and Infinity*] … , p. 258.
68 *Ibidem*, pp. 258–259.

2. I object to the statement that will is not reason. Will pursues reason. Will is reason in pursuit of itself or creating itself; Levinas refers here to Spinoza and Hegel.
3. I object to the statement that my 'objection' is a usual protest of an individual who rejects the system and reason (as a pure arbitrariness that cannot be silenced by a persuasion of a calm discourse).
4. Objection does not involve withdrawing from being (Levinas writes about 'turning a blind eye to being' or even about 'banging one's head against the wall while trying to overcome awareness of one's insufficiency, transforming humiliation into desperate pride').[69]

Where is the source of objection?

1. Objection emerges from a certainty of a surplus which a separated and craving existence constitutes with respect to the wholeness of being (motionless being or being in the act).
2. Objection stems from a surplus actualized by being with infinity. The surplus is of a particular, due to an 'incessant', character.
3. Objection 'Originates in a certainty that the ideal of being, which is perpetually realized and thinks exclusively of himself, cannot be an ontological example for life, for becoming what lives on constantly renewed Desire, a social relation'.[70]

The certainty of a surplus notion plays, as it seems, a key role, since it leads us to the very sense of a human Individual's life – an Individual who is personal in all respects. An individual life and, to be more specific, possibilities which an individual life offers, cannot be reduced ('belittled' according to Levinas) to possibilities available to being an individual existence, a person, 'I'. An Individual acts independently of universality, of what is universal and how it is universal. 'An individual and personal existence is indispensable for Infinity to actualize as infinite', Levinas writes.[71] The surplus itself is manifest through being with the Infinity – being of an 'incessant' character.

Taking the above statements into account, it seems that one may suggest that the 'certainty of a surplus' notion, characteristic of an excendent dialogue, will lead to a dialogue saturated with 'reflective and finite freedom' which Levinas explains as follows: 'Thus, it is not freedom that accounts for the transcendence of the Other, but the transcendence accounts for freedom – transcendence of other man with respect to me, an infinite transcendence and, therefore, one of not the same significance as my transcendence to him'.[72] Accordingly, freedom as such

69 *Ibidem*, pp. 259–260.
70 *Ibidem*, pp. 259–260.
71 *Ibidem*, p. 260.
72 *Ibidem*, p. 269.

can reveal itself only beyond a totality. The particular, Levinasian 'beyond totality' opens up through the transcendence of the Face. In order for any relation, a dialogue between any beings separated from each other to be eventually initiated, they have to be partially independent and partially linked by a given relation.[73] It seems to have consequences for the notion of an identity of an individual, so important to postmodernity. The Identity of the Individual, 'I', who participates in a dialogue marked with excendence, is never the same. The Identity of the Individual entails that the individual is *identical*. To put it differently, 'I' identifies himself as if from within and escapes identification from without, through the usual indications.[74] The reduction of a convention, according to Løgstrup, is the last of notional hybrids' parts whereby I suggest a potential direction for an excendent dialogue.

This remarkable Danish philosopher believes that what characterizes our civilization is the lack of attention to and care for the Others in everyday life.[75] Løgstrup blames a social convention (a convention in this book will be reflected in norms – above all in the part dedicated to Reason, as well as to Myth and Reason, in the form of an analysis of the human right to science and culture) for this state of affairs. The Individual is marked with a reduced trust and with a reduced requirement of care that we should give to Others. Løgstrup reminds us that an original aim of conventions was to unite people, bring them closer together. Nevertheless, their actual influence has been the opposite. People become more and more strangers to one another as they behave in compliance with etiquette or conventions in order to drift apart, hide and seclude themselves. Løgstrup draws our attention to one more fact (which many view as a benefit in our postmodernity) related to the characteristic features of conventions, namely that conventions (such as norms and an exemplary right to science and culture) provide us with very precise guidelines on how we should behave, what we should do and what we should refrain from doing, what we should defend and how and what we should not focus on at all and so on. As a result, in reality norms relieve us from some responsibility which does not bother us any more. The consequences are disastrous, since more and more frequently we comply with conventions by taking no care of the Others. A convention releases us in a way from human care and attention.[76] We are, therefore, not absorbed in truth but we focus on extremities which are brought about by a convention. Obviously, in consequence, we ignore the truth included in convention itself, in its Text, but I will elaborate on this in subsequent parts of the book.

Norms as an instance of conventions result in our lives becoming safer and never restless. We are not restless. Analyses of Løgstrup bear a close resemblance to the description of a self-sufficient petit bourgeois of modernity created by Levinas and presented at the beginning of the text. A moral self of a petit bourgeois of modernity is at least completely dormant or non-existent. Such an Individual has

73 *Ibidem*, p. 266.

74 *Ibidem*, p. 346.

75 K.E. Løgstrup, 'The Ethical Demand' … , p. 121 et seq.

76 *Ibidem*, p. 121 *et seq.*

(in his opinion) a peaceful conscience due to the following everyday reflections: 'but everyone behaves like this', 'why should I be different?'. This is a medicine of a self-sufficient petit bourgeois of modernity for a dormant or even non-existent moral self, an unaroused moral self, or even a non-sobering moral self. As Bauman points out, this comes as a result of an increase in the role of conventions (norms). The Individual is deprived of (better: loses) autonomy.[77] It seems, thus, that one may suggest a statement that an excendent dialogue, more precisely an atmosphere of the dialogue, should be dominated by an independent and autonomous Individual (and, consequently, this is 'basically non-social moral self').[78]

Bearing in mind all notional hybrids inspired by the philosophies of Levinas and Løgstrup, one can make a final suggestion that they contribute in different ways to restoring the possibility of expression in which the Individual, forsaking the relation of reciprocity, reveals itself as unique and one of a kind. We learn from Levinas that 'justice involves restoring the possibility of expression'.[79] Levinas calls a relation the Face in a straightforward way (significantly, conceived as a relation epitomized in a word) – a Desire which is filled with goodness and justice.[80] He suggests that a primary aim of an excendent dialogue will be a pursuit of goodness and justice jointly understood as the right to speak; Levinasian Face is the one which asks for goodness but demands justice.

However, considering the above discussion, one should postulate that in the present postmodernity the Face will also be the one which asks for mercy (derived from Kołakowski) but demands solidarity (derived from the thought of Bauman). Furthermore, one can suggest that *de facto* what unites a request and a demand is expressed in the philosophy of good hope of Kępiński. And such will be a dialogue. Levinas argues: 'In a political life people are understood exclusively on the basis of their works. It is a humanity of mutual relations, a humanity which comprises individuals mutually replaceable. Replacing some people with other – a source lack of respect – allows exploitation'. In postmodernity, it will be solidarity more than justice that will rely on restoration of the possibility of expression, in which a person forsaking relations of reciprocity is manifest as unique and exceptional. Solidarity will constitute the Levinasian right to speak in postmodernity. As Levinas writes: 'Metaphysics thus brings a fulfilment of "I" as a unique and exceptional being in relation to whom state affairs should situate themselves in the right place and should be conducted with respect to this being'.[81] An excendent dialogue will, therefore, lead to allowing social plurality and Levinasian face to

77 Z. Bauman, *Etyka ponowoczesna* ... , p. 121.

78 L. Dumont, *Essays on Individualism: Modern Theory in Anthropological Perspective* (University of Chicago Press, Chicago 1986), p. 25 *et seq*.

79 E. Levinas, *Całość i nieskończoność* [*Totality and Infinity*] ... , p. 358.

80 *Ibidem*, p. 356.

81 *Ibidem*, p. 362.

face relation that will never be a kind of coexistence. It is a source happening, a manifestation of a being to whom all possible relations should be referred.[82]

'A Dialogue of Saints' (i.e. Speaking from within the Metaphor) as a Call for Anti-Adiaphorization of Human Behaviours

If I was asked to translate the name of an excendent dialogue into the language of the metaphor (or, as Tischner wants: 'speaking from within the metaphor')[83] I would use the notion of 'a dialogue of saints'. As Bauman brilliantly puts this: 'saints are saints, since they do not hide behind the broad back of the law'.[84] Metaphorically speaking, it would be 'a dialogue of saints' as its aim is not a constant meeting or satisfying of every-day reality, or normality, but being ahead of every-day reality and normality and rising above them – even in coexistence with an impulse of utopia. This is a dialogue orientated towards something better than a being, towards something which literally has no entity of its own. A dialogue orientated not towards 'being with' but towards 'being for' and 'what rises above and is ahead of normality sets a horizon of what is normal'.[85] Then, the heroism of saints and, here, a heroic ethics of the Other will set the horizon of what should be but what is still not normal for our civilization. What should be normal is, consequently, restored in a heroic expression: 'I am for the Other' signifies 'I take responsibility for the Other'.

One of the saints of whom one will never cease thinking about was Janusz Korczak, a Polish paediatrician, a teacher in an orphanage in Warsaw during the interwar period; he could be depicted as a 'philosopher of a dialogue with a child'. He was killed in Auschwitz with children deported by the Nazis during World War II. He refused to 'being saved' in exchange for working for the Reich as proposed to him by the Germans.[86] Why does a brief presentation of Korczak serve as an introduction to my discussion of an excendent dialogue as a 'dialogue

82 *Ibidem*, p. 368.

83 J. Tischner, *Filozofia Dramatu* [*Philosophy of Drama*] (Wydawnictwo Znak, Krakow 2012).

84 Z. Bauman, *Etyka ponowoczesna* [*Postmodern Ethics*] … , p. 124.

85 *Ibidem*, p. 124.

86 Janusz Korczak, the pen name of Henryk Goldszmit (1878 or 1879 – August 1942), was a Polish-Jewish educator, children's author and paediatrician known as Pan Doktor ('Mr. Doctor') or Stary Doktor ('Old Doctor'). After spending many years working as director of an orphanage in Warsaw, he refused freedom and stayed with his orphans when the institution was sent from the Ghetto to Treblinka extermination camp, during the Grossaktion Warsaw of 1942.

> He told the orphans they were going out in to the country, so they ought to be cheerful. At last they would be able to exchange the horrible suffocating city walls for meadows of flowers, streams where they could bathe, woods full of berries and mushrooms. He told them to wear their best clothes and so they came

of saints'? For the simple reason that the figure of Janusz Korczak exactly epitomizes the saintly characteristic of an excendent dialogue analysed above. The manner in which Korczak took responsibility for children by bringing them up and, consequently, holding their hands is an illustration of fulfilling a heroic order of the Other, serving as an example of being without expecting reciprocity.[87] An illustration of a similar 'being for' who gave with his life is the aforementioned Danish professor of philosophy, Knud E. Løgstrup who, during World War II, was active in the resistance movement and who, along with his wife, helped to rescue Jewish refugees from Denmark and was forced to go underground.

It is a foregone conclusion that saints are people unique in all respects because they do something that others would not be capable of and they do it in a manner which others, presumably, would not think of or they might think of but are too weak spiritually. Obviously, saints cannot demand such actions from others. Saints can demand 'saintliness' only from themselves. They fail to treat their deeds as a 'universal norm' – and that is precisely what makes them a saint, Bauman says.[88] 'I', who is a saint, may demand such deeds only from himself; and here a demand begins and here it ends. Do saints demand from themselves something which to others is utopian in all respects? Of course! Saints blaze a trail against self-sufficiency; they blaze a trail for those who are fearful as their moral selves 'have not sobered up yet'. It seems, then, that what leads a saint 'I' in postmodernity is thinking according to active utopia as a utopia based on morality; and, as we know, humanity itself does not need an element of reciprocity at all, it needs asymmetry.

Accordingly, a lack of an excendent dialogue will result in adiaphorization of human behaviours. The subject of adiaphorization was elaborated on in an immensely interesting way by Zygmunt Bauman.[89] What, in the Middle Ages, the Church regarded as adiaphoric meant that in such a case the Church took no position. In other words it was neutral from the stance of the doctrine. Bauman applied this term in respect of human behaviours. Adiaphorization, in this sense, signifies that some types of human behaviours become morally neutral; it releases them from moral judgements. A Baumanian example of the adiaphorization mechanism is a system aimed at bureaucracy. In accordance with the bureaucratic order, if 'I' acts by abiding by an established procedure, by a prescribed routine, I abide by legal acts accurately, so I am liberated from moral problems and pricks of conscience. If, then, as a consequence of my actions compliant with the rules, someone will suffer, someone will be deprived of his parental rights to his child, someone will have no access to a life-saving medicine, someone will have no access to books, information or knowledge – this is no fault of a particular 'I'. Thus, the correctness

out into the yard, two by two, nicely dressed and in a happy mood. The little column was led by an SS man ... – Władysław Szpilman, *The Pianist.*

87 See among many of his works: J. Korczak, *Prawo dziecka do szacunku* [*A Child's Right to Respect*] (Warsaw 1929).

88 Z. Bauman, *Etyka ponowoczesna* [*Postmodern Ethics*] ... , p. 80.

89 *Ibidem*, pp. 19–29.

of my actions' morality is determined exclusively by compliance with a procedure, a procedural rationality and not moral considerations.[90]

Taking into account the above statements, one may contrast the excendent Individual with the adiaphoric Individual. The adiaphoric 'I' (here, a contemporary petit bourgeois of Levinas) escapes from moral responsibility. The escape is epitomized by adiaphorization. Consequently, issues that used to be moral are redefined as technical problems. Greater and greater fields of human behaviour are completely excluded from any moral discussion.[91] As Bauman emphasizes in his interview, a contemporary life generally tends to cut effects off causes and treats life as a set of episodes. He calls it 'inconsequentiality'. Bauman believes that adiaphorization is an effect of a division of life processes into separate episodes. Whereas the cruelty of an episode is that one never knows for sure if a particular encounter was truly only an episode, its echoes may return. A harmed patient may appear, a mother ill with HIV may appear with a child, or a poorly educated, passive or defenceless society may emerge. Bauman states: 'It is a bit like in a Tom & Jerry cartoon. The characters of these short films are constantly killing each other, but immediately rise from dead and the action of the film continues as if nothing happened, as if nothing irreversible and for real happened ...'.[92]

90 Z. Bauman, *Wywiad z Baumanem* [*An Interview with Bauman*] ... , pp. 19–29.

91 *Ibidem*, pp. 19–29. Bauman argues as follows:

> Adiaphorisation affects also the everyday life; it does not stop at the sphere of public or professional life. It is present, for instance, in the abandonment of obligations arising from sexual relations, in a change of rules and criteria of partnership as well as marital and family life. If, in the nineteenth century, adiaphorisation embraced the functions of a soldier, an office clerk and other public activities – while private life was to be subject of moral regulation – nowadays we observe adiaphoric tendencies in private life as well.

92 *Ibidem*, pp. 19–29.

Chapter 3
Excendence Stance on Thinking: Text

Augustinian *Verbum* or of Non-Self-Sufficiency: Towards *Quiddam Mentis Nostrae*

At the centre of the discussion on thinking in excendence terms has so far been the Individual and the Speech. Now, attention will be focused on the Conventions in the written form (that is the Text, the Word). I am specifically referring to the Conventions which a contemporary, Levinasian self-sufficient man (that is the adiaphoric Individual) conforms with (and I think who is even partially addicted to it) to such an extent. A specific instance of the Conventions will be provided in the subsequent parts of the book by regulations and interpretations directly relating human right to science and culture. The discussion will revolve around the Text whereby the Convention is generally expressed. What follows is a fundamental question of how the Text should be interpreted to prevent adiaphoric behaviour in the postmodern society (or at least to reduce it). To put it differently, how to read the Text (here, human rights on a specific example of the right to science and culture), how to interpret it, how to analyse it to prevent escapes from moral responsibility in social life in the postmodern era, to put an end to cutting effects off causes and treating life as a set of Baumanian episodes?

I will start the discussion with Augustinian hermeneutics (and its brilliant interpreter, Jean Grondin) stating that a desire to understand the Text is not a cold and purely epistemological process between a subject and an object, but something which proves the anxiety of the Individual reading the Conventions. It is precisely the Augustian idea which will enable Gadamer to go beyond understanding of language typical of Greek ontology and characterized by its nominalistic and technical understanding. I refer, here, to liberation (to an escape) from a *stricte* ontological understanding of a Text. Augustinian idea of *Verbum*, as Grondin points out, could do justice to the tradition of language existence. Universalism of hermeneutic access to language is expressed in conceiving the word as a processual incarnation of the spirit. Consequently, a 'particular something' is present in the word and yet it refers to what is Other.[1]

---

1 J. Grondin, *Wprowadzenie do hermeneutyki filozoficznej* [*Introduction to Philosophical Hermeneutics*]. Myśl Filozoficzna (Wydawnictwo WAM, Krakow 2007), p. 47. cf. also J. Grondin 'Unterwegs zur Rhetorik'. Gadamers Schritt von Platon zu Augustin in 'Wahrheit und Methode', in: G. Figal, J. Grindin and D. Schmidt (eds), *Hermeneutische Wege* (Tubingen 2000), pp. 207–218.

Augustine assumes that Scripture is, by definition, clear to every reader. However, in fact, everything is dependent on the 'spiritual disposition of an interpreter' which may vary. Augustine claims that if the disposition is to be closest to the ideal, it should be based on three foundations of faith, hope and love. However, of the utmost importance for Augustine is love. Grondin, analysing Augustine's thought, writes as follows:

> Everything is dependent … primarily on love [*caritas*]. He who wants to proceed to reading Scripture with love and attention will first read all canonical books, thereby achieving at least familiarity with them even if he cannot understand everything.[2]

It follows that the principle of love (thus including the principle of care and goodness) becomes a kind of a lodestar for an interpreter of the Text, for every researcher thereof. As a way of introduction, Augustine prescribes to an interpreter a particular 'attachment' to the language of all Books constituting a particular Text (Augustine, obviously, refers to Scripture as the Bible) or related to the Text and only then an attempt at understanding obscure passages with reference to the language used in other Texts constituting a particular Text. One can come to the conclusion that, in all actions compliant with the rules, light which is indispensable to comprehend obscure passages of the Text must come from God.[3] An interpreter of the Text is, therefore, referred to something else than what exists in the word. In the case of Augustine it is God.

In this way an interpreter will become attached to the language of the Text and will achieve an ability to understand obscure passages by means of clear passages. Accordingly, the ambiguity of the Text is a foundation for the necessity of hermeneutics, which was not yet called by its name in Augustine's writings and that derives, in his opinion, from the confusion of a proper and metaphorical sense. Apart from the rule of love that Augustine relates to systematically and everywhere, there is also a general principle asserting that obscure passages in the Text should be explained, where it is possible, by clear, parallel passages.[4] Augustine argues that source speaking or thinking is something internal, it is a speech of the heart. This internal language possesses no sensual or material form, but it is purely intellectual or universal. It therefore has yet to take the form of a particular, sensual or historical language. As Grondin points out: 'When we hear a human word in a specific language, it is self-evident that we do not pursue its particular, accidental

---

2 *Ibidem*, p. 48. cf. also St Augustine *O Trójcy* Świętej [*Of Holy Trinity*], 1, 2, translated by M. Stokowska (Poznan 1963), p. 80: 'Scripture adjusting to the mode of thinking of the little people …'. cf. also St Augustine *O nauce chrześcijańskiej* [*On Christian teaching*]. *De doctrina christiana*, Introduction and commentary translated by J. Sulowski (Warszawa 1989).

3 J. Grondin, *Wprowadzenie do hermeneutyki filozoficznej* [*Introduction to Philosophical Hermeneutics*] … , p. 47.

4 *Ibidem*, p. 49.

form, but the word [*verbum*] or a sense epitomized in it, naturally in an imperfect manner, as is each epitomization of the spirit in the case of man'.[5] Thus, the word is a reflection of something not certain and not something related to self-possession as we 'do-not-self-possess' the word. Consequently, the word is no mirror image of understanding the certain but a reflection of understanding something uncertain, imperfect and even, I think, infinite. We, interpreters, can therefore reach the true, human word [*verbum*] if we cross the sensual and language.

This leads to a pre-eminent tenet for this book that the word is not self-sufficient; the word in itself is not self-sufficient, just as a man, as the Individual discussed in preceding parts of this book. The word that an interpreter wants to reach, the *verbum*, is devoid of sound and, despite this, is present in each speaking and precedes all characters it can be translated into. A question arises: What does a researcher of the self-sufficient word utilize when it is to be interpreted? An interpreter of the Conventions seems to apply a particularly unclear knowledge, 'something unspecified in our minds' [*quiddam mentis nostrae*] to help thoughts in their expression. The 'something unspecified in our minds' is not completely formed; it fails to originate from a clear vision, but is rather derived from infinite formation [*hoc formabile nondumque formatum*].[6] While Augustine refers to the word of God and the presence of God, what could a postmodern man (a Levinasian petit bourgeois of modernity) refer to when reading the Conventions to eliminate or minimalize adiaphoric behaviours? To put it differently, how to interpret them in order to invite morality? Considering the above assertions, this book postulates a preliminary (supplemented at the end of the discussion on the Speech) tenet on non-self-sufficiency of the word (a tenet on non-self-sufficiency of man was postulated in preceding parts of the work) which constitutes one of the principal assumptions for elimination or minimalization of adiaphoric behaviours of contemporary people. The proposed 'tenet on non-self-sufficiency' of the word comprises understanding of the Text (of the word) described in the following manner:

1. The understanding of Scripture is not a purely epistemological process between a subject and an object but something which proves the anxiety of the Individual reading the Conventions.
2. The word is no mirror image of understanding the certain and final, but a reflection of understanding something uncertain.
3. The 'particular something' is present in the word which, however, refers to what is Other.
4. The principle of love (thus including the principle of care and goodness) becomes a kind of a lodestar for an interpreter of Scripture, for every interpreter.
5. The source of the word is in 'something unspecified in our minds' [*quiddam mentis nostrae*].

5 *Ibidem*, p. 5.
6 *Ibidem*, p. 51.

Gadamerian Surplus of Meaning

Accordingly, each word and each utterance should aspire to truth and, for this to happen, its interpretation has to be liberated from an ordinary plane of utterance, an ordinary affirmative sentence. If one intends to grasp a word or an utterance in its truth, one should not focus solely on characters, but should take into consideration a whole which the utterance or the Texts open. In a lecture from 1957 entitled 'Was ist Wahrheit?' [What is Truth?] Gadamer intended to liberate language aspiration to truth from the plane of utterance by stating: 'No utterance exists which can be captured solely in the content it conveys if one intends to capture it in its truth. Each utterance is motivated. Each utterance has assumptions which it fails to express'.[7] Thus, as Marek Zirk-Sadowski eloquently emphasizes, each Text in Gadamer's view will be a text equipped with 'a surplus of meaning'.[8] Each word, each Text, each Convention is to be therefore understood 'in surplus', so always 'not-in-insufficiency'. This 'surplus of meaning' seems to have a significant bearing on the issue, as it intensifies a surplus of truth pursued in the word. Gadamerian zero point fails to exist, just as Gadamerian basic sentence or an ordinary 'translation' of the language of reality.

Following in the footsteps of the analysis of Marek Zirk-Sadowski it can clearly be noticed that meaning is not something which can be discovered in a recurrent manner. One cannot go beyond one's situation in order to see the meaning of the word in a pure way. Meaning is inseparable from interpretation, it is an interpretation. Meaning is *de facto* interpretation. Meaning is thus unique. Consequently, according to Gadamer, it is not the case that, as Dilthey argued, an understanding of the text is empathizing of one individual with the other. Gadamerian understanding of the Text entails rising to a higher generality by overcoming not only one's own but, what is crucial, other's particularism as well.[9] Gadamer's partner in his particular hermeneutic conversation is a written Text. A written Text is subject to interpretation (i.e. particular understanding). Thus, as in a real conversation, the text takes the floor only through one of his partners (an interpreter, a researcher of the Text). It is due to an interpreter that the characters of the text are transformed again into sense. What follows is that each understanding becomes an interpretation happening in the language.[10]

7 *Ibidem*, p. 53.

8 M. Zirk-Sadowski, *Wprowadzenie do filozofii prawa* [*Introduction to Philosophy of Law*] (Kantor Wydawniczy Zakamycze, Krakow 2000), pp. 88–87. See also a second edition of the book: M. Zirk-Sadowski, *Wprowadzenie do filozofii prawa* [*Introduction to Philosophy of Law*] (Wolters Kluwer Polska, Warszawa 2011).

9 *Ibidem*, pp. 87–88.

10 P. Dehnel, B. Sierocka, 'Rozmowa którą jesteśmy' [Conversation which we are], in: H.-G. Gadamer, *Język i Rozumienie* [*Language and Understanding*] (Fundacja Aletheia, Warszawa 2003), p. 162.

Understanding the Text and the word included in it is, simultaneously, understanding 'something unspecified in our minds' [*quiddam mentis nostrae*]. Grondin puts this as follows:

> As a consequence, the foundation of language universality is not in the spoken language but in the 'inner word' as one can describe it, obviously in a clumsy way, quoting Augustine. Yet it is not tantamount to ignoring a specific language. It only entails situating language in its proper hermeneutic horizon. The word of the 'spirit' may not be heard, still we have to account for it if we want to understand that which is linguistic.[11]

As a result, Gadamer says that the situation of understanding itself is a position which limits the ability to see. Gadamer calls this limitation a horizon.[12]

Gadamer's Communication with the Text

Since, if the Text is the ideal for an encounter with other man in the philosophy of a dialogue, then Gadamer in his 'Truth and Method' argues that an encounter with tradition, with the Text of culture originating in the past – in our case with the Convention – has the structure of a dialogue. The analogy may mislead us into thinking that Gadamer treats being with the Text and interpretations of the Text as an encounter with its author mediated by the Text and an attempt at reconstructing the author's intention. Nonetheless, far be it from Gadamer to conceive of dialogism of hermeneutic experience in this manner. The object of the experience is a written Text. Gadamer is certainly an anti-psychologist and reiterates on numerous occasions that we communicate with the Text and not with its author.[13]

---

11 J. Grondin, *Wprowadzenie do hermeneutyki filozoficznej* [*An Introduction to Philosophical Hermeneutics*] ... , p. 53.

12 M. Zirk-Sadowski, *Wprowadzenie do filozofii prawa* [*An Introduction to Philosophy of Law*] ... , pp. 88–89. As Marek Zirk-Sadowski reminds us, traditional hermeneutics posited walking out of one's own situation and entering a horizon of an analysed epoch. Presently, modernity is the horizon for us. Marek Zirk-Sadowski advances a thesis that our common modernity is not a closed form, it is a becoming, a shaping by the future, i.e. a merging of horizons which apparently exist for themselves. Understanding conceived in this manner is a process of horizons merging. The text itself cannot be read by a neutral interpreting subject, but it is always interpreted already with some expectations. Consequently, there always exists the so-called draft sense of a read text. A provisional understanding of a text exists that is related both to each of its parts as well as to the whole.

13 K. Rosner, 'Dialog jako temat filozofii współczesnej: Buber, Gadamer, Habermas' [Dialogue as a Subject of Modern Philosophy: Buber, Gadamer, Habermas] in: *Dialog* [*Dialogue*]. *Idea i Doświadczenie* [*Idea and Experience*] (Wydawnictwo Uniwersytetu Gdanskiego), p. 21.

Thus, the Text and its meaning become independent both of their author and of the original recipient to whom it was addressed in the moment of creation. This is the case as the Text lives its own life. Although we have the situation of an encounter here, it is an encounter between an interpreter and the Text. From Gadamer's perspective, writing represents a hermeneutic problem in its pure form, distant from all that is psychological. Rosner states as follows:

> An interpreter, to be able to express the meaning of the text and for the text to be able to talk to him, has to translate it into his own language, that is relate it to the set of linguistic meanings which he himself uses. ... In the process of interpretation, an interpreter's notions are accompanied by his bias, prejudice and historical horizon. This fact fails to impede the process of understanding, on the contrary, it is a condition of its feasibility.[14]

Accordingly, not only the object of interpretation but an interpreter as well, are historical – and, what follows, an interpreter of the Text, is historical. He is situated within the tradition and the very 'encounter with the Text', an interpretation is not an encounter of pure reason with something that originates in the tradition, it is an encounter of two historical horizons. The encounter of two historical horizons in postmodernity, while interpreting the human right to science and culture, could account not only for the history and development of intellectual property law in the direction of its unimaginable expansion (as a basically feudal law) but also in the direction of other alternatives derived from knowledge commons, which will be dealt with in subsequent pages of the text within parts focused on *Reason* and *Myth and Reason.*

The Gadamerian figure of 'merging of horizons' may be considered as a fundamental and universal figure of the process of understanding as such.[15] Gadamer adopts an ongoing character of 'a conversation with tradition' process. The process involves an incessant going beyond itself of understanding (its permanent self-transcendence), it is simply the manner in which understanding happens. As a result, only in the light of this can self-understanding, its new, 'merged' unity with itself, take shape. Thus, only in this sense, i.e. as the other side of a process of an incessant self-differentiation of understanding in the perspective of understood 'thing', may a figure of 'horizons merging' be considered as a fundamental and universal figure of the understanding process as such.[16]

---

14 *Ibidem*, p. 21.

15 M. Zirk-Sadowski, *Wprowadzenie do filozofii prawa* [*An Introduction to Philosophy of Law*] ... , pp. 88–89.

16 P. Dybel, Granice *rozumienia i interpretacji. O hermeneutyce H.-G. Gadamera* [*The Limits of Understanding and Interpretation. On H.-G. Gadamer's Hermeneutics*] (Towarzystwo Autorów i Wydawców Prac Naukowych, UNIVERSITAS, Krakow 2004), p. 317.

Gadamerian duality or ambiguity is based on a premise that we understand anything insofar as we understand the 'anything' in a different manner.[17] Understanding is, therefore, understanding insofar as it constantly becomes different in relation to itself. Thereby all mediation of understanding (that is 'merging') with itself becomes possible only in light of an incessant alienation from itself. That is why of utmost importance is, at this point, Gadamer's assertion that the moment of 'otherness' in the testimonies of cultural past and the moment of 'belonging' of a researcher or an interpreter-humanist to the tradition are in permanent tension. It is the process of understanding that activates (understanding becomes) the extraordinary tension.[18] The researcher of the Text acts here in the capacity of a particular mediator. His aim is to mediate between the otherness of the sense and his own self-understanding. He is, thus, a hermeneutist who mediates between modernity and the past in a particularly unique way.

Openness as a Condition of an Authentic Experience of the Text

Each encounter with the Text originating in the past therefore includes the tension between the Text itself and the presence of an interpreter of the Text. The task of hermeneutics is exactly to reveal this tension.[19] Thus, if the Text is to have something to say to an interpreter, it has to confront him with his own presuppositions and his own situation. An interpreter omits to limit himself to the identification of the meaning of the Text and the historical interpretation itself orientated to reconstruct the Text, which Gadamer calls subjectifying and contrasts it with a hermeneutic interpretation that starts a conversation with the text and lets it speak to us. The relation of the Text's meaning to itself, to one's own situation, Gadamer calls application. Application constitutes an integral part of the hermeneutic process, since an interpreter has to relate the text to himself if he is to understand it at all.[20]

As Rosner aptly points out, a hermeneutic experience, i.e. hearing everything that the text has to say, requires openness. Openness is the opposite of dogmatism.[21] Openness is a condition of an authentic experience. We have to relate the Text to our world, to our unique postmodern modernity, for the Text to speak to us. In other words, we have to relate it to our world and to our historical horizon. We have to refrain from our own bias and prejudice and assume an attitude open to the message

---

17 K. Rosner, *Dialog jako temat filozofii współczesnej: Buber, Gadamer, Habermas* [*Dialogue as a Subject of Modern Philosophy: Buber, Gadamer, Habermas*] … , p. 317.

18 P. Dybel, *Granice rozumienia i interpretacji. O hermeneutyce H.-G. Gadamer* [*The Limits of Understanding and Interpretation. On H.-G. Gadamer's Hermeneutics*] … , pp. 317–318.

19 K. Rosner, *Dialog jako temat filozofii współczesnej: Buber, Gadamer, Habermas* [*Dialogue as a Subject of Modern Philosophy: Buber, Gadamer, Habermas*] … , p. 23.

20 *Ibidem*, p. 23.

21 *Ibidem*, pp. 23–24.

of the Text. Being open entails being able to confront our own presuppositions with presuppositions contained in the text. It is only by assuming such an attitude that we can understand that a product of a culture from the past is not an object at all but a relation linking the reality of history with the reality of an interpreter. In Gadamerian hermeneutic interpretation a fusion of horizons takes place – of the past horizon and of our contemporary horizon – which is not motionless but is in constant motion, it is continuously formed *inter alia* by being with tradition and by interpreting its Texts. By confronting our presuppositions with the message from the Text, we can confirm or reject them, thereby broadening our horizons, our understanding of ourselves and of the world. A hermeneutic interpretation, thanks to its characteristic feature of openness, turns out to be a path to broadening our self-consciousness. Such an interpretation becomes a creative activity for us and enriches us as individuals. We therefore aim at an understanding of 'recovering notions from historical past' so that the notions can find their own place in our contemporary thinking and understanding of a particular issue. And this seems to be the essence of a Gadamerian fusion of horizons, because the reconstruction of the question to which the Text is a response becomes our own questioning.[22]

Rosner comes to the following conclusion: 'The analogy between an interpretation and a dialogue which concludes Gadamer's discussion on hermeneutic experience leads in the same direction as Buberian encounter with the Other. In both cases the Other or the text is not to be objectified and is allowed to speak to us'. ' … an expression of such a community with the tradition is also an encounter with the text, the result of an interpretation. Gadamer emphasizes that the meaning of the text is not something ready, something which we identify during an interpretation, but it remains in the process of interpretation'. ' … The fusion of horizons which takes place in the process results in the fact that after it finishes an interpreter is not the same any more. From the viewpoint of an interpreter, a hermeneutic experience is a phase in the development of self-consciousness'.[23]

The thought on *verbum interius* warns us against considering linguistic characters as something final. They are a mere imperfect interpretation, which is dependent on a subsequent process of speaking, until the whole idea unveils. According to Grondin, the most prominent principle of philosophical hermeneutics was formed by Gadamer in 1993 and states as follows: 'We can never say fully what we would like to say'.[24] The Text containing the word and the utterance have

---

22 H.-G. Gadamer, *Prawda i Metoda. Zarys hermeneutyki filozoficznej* [*Truth and Method. An Outline of Philosophical Hermeneutics*] (Wydawnictwo Inter Esse, Krakow 1993), p. 348.

23 K. Rosner, *Dialog jako temat filozofii współczesnej: Buber, Gadamer, Habermas* [*Dialogue as a Subject of Modern Philosophy: Buber, Gadamer, Habermas*] … , p. 25.

24 L.E. Hahn (ed.), 'The Philosophy of Hans-Georg Gadamer', *The Library of Living Philosophers, vol. XXIV* (Chicago, Illinois 1997), p. 496. cf. also J. Grondin, *Wprowadzenie do hermeneutyki filozoficznej* [*An Introduction to Philosophical Hermeneutics*]. *Myśl Filozoficzna* [*Philosophical Thought*] (Wydawnictwo WAM, Krakow 2007), p. 54.

limits originating in our, by definition, historical finitude and in our dependence on the abundance of already existing, but always open language. The Text has its own limits. Gadamer elaborated on the thought in his brilliant essay 'Limits of Language'. Western thought stopped in the development of thinking on the Text at an affirmative sentence. It focused logistically on what has a structure of a sentence. What Western thought failed to consider – in Gadamer's opinion – is a particular character of the word as the utterance and its dependence on what is earlier, namely, on the question.[25]

The 'Insufficiency of the Word' is an Openness of the Adiaphoric Individual to Language and Understanding of the Text

The utterance, according to Augustine and Gadamer, will never tell us everything that it has to say. In 'Limits of Language' Gadamer argues:

> Plato called thinking an inner conversation of the soul. The expression conveys accurately what is the essence of thinking. It is called a conversation since a question and a response are here, because one asks oneself as one asks the other person and says something to oneself as one speaks to the Other. It was already Augustine who drew our attention to this mode of speaking in which one remains in a conversation, in a way, with oneself. Even if one holds a conversation with another person, one has to – as long as one thinks – remain in a conversation with oneself. Language, therefore, actualises itself not in sentences, but in a conversation, in the unity of sense arising from the word and the response. It is only in this situation that language achieves its fullness.[26]

Society, in principle, has normative and conformist functions. But against all conformisms, language lives and changes. New phrases and modes of expression emerge, which come as a result of our life changes and of our experience. In this way, Gadamer states, an antagonism never disappears, an antagonism that makes language something universal and, despite this, allows emerging of new impulses serving transformation of this universality. It is self-evident to Gadamer that the life of language laden with tension is characterized by 'an antagonism between conventionality and revolutionary negation'.[27] In our times a deliberate and conscious regulation of language takes place. This is a deliberate instrument of politics and of a technology civilization. How, then, to co-determine social

25 H.-G. Gadamer, 'Granice Języka' [The Limits of Language] in: *Język i rozumienie* [*Language and Understanding*] (Fundacja Aletheia, Warszawa 2003), pp. 25–40.

26 *Ibidem*, p. 38. H.-G. Gadamer, *Prawda i Metoda* [*Truth and Method*], *Zarys hermeneutyki filozoficznej* [*An Outline of Philosophical Hermeneutics*] (Wydawnictwo Inter Esse, Krakow 1993), p. 359.

27 *Ibidem*, pp. 12–13.

life, Gadamer asks? How, through sharpness of insight and critical judgement, to co-determine social life? On a more contemporary note, one can continue by asking how to release the Text from certain Baumanian 'positions', certain politics and certain economy that treat the Text logistically, technically and contribute to adiaphoric human actions?[28] The insufficiency of the word seems to be a turning point for adiaphoric 'I', since it opens him up to such an understanding of the Text which leads it towards a successful conversation.

Another burning question arises at this stage, intimately connected with the philosophy developed by Gadamer – what does a successful conversation look like? Gadamer's conversation is not a speaking beside oneself. A conversation is no polemical discourse (a polemical discourse seems too obvious to legislators or politicians of our times). Conversation reveals a common aspect of what is being talked about. The reality of human communication determines the fact that a conversation fails to contrast opinions of one and of the other party polemically and it also omits to add from itself as in a simple calculation. A conversation transforms both opinions completely. Philosophy, according to Gadamer, should be a conversation and, in fact, a hermeneutic conversation. It should be a starting of a hermeneutic conversation. Philosophy (also philosophy of human rights and an exemplary right to science and culture) can be a monologue of the reason that devises theories. It is required by a discursive nature of truth. This is a brilliant thought of Gadamer.[29]

A conversation, in Gadamer's terms, always teaches and never ends. It teaches us that unquestionable truths are invalid if they are imposed (they may not be valid at all). Gadamer teaches us conversation with oneself. He believed that a hermeneutic philosophy entails the tenet that we can never succeed in finding words to express the original things and, the more so, the final things. Thus, if we make this assumption, then, concurrently, the achievement of an understanding of cardinal principles, original 'understandings', definite sources of sense, i.e. everything Western metaphysics has dreamt of, suddenly becomes very problematic. It becomes significant and problematic because of great Gadamerian hermeneutics. Gadamerian hermeneutics is characterized by the fact that no-one and nowhere can specify the final interpretation. Our words will always be entangled in a context. Our words can take on a new meaning only in this specific context or in specific contexts. Our every expressed word lives in a context of other words, moreover, in relations with other words, moreover, in mutual interweaving and in mutual taking oneself up anew in a constant motion and no statics. This situation of a conversation is, for Gadamer, the one in which the life of the word fully realizes itself . Our words reveal their meanings only in a conversation. Not earlier. A conversation is thus treated as a process of communication.[30]

28 Z. Bauman, *Etyka ponowoczesna* [*Postmodern Ethics*] … , pp. 72–73.

29 P. Dehnel and B. Sierocka, *Rozmowa którą jesteśmy* [*Conversation which We Are*] … , p. 162.

30 *Ibidem*, pp. 161–162.

It is a conversation that guides people and decides about us – this is the purpose of Gadamerian conversation. The more authentic a conversation, the less it depends on the participants of the conversation themselves and on the fact of its *holding*. A conversation *is never held* because we should be engaged in Gadamerian conversation, we should be guided. It is only then that a conversation will convey its own truth, that is, it will be discovering and releasing something which from now on begins to exist independently. It is characteristic of such a hermeneutic conversation that it always leaves the possibility of a communication continuation. On this account, Gadamer rules out the existence of the so-called original or final word. Words exist, become, happen, have no precedence, no priorities; they merge, come and go, return, weigh and continue for the future. Other words can emerge in every moment and each thought becomes an opening to something new, frequently fuller and more interwoven in modernity or even in the future. Gadamer's partner in this particular hermeneutic conversation is, obviously, a written Text. The Text is subject to interpretation (that is to a particular understanding). What follows is that, as in a real conversation, the Text takes the floor only through one of the partners (through an interpreter). An interpreter is credited with transforming characters of writing back into sense. As a result, understanding becomes interpretation taking place in a language.[31]

A successful conversation, in the philosophy of this great German thinker of the last century, transforms both opinions completely. In a successful conversation one cannot return to the initial controversy. Gadamer claims that it is only a community which is so universal that there exists not only my or only your opinion but a universal interpretation of the world which makes social ethics and solidarity possible. What is right and constitutes law in force, according to Gadamer, requires, in fact, a community that emerges in people's understanding of each other.[32] This unique thinker states that a community of opinion is constantly taking form in a conversation and, subsequently, is dissolving in a silent agreement and self-understanding. Gadamer seems justified to say that all non-verbal forms of understanding are reciprocally orientated to understanding, realizing themselves in speaking and in a conversation. Gadamer assumes a universalism of understanding, that understanding is universal. He states that understanding constellations and the order of our world, a mutual understanding of one another in the world, assumes with all certainty both a critique and fighting what has become ossified or alien, as well as an acceptance or a defence of the existing *status quo*. This duality is manifest in the manner in which we speak to each other and build agreement.[33]

It is particularly noticeable in the present society that, along with new goals and new aspects, a new language is worked out and manifests itself. It is not entirely a new language, but it becomes something more than a new manner of expressing old concepts. The language causes disruptions in communication. But, simultaneously,

31 *Ibidem*, p. 162.

32 H.-G. Gadamer, *Język i rozumienie* [*Language and Understanding*] … , pp. 10–11.

33 *Ibidem*, pp. 10–11.

it leads to overcoming disruptions in the communicative processes. That is the ideal purpose of all communication. At times, it may prove to be unattainable, for example, in the case of a pathologic breakdown in communication between people. According to Gadamer, conflicts of social interests prevent communicative processes to the same extent in which it happens due to mental illnesses. In the case of the latter, a therapy involves linking an ill person to a social community of agreement. The sense of the ideology critique is to correct false consciousness and, thereby, create a proper communication anew. Particular cases of a deeply disrupted agreement may cause the necessity to develop one's own forms of its reconstruction based on a complete knowledge of disruptions (so important in the context of society's reflectivity paradigm, which will be elaborated on in the part dedicated to *Reason* as well as *Myth and Reason*).[34] They, thereby, confirm a constitutive function of agreement as such.[35]

The Gadamerian word as a word that is the smallest unit of sense is not a word at which identifying parts of speech finishes as last element. The original word fails to exist. A sense of a particular word is based on a system of words. I cannot also say 'I introduce a particular word'. It is not people that introduce words – they propose a phrase or through definitions transform a professional phrase at most. Its becoming a word is independent of the people – it is not within their power, because a word introduces itself. In Gadamer's view, it becomes a word only when it is put into communicative circulation. Thus, it is a false scenario in which we, speakers of language, keep words in our pockets, take them out only when we need them – and then put them back, as if the use of language was a free act of a language speaker. Language delineates language usage by itself. Language usage signifies that language itself refrains from an incorrect use. By that, I mean claims of language which are irreducible to an individual and subjective judgement. As Gadamer asserts: 'It is we who talk, none of us and yet we all – this is the manner in which language is present'.[36]

Language entails that words lack in explicitness, contrary to their defined meanings and the scope of their meanings is subject to constant change. Such fluctuation, in Gadamer's opinion, constitutes a particular risk of language. It is only in the course of speaking, in constructing linguistic context that the moments of speech are established conveying sense, correcting and ordering one another. Even the phrase 'language usage' implies situations which do not tally with the essence of our linguistic experiencing of the world. Gadamer states that the word never liberates itself entirely from polisemy characteristic of it, even if each time the context makes sense unambiguous. What is present is not only the sense which

34 cf. in the context of a dialogue's conditions Z. Brodecki and A.M. Nawrot, Świątynia *w cyberkulturze. Technologie cyfrowe i prawo w społeczeństwie wiedzy* [*Temple in Cyberculture. Digital Technologies and Law in Information Society*] (Wydawnictwo Uniwersytetu Gdanskiego 2007), pp. 83–85.

35 H.-G. Gadamer, *Język i rozumienie* [*Language and Understanding*] … , p. 12.

36 *Ibidem*, pp. 21–22.

is attributed to the word in a specific utterance. Co-existent is also that which is other, as well as a presence of all which, by coexisting in this way, determines the evocative power of a living language.

There is always more and more to say in the direction determined by speaking. Every speaking opens up to its continuation. This justifies the Gadamerian premise that language goes beyond itself in a conversation.[37] Gadamer rightly emphasizes that if the phenomenon of language is not viewed from the perspective of an isolated sentence, but of the totality of our being in the world which is also living in a conversation, then one can understand better why the phenomenon of language is so enigmatic – attracting and repelling. In the Gadamerian vision this being in the word – the fact that we are not directed to it as to an object – is a basic way in which all linguistic behaviours are affected. Language has the power of concealing and self-concealing, hence what happens within it is protected from its own reflection and remains somewhat hidden in what is unconscious. The identification of this concealing–unconcealing essence of language makes us go beyond the dimension of sentence logic and toward broader horizons. Gadamer persuades us that we live in language. Language is a kind of a guarantee of what is talked about.[38]

Yet language conceived in this manner realizes itself not in sentences but in a conversation, in the unity of the sense originating from the word and a response. Only in this process does language achieve its fullness.[39] Language itself should be perceived not only as a structure which consists of words but, above all, as a form of communication. Consequently, a broad understanding (comprehension) of language emerges.[40] It is in the mirror of language that all that is, is reflected, Gadamer states and language is not a mirror and what we see in it is no reflection of our *being* (and *being* in general). Language is an interpretation and experiencing of what is happening to us, both in interrelation of work and power as well as in everything else which constitutes our world. Language is also no lost and found subject of all processes or socio-historical actions, a subject which we can see with all its achievements and objectivizations. Language is a kind of a game in which all of us participate. No-one has priority in this game. Everyone is in it constantly and everyone is constantly given motion. Gadamer maintains that this happens when we understand and also when we recognize or expose appearances distorting our social reality. Everything becomes clear when we have already recognized something which seemed odd and incomprehensible to us, when we combine it with out a linguistically ordered world.[41]

37 *Ibidem*, pp. 21–22.

38 *Ibidem*, pp. 23–24.

39 H.-G. Gadamer, *Granice Języka* [*The Limits of Language*] … , p. 38.

40 *Ibidem*, p. 25.

41 H.-G. Gadamer, 'Retoryka, Hermeneutyka i krytyka ideologii' [Rhetoric, Hermeneutics and Ideology Critique] in: *Język i rozumienie* [*Language and Understanding*] (Fundacja Aletheia, Warszawa 2003), pp. 88–89.

The Gadamerian Moment of 'Perfection Presumption'

An initial discussion was aimed at proceeding to the analysis of the 'phenomenon of authority recognition' of key importance to Gadamer and a related 'condition of perfection presumption' as a condition of understanding anything. There exists a particular moment in Gadamerian hermeneutics which he calls the 'perfection presumption' [in German: *der Vorgriff der Vollkommenheit*]. Gadamer views it as a preliminary presumption we make during a conversation with others (or in the course of being with messages of tradition) when we strive to understand words or the sense of a cultural product conveyed to us. We therefore assume that the sense of a given utterance has been told to us in the 'most perfect possible' way. Gadamer also believes we should assume that the very truth of the utterance is perfect as well, i.e. what was spoken in the utterance (truth of an utterance).[42]

In this context two quotations from Gadamer's *Truth and Method* are of utmost importance:

> The perfection presumption includes not only a formal aspect that a text is to express its opinion in a perfect way, but also that the content conveyed by the text is a perfect truth.[43]

> Hence the perfection presumption is made when we read a text and only if it proves to be insufficient, that is a text fails to become understandable, do we begin to doubt about the message and try to find a way to heal it.[44]

According to Gadamerian thought we will be able to take a critical stance on something if the 'perfection presumption' is fully met. This comes as a result of the fact that only then can we state that the utterance of the other (the Other), of what the text says, fails to attain the preconceived ideal of perfection. If, then, as Dybel stresses in his most absorbing monograph entitled 'The Limits of Understanding and Interpretation. On Hermeneutics of H.-G. Gadamer', we disagree with the spoken text, it means that the utterance omits to say what we would expect of it in a 'perfect' way, or even that it is false or erroneous. Accordingly, if we failed to apply the 'perfection presumption' as if in advance, we would not be able to understand anything from (for instance) a given text at all. As Dybel aptly notices, only when we relate a particular 'perfection presumption' to the content of an utterance do we open up 'in source terms' to what it says, to its truth. Thus, only in this moment we can determine if the truth corresponds to our expectations of 'perfection' related

42 P. Dybel, *Granice rozumienia i interpretacji O hermeneutyce H.-G. Gadamera* [*The Limits of Understanding and Interpretation. On Hermeneutics of H.-G. Gadamer*] ... , p. 324.

43 H.-G. Gadamer, *Prawda i Metoda. Zarys hermeneutyki filozoficznej* [*Truth and Method. An Outline of Philosophical Hermeneutics*] ... , p. 280.

44 *Ibidem*, p. 280.

to it. The perfection presumption becomes a kind of a background, as Dybel is at pains to emphasize, an essential and indispensable background.[45] In reference to the background, a reflection on the sense and wisdom of an utterance or a cultural product becomes possible. Importantly, with presumptions of this kind, one fails to determine anything in a final way because the values of substance of what is understood in this case are not at issue. At issue is a 'formal presumption of all understanding', on which Gadamer writes in 'Truth and Method'.[46]

Consequently, only in light of perfection conceived in this way can one understand a positive function of authority recognition of *a person* in the process of seeking truth. Dybel writes as follows:

> It happens when we conclude that someone's opinion, remark or suggestion reveals before us a brand new perspective of understanding of a given thing, a perspective we would never achieve by ourselves. In this situation, an opinion of the person seems 'perfect' to us, not in the sense of confirmation of our achievements [to date], but in the sense of an opinion that exceeds these expectations in what it says. That entails we can learn something new on this basis. Considering this opinion as more apt than ours, we thereby open up to the truth contained in it, which goes beyond the horizon of our understanding.[47]

In this case, the recognition of someone's authority does not involve thoughtless acceptance of this opinion as right only because it has been voiced by the person, but signifies opening to what is other, what exceeds the current horizon of our understanding. Our readiness to accept our 'inferiority' to the Other omits to constrain us and to captivate us, but allows opening fully to the truth of what was spoken by the other. However, it would be impossible if we took a position of a 'critical distance' to his utterance in advance. The phenomenon of someone's authority 'recognition' is not a proof of our 'conservatism' and uncritical 'conformism', but an act of the reason itself, thanks to which we are able to learn something new.[48]

The phenomenon of authority recognition offers the adiaphoric 'I' a unique opportunity to learn something new about the Text – during the process of seeking the Truth. The opinions given by the Authority (the Other) can have advantage over our understanding and thus we can learn something from the Other (the Other), we can open to something Other. As Dybel stresses in his unique analysis of Gadamer's philosophy, the centre of our attention should constitute here the word 'can' – everything revolves around it. 'Can' is not an abstract possibility

45 P. Dybel, *Granice rozumienia i interpretacji O hermeneutyce H.-G. Gadamera* [*The Limits of Understanding and Interpretation. On Hermeneutics of H.-G. Gadamer*] ... , p. 324.

46 *Ibidem*, p. 325.

47 *Ibidem*, p. 326.

48 *Ibidem*, p. 326.

but a real chance which we should seize. Summing up what other – the Other – authority says, there is no reality in a previously given, self-evident form, but he demands from us 'making an effort of going beyond patterns of thought which define our traditional understanding'.[49]

Elaborating on the Gadamerian phenomenon of 'authority recognition', Dybel aptly perceives its significance as a constitutive moment of human understanding. As a result, the Gadamerian phenomenon of 'authority recognition' is not arbitrarily accepted, interpretive dogma or a specific methodological suggestion. I refer here to a kind of inquiring self-awareness.[50] The components of this self-awareness cannot be explicated and justified in a manner similar to how one can justify tenets of a theory or a method. As a consequence, what authority will say will have a status of 'other truth'. The truth may seem difficult to accept to us, 'incomprehensible due to its otherness'. But the Truth has a potential of opening before us (saying before us) a perspective of going beyond the current horizon of understanding. Interestingly enough, it seems that in Dybel's interpretation this requirement is related to the heroic order of the Other. 'Other truth' is present, though expressed in a completely different (philosophically) manner; it also emanates from the Face of the Other.

In Gadamer's view, the revision of writing each time requires an interpretation in the sense of an explanatory understanding, just as the revision of the word requires it, a word which is spoken to someone. The essence of Gadamerian thought on the art of hermeneutics constitutes, therefore, the taking up of what someone actually wanted to say. It will be critical to differentiate this from a mere attribution to someone of something he wanted to say. As a condition *sine qua non* Gadamer considers merging the horizon of one person with the horizon of another person in each understanding. Nonetheless, this fails to entail a motionless or an identifiable One, but the merging is effected in a constant dialogue. Gadamer continues that one should strive to understand the Other, which involves that one should be ready to allow for the fact that one is mistaken – then understanding occurs.[51]

Understanding as a State of Anticipation in Gadamer's Philosophy

The adiaphoric Individual, therefore, has chances to understand the sense of the Text, which has nothing in common with a pure and objective understanding. Such an understanding of the Text does not exist. Understanding involves the application of the sense to our situation and to our problems. As Grondin rightly points out, for Gadamer understanding and application converge. Grondin demonstrates this on a negative example of non-understanding. ' … if we cannot

49 *Ibidem*, p. 327.

50 *Ibidem*, pp. 328, 330.

51 H.-G. Gadamer, 'Romantyzm, Hermeneutyka, Dekonstrukcja' [Romanticism, Hermeneutics, Deconstruction] in: *Język i rozumienie* [*Language and Understanding*] (Fundacja Aletheia, Warszawa 2003), pp. 149–151.

understand a text, this is because it tells us nothing or has nothing to say. There is thus nothing strange in the fact that understanding both in each epoch and in the case of each individual looks different'.[52] Understanding is therefore a creative procedure including application.

Gadamer conceives of tradition as a 'limitless horizon of the sense'. We are always open to this horizon in our understanding in advance. Only in light of this understanding can we understand 'anything' as 'something'. In analysing a Gadamerian approach to the notion of tradition, we should regard tradition as a 'question'. This is a question which we are asked by specific cultural testimonies of past epochs. Tradition opens us to specific 'things' understood by us, e.g. justice and beauty. The 'things' never occur in isolation from the context of a specific historical perspective.[53] Dybel writes as follows:

> We are not open to the 'things' as to pure and identical notions that can be explicitly distinguished from [pre]judgments in light of which they occur and which are closely related to singularity of a historical context. In this sense, a universal moment ['about what' of understanding as a 'thing'] and a particular moment ['what' of understanding, a historical mode in which one understands its 'thing'] are here intertwined, implying each other.[54]

The manner advanced by Gadamer, in which a person who understands relates to tradition when he encounters I as You that asks the person a question, is unique in its construction. This uniqueness combines with the manner of depicting tradition encountered not only as a partner in a conversation (who in his speaking 'starts to talk' to him about a 'thing') but above all as a partner (tradition) who, in its 'starting to talk', opens him up to the 'thing' as such. Tradition is above all such a partner. In this ontological sense, tradition constitutes 'authority' to him as it is such an Other (the Other as tradition). Only in relation to the Other–Tradition can one understand anything. Tradition becomes 'perfect' authority. Tradition is, in other words, certain, unique 'You' without whom an Individual 'talked to' would not be able to understand anything at all.[55]

---

52 J. Grondin, *Wprowadzenie do hermeneutyki filozoficznej* [*An Introduction to Philosophical Hermeneutics*] … , p. 145.

53 P. Dybel, *Granice rozumienia i interpretacji O hermeneutyce H.-G. Gadamera* [*The Limits of Understanding and Interpretation. On Hermeneutics of H.-G. Gadamer*] … , pp. 333–334.

54 *Ibidem*, p. 334.

55 *Ibidem*, pp. 334–335. In this context Paweł Dybel expounds on his thought as follows:

> Tradition encountered as authority is a distinguished Other in Gadamer's concept who, by 'starting to talk to' us, not only tells us something, but also brings us to the field of understanding and speech'. As Dybel continues, Gadamer, here as the author of 'Truth and Method', ' … seems to be close to a Lacanian understanding of language as the Great Other, although naturally

If he wants to understand a text from the past, the adiaphoric Individual has to translate it into his own, particular situation. In order to do so, he has to be able to hear in the Text a linguistic response to questions of times in which he lives, such as our postmodern times. Before the times which are now contemporary, a conversation started for the adiaphoric Individual. Understanding will be its continuation. Understanding as suggested here and now by the adiaphoric 'I' will be a continuation of the conversation from the past, from tradition. I will therefore understand the text if I continue a conversation about the text, which has started long before me. The Individual thus encounters a new sense. Thanks to these encounters, the Individual assumes in this way and modifies in himself some aspects of the sense conveyed to him by tradition and modernity.[56] Now the Text will be able to speak only through questions which the adiaphoric Individual asked the text today. Consequently, in the dialogue suggested by Gadamer, there exist 'no' utterances, but questions and responses which provoke new questions again.[57]

And we return here to the most prominent notion for the discussion so far, i.e. the teaching on Augustine's *verbum interius* which claims that the words we use, simply because they come to our minds, cannot exhaust what we have 'in our souls', i.e. the conversation that we are.[58] Given the above assertion, it seems justified to return to the question posed in the introduction to the discussion on the Text, namely: How to interpret the Text to avoid escapes from moral responsibility in the social life, cutting effects off causes and treating life as a set of episodes? In an attempt to answer these questions, one should first return to the attempt of designing a preliminary premise on non-self-sufficiency of the word, which, in my opinion, constitutes one of the cardinal tenets of eliminating or minimalizing adiaphoric behaviours of modern people.

Considering Gadamerian hermeneutic philosophy and the discussion conducted in the chapter on thinking orientated to excendence in the context of the Speech, I suggest the following extension of assumptions, focusing on the notions of language and understanding:

1. Understanding the Text is not a purely epistemological process, which occurs between a subject and an object, but which proves the anxiety of an Individual reading the Conventions.

---

his concept of language is based on totally different premises. Similarly, as in Gadamerian tradition conceived as You, who asks and only in light of whose question 'I' can – by responding to him – understand anything; in Lacan, only when a subject relates to the field of the Great Other, is he able to say anything (just as he can build his individual and cultural identity).

56 cf. R. Deazley, *Rethinking Copyright. History, Theory, Language* (Edward Edgar Publishing, Northampton 2006), pp. 1–9.

57 J. Grondin, *Wprowadzenie do hermeneutyki filozoficznej* [*An Introduction to Philosophical Hermeneutics*] … , pp. 145–148.

58 *Ibidem*, p. 149.

2. *Extension:* An utterance has its limits. The words we use, simply because they come to our minds, cannot exhaust what we have 'in our souls', i.e. a conversation which we are.
3. The word is no mirror image of a certain, final understanding, but a reflection of understanding of something uncertain.
4. *Extension: vide* extension from point (1).
5. The word contains the 'particular something' which, however, refers to what is Other.
6. *Extension:* The distinguished Other is Tradition encountered in the Text.
7. Tradition has to be treated as Authority. The Other by 'starting to talk to' the Individual, not only says something to him, but also brings him by what he speaks to the field of understanding and speech.
8. The principle of love (thus including the principle of care and goodness) becomes a particular lodestar for an Interpreter of the Text, for each Interpreter.
9. *Extension:* Linguisticality of understanding itself is expressed in a particular pursuit which the Individual should bring himself up to take. It is connected with a constant (never breaking off) pursuit of a language appropriate to express what we have in our souls and what we want to say. The Individual by means of the word found expresses what exists.
10. The source of the word comes from 'something unspecified in our minds' [*quiddam mentis nostrae*].
11. *Extension:* It is important to find what is constitutive of a hermeneutic aspect of understanding. What is constitutive is that understanding is an on-going process of 'adding to the word' and pursuing a communicable language and it should be perceived as this process. As the process, which is an appropriate realization of an inner word [*verbum interius*], justifies the universality of hermeneutics.

It is noteworthy that what is common to this extended construct, to an extended call (and what links it with dilemmas of the Individual and the Speech) is a utopian impulse present in it and associated with *verbum interius*. It seems that, on the basis of an analysis conducted in the chapter, one can propose a utopian character of *verbum interius*. The Text, similar to the Individual and the Speech, is not self-sufficient and this non-self-sufficiency supports a utopian element. Its utopian character stems from the fact that Gadamerian words which we use simply because they come to our minds cannot exhaust what we have 'in our souls', i.e. the conversation which we are.[59] To put it differently, the more non-self-sufficient the Text, the greater possibility of utopia's development in horizons' merging.

To the postmodern adiaphoric Individual or to the self-sufficient Individual, the text in Gadamer's terms is an abstract perfection of language, a self-alienation. Overcoming this perfection by reading the text (reading of the text with

---

59 *Ibidem*, p. 149.

understanding) is the most important task of hermeneutic understanding. The task will be completed when the Individual is able to transform the text into language. Gadamerian language is always a metaphoric language of a conversation. The Individual cannot view language as a limitation or an impediment. Language is not a copy of meaning or an outer border. Gadamer conceives of language as a medium in which understanding is effected. It is a place in which all and thus unique, sense is created. Following the Gadamerian path, the Individual can go beyond language, can leave the space of writing, the space of the Text. One can imagine such a reading of the Text with understanding in which notions would speak in the authentic voice of a conversation again. In a conversation, as the Greeks argued, the most intimate closeness would exist between the word and the notion.

The essence of Gadamerian conversation is communication. There is no issue which we could not agree upon. As Dybel argues:

> A political discourse analysed from this perspective, in which a fundamental principle is defending one's stance 'at all costs', regardless of how serious and overwhelming the arguments the opponent presents, constitutes a degenerated and grotesque form of a conversation with tradition which is conducted in the experience of the humanities. This constitutes a demagogic discourse in the Old Greek understanding of the word. It fails to involve an opening to the arguments of the opponent, or even the 'thing' which is debated on, but it involves forcing one's own viewpoint through at all costs in the name of a particularistic interest of a political party one represents.[60]

It seems that endowing *verbum interius* with a utopian character will bring hope for such a political discourse, in which one can at last be supported by the word liberated from constraints of the Text and where thinking in terms of excendence will be acknowledged, keeping in mind going beyond the space of the Text. After all, the 'particular something' which refers to what is Other, is present in the word.[61] It is so important to postmodernity that neither the Text, nor the Individual, nor the Speech are and will ever be self-sufficient. And if interlocutors think so, there is no hope for a utopian impulse in human right to science and culture. The hope of postmodernity is related to Levinasian and Gadamerian 'non-self-sufficiency' of the Individual, the Speech and the Text *sensu largo*, which refer to what is Other and even utopian.

---

60 P. Dybel, *Granice rozumienia i interpretacji. O hermeneutyce H.-G. Gadamera* [*The Limits of Understanding and Interpretation. On Hermeneutics of H.-G. Gadamer*] … , p. 337.

61 J. Grondin, *Wprowadzenie do hermeneutyki filozoficznej* [*An Introduction to Philosophical Hermeneutics*] … , p. 47.

PART II
The Reason

That which is wise, logical, essential and rational is nothing else than a result of a consolidation of our passions, emotions and desires. I consider the human mind as nothing else than our emotions crystallized into solid, psychological and logical forms; emotions and passions which fossilized and, as such fossils, seem unshaken, essential and unquestionable. I would perceive each essential truth of the reason as based on real, irrational – although to a certain extent regular – human emotions. And only such reason I would like to defend, not the fancy reason of philosophers and mathematicians who take their own desires and fears – as well as regularities which theirs fears are subject to – for an objective, absolute and supraindividual reason.

Zygmunt Bauman
An excerpt from an interview given in 1994 in Leeds, England

Chapter 4
Thinking in Paradigms: Post-Analogue Society in the Era of Postmodernity

Consequences of the Year 1903

It was precisely the year 1903 which witnessed an explosion of interest in recently invented manned flight technology. It was comparable with the present explosion of interest in the Internet and cyberspace. The fact that, on 17 December 1903, the Wright brothers proved on a windy beach of North Carolina in less than 100 seconds that a vehicle heavier than the air can fly on its own marked a breakthrough in technological development for the whole of humanity.[1]

Under American law in force at the time the Wright brothers constructed an aeroplane, a land owner owned not only the surface of his land, but also the whole area stretching below, as far as the centrosphere and the whole space above the land, extending to 'an indefinite extent, upwards'. Over the years scholars pondered how to best interpret the idea of the right to land stretching to the heavens. Laymen of the time even asked: Does it entail owning the stars? Can passing geese (owners of the geese) be punished for deliberate and regular trespassing on the land? (the question may sound naïve but it *de facto* conveys perfectly the atmosphere of shock, which an entirely new technology brought with changes in its wake). If, thus, my land reaches to the sky, what then happens when aeroplanes of a specific airline fly over my field? Do I have the right to forbid them from doing so? Are they allowed to enter into an exclusive contract with a specific air carrier?

These questions lead directly to the case of Thomas Lee and Tinie Causby – a federal court case from 1945. The key facts are as follows: the Causbys, farmers from North Carolina, suffered losses in chicken numbers due to low flying military aircraft: scared chickens rushed and hit their barn wall. The Causbys filed a suit in which they accused the American government of illegal trespassing on their property. The aeroplanes, obviously, never touched their land. However, if, as the lawyers of the Causbys claimed, their land stretched to 'an indefinite extent, upwards', the government had actually trespassed the borders of their property and the Causbys demanded that it immediately be ceased. The Supreme Court held in the case. First the Court took note of the fact that 'it is ancient doctrine that common law ownership of the land extended to the periphery of the universe'.

1 A sub-chapter inspired by the Introduction in Lawrence Lessig's book, *Free Culture. The Nature and Future of Creativity* (Penguin Books, London 2005), pp. 1–13.

Judge Douglas took the following position on the above doctrine in his ruling, in one paragraph doing away with hundreds of years' tradition of right *in rem*:

> [The] doctrine has no place in the modern world. The air is a public highway, as Congress has declared. Were that not true, every transcontinental flight would subject the operator to countless trespass suits. ['Common sense revolts at the idea' adds Lessig[2]] To recognize such private claims to the airspace would clog these highways, seriously interfere with their control and development in the public interest and transfer into private ownership that to which only the public has a just claim.[3]

Summing up, in this manner 'private interests' were not allowed to take precedence over a self-evident benefit for the whole community.[4] Keeping in mind the above example, it would seem that certain ideas perished and would never come back, or that the vision of creativity will control the future ideas.[5] Nevertheless, it turns out in practice that these ideas are sustained as a result of an extraordinarily strong 'position', a policy, an economy and so on.[6] Subsequently, ideas of this kind reveal their whole potential and their consequences in the present postmodern and postanalogue society – in this text, in the form of a right to intellectual property, a right almost as feudal and expansive in its postmodern variety.[7]

2 L. Lessig, *Free Culture* … , p. 2.

3 *USA v. Causby*, U.S. 328 (1946) pp. 256, 261. The Court did not hold that it can be considered as 'expropriation', even if the Court's use of the land caused a decrease in value of the Causbys' land. I refer here after Lessig to the text of Keith Aoka, '(Intellectual) Property and Sovereignty: Notes Toward a Cultural Geography of Authorship', 48 *Stanford Law Review* (1996), pp. 1293, 1333.

4 *Ibidem*, p. 2. This is otherwise an example of the genius of the *common law* system, as it is expressed in the ability to adjust the law to the technology of a given epoch.

5 L. Lessig, *The Future of Ideas. The Fate of the Commons in a Connected World* (Vintage Books, New York, 2001), p. 17. See also L. Lessig, *Code version 2.0* (Basic Books, New York 2006), p. 313–324.

6 Z. Bauman, *Etyka ponowoczesna* [*Postmodern Ethics*] … , pp. 72–73. cf. also M. Fouad Makeen, *Copyright in a Global Information Society. The Scope of Copyright Protection Under International US, UK and French* Law (Kluwer Law International, the Hague, 2000), pp. 2–30. cf. also K.E. Maskus, *Intellectual Property Rights in the Global Economy* (Institute for International Economics, Washington), pp. 27–239.

7 cf. X. Li and C.M. Correa (eds), *Intellectual Property Enforcement* (Edward Elgar, Cheltenham, UK 2009), see Preface. See also D. Bainbridge, *Intellectual Property* (Pitman Publishing, Harlow 1999), pp. 3–26 (on what is intellectual property law), pp. 29–36 (on background and basic principles of copyright), L. Bently and B. Sherman, *Intellectual Property Law* (Third Edition, Oxford University Press, Oxford 2009), pp. 3–5 (on justifications for intellectual property), pp. 31–329 (on copyright), pp. 335–602 (on patents).

Hornborg's Path on Structure

A Swedish scientist, Alf Hornborg from Lund, authored a unique book entitled *Global Inequalities of Economy, Technology and Environment* and a no less telling article 'Challenges in Conceptualizing Environmental Load Displacement and Ecologically Unequal Exchange in the World-System'.[8] These two works are of a truly groundbreaking character for world science, owing to the fact that they advance a theory positing that structures do not consume 'energy' which cannot be created or destroyed – but they consume 'order' that can be extracted from energy. Energy constitutes an indicator of a degree of order and information it contains. The 'order' included in energy can be 'incorporated into' an order of material structures or transformed into radiation. Hornborg argues that we are – as humans – 'caught in a collective illusion about the nature of modern technology that prevents us from imagining solutions to our economic and environmental crises other than technocratic fixes'. He demonstrates how the power of the machine generates increasingly asymmetrical exchanges and distribution of resources and risks between distant populations and ecosystems and thus an increasingly polarized world order. The author challenges us to reconceptualize the machine – 'industrial technomass' – as a species of power and a problem of culture. Hornborg shows how economic anthropology has the tools to deconstruct the concepts of production, money capital and market exchange and to analyse

8 A. Hornborg, *Global Inequalities of Economy, Technology and Environment* (AltaMira Press, US 2001), pp. 2–264. See also A. Hornborg, Challenges in Conceptualizing Environmental Load Displacement and Ecologically Unequal Exchange in the World-System, 50(3–4) *International Journal of Comparative Sociology* (2009), pp. 237–262. The article's abstract:

> This article discusses various ways in which conventional discourse on sustainability fails to acknowledge the distributive, political and cultural dimensions of global environmental problems. It traces some lineages of critical thinking on environmental load displacement and ecologically unequal exchange, arguing that such acknowledgement of a global environmental 'zero-sum game' is essential to recognizing the extent to which cornucopian perceptions of 'development' represent an illusion. It identifies five interconnected illusions currently postponing systemic crisis and obstructing rational societal negotiations that acknowledge the political dimensions of global ecology: 1) The fragmentation of scientific perspectives into bounded categories such as 'technology', 'economy' and 'ecology'. 2) The assumption that the operation of market prices is tantamount to reciprocity. 3) The illusion of machine fetishism, that is, that the technological capacity of a given population is independent of that population's position in a global system of resource flows. 4) The representation of inequalities in societal space as developmental stages in historical time. 5) The conviction that 'sustainable development' can be achieved through consensus. The article offers some examples of how the rising global anticipation of socio-ecological contradiction and disaster is being ideologically disarmed by the rhetoric on 'sustainability' and 'resilience'.

capital accumulation as a problem at the very interface of the natural and social sciences. His analysis provides an alternative understanding of economic growth and technological development.[9] We assume here that 'the act of order production' or of 'order reproduction' can each be creative acts present in our society. Thus, each act of 'order production' is in its essence a destructive event since; on a local scale (on a given geographic or social area), it results in a lesser increase in order than its decrease from the sum of the order's global resources. This involves, in order to translate it into an appropriate language for the purposes of this book, that any modern efforts of order creation in a society 'already updated' (our 'western' or 'modernized' society) succeeded only through a blatantly unequal distribution of world energy resources.

We are dealing here with something that may be to a certain extent and in Baumanian terms, called a 'private, corporate morality' which, in practice, has nothing in common with a description presented on the previous pages of this discussion of moral community or perspective on the Other. In other words, this kind of morality may grow stronger due to regular robbing, 'remaining', 'backward', 'unmodernized' (and 'Other') part of the world of its 'order potential' – of its share in global resources use. One might say corporate social responsibility is not enough; it seems cultural corporate social responsibility is here at stake.[10] Accordingly, given Hornborg's works, it should be stated that economic growth is not about increasing a total sum of order, but on expropriation and redistribution of the order.[11] To put it differently, private, corporate morality will not be affected by creating more order, but by sharing it – thus the emphasis on cultural aspects of the topic will be eventually required. This brief introduction leads to an analysis of the following paradigms: the well-being, the reflectivity, the knowledge commons, the pooling, the Open Source and the rule of balancing. It seems that one may suggest that these paradigms are 'representative *sensu largo*' of a 'total sum of order of the postanalogue society' in the postmodern era, which seeks opportunities to redistribute the order.

The Well-Being Paradigm

Perhaps in order to describe the meaning of the well-being many of us would cite 'Irish Blessings': 'May you always have walls for the winds, a roof for the rain, tea beside the fire, laughter to cheer you, those you love near you and all your heart might desire'. Others would rather equate the notion of well-being with

9 A. Hornborg, *Global Inequalities* … , pp. 2–64.

10 See also W.M. Cohen and J.P. Walsh, 'Access – or Not – in Academic Biomedical Research Pluralism', in: R.C. Dreyfuss, H. First and D.L. Zimmerman, *Working within the Boundaries of Intellectual Property. Innovation Policy for the Knowledge Society* (Oxford University Press, Oxford 2010), pp. 3–28.

11 Z. Bauman, *Etyka ponowoczesna* [*Postmodern Ethics*] … , pp. 329, 331.

virtues like being kind, generous, just, hospitable and courageous. The French could stand for liberty, equality and fraternity. Environmentalists would underline sustainability. Indians might defend inner strength and wisdom. The Swedish might choose equality. Communitarians would vote for common good. Liberals might decide to make liberty a priority and Europeans would perhaps vote for freedoms, citizens' rights and justice and so on.

In general the notion of well-being describes what is 'ultimately good for a person'.[12] The modern conception of well-being is based on an assumption that the greater the freedom of choice people have in planning the course of their lives the better off they are and that people know what is best to enhance their well-being. However, the concept of human well-being is an ambiguous one. It has numerous and often competing interpretations and it lacks a universally accepted definition. Terms such as, for example, income, security, life satisfaction, good life, sustainable development, knowledge and culture, health and population, wealth, happiness, prosperity, human development, equity, freedom and governance, peacefulness, empowerment, resource use, utility and needs fulfilment are often used interchangeably with well-being or perceived as constituents of well-being.[13]

Human well-being is a core global issue. Achieving and sustaining higher levels of well-being is a challenge for both individuals and nations. There are three main theories of well-being that have been distinguished and that are cited as standard theories: (1) hedonist theories, (2) desire theories and (3) objective list theories. According to the simplest form of hedonism, human beings always act in pursuit of what they believe will give them the greatest balance of pleasure over pain.[14] However, since pleasure and pain are inside people's heads and are also hard to measure, economists began to see people's well-being as consisting in the satisfaction of preferences or desires that could also be ranked ('the value of preference satisfaction'). Objective list theories are usually understood as theories which list items constituting well-being that consist neither merely in pleasurable experience nor in desire-satisfaction. For example, according to the recently developed theory by Hurka (the 'perfectionism theory' influenced by Aristotle), what makes things constituents of well-being is their perfecting human nature.[15]

12 *Stanford Encyclopedia of Philosophy*, 6 November 2001. Electronic copy available at www.plato.stanford.edu/entries/well-being/, visited on 30 July 2011. See also V. Arnason, 'Universalism in Ethics and Cultural Diversity', in: Bexell G. and D.-E. Andersson (eds), *Universal Ethics. Perspectives and Proposals from Scandinavian Scholars* (Martinus Nijhoff Publishers, Kluwer Law International, The Hague/London/New York 2002), pp. 18–19, p. 21.

13 W. Glatzer, 'Quality of Life in the European Union and the United States of America: Evidence from Comprehensive Indices', 1:169–188 *Applied Research in Quality of* Life (2006), pp. 170–175.

14 N. White, *A Brief History of Happiness* (Blackwell Publishing, UK/USA 2006), pp. 41–75. See also M. Chekola, 'Book Review: Plurality of Aims and Desires versus Overall Judgments', 8 *Journal of Happiness Studies* (2007), pp. 149–154.

15 T. Hurka, *Perfectionism* (Oxford University Press, Oxford 1993), pp. 31–33.

It is interesting to note that some of the modern philosophers reject the 'virtue' aspects of well-being and instead they focus on the 'self-fulfilment' aspect. Haybron is one of them. In his view the notion of well-being consists of attunement, engagement and endorsement.[16] While an 'attuned' person is a person who has peace of mind, a high level of confidence and is 'uncompressed' (does not lead a harried life feeling emotionally deflated), engagement refers to exuberance, vitality and flow and endorsement could be discussed in terms of joy and cheerfulness. Thus, according to Haybron, well-being is an emotional state comprised of high levels of attunement, engagement and endorsement.

However, since all these concepts might disagree about the content of well-being, the primary idea of what is good is ultimately the development of human nature. This is very close to the above-mentioned 'objective list theories' as well as Haybron's theory (particularly while mentioning engagement as one of the aspects of self-fulfilment). Therefore, if we could agree that a part of human nature is to acquire knowledge, then a perfectionist should claim that knowledge is a constituent of well-being. Moreover, the aspect of engagement also seems to be met.

Well-being is multidimensional.[17] Identifying an exhaustive list of dimensions is a challenging task. Also, obtaining general agreement on the list and the relative importance of each component would appear to be an impossible one. Today knowledge and culture are among the most frequently mentioned dimensions of human well-being. Both knowledge and culture are the conditions for human well-being presented in the Human Well-Being Index (HWI). Knowledge ('to acquire knowledge') is also present as a goal in the Human Development Index (HDI). Also education is mentioned in the weighted Index of Social Progress (WISP).[18] It seems that HWI describes knowledge in the broadest sense. According to this Index, knowledge is a dimension of well-being that affords people to have the capacity to innovate and cope with change, live well in a sustainable fashion and fulfil their potential whereas culture is concerned with avenues for creative growth and self-expression.[19]

What makes society well and sustainable? According to Prescott-Allen a society can be well and sustainable only if both people and the particular ecosystem(s) are well. What is crucial is the relationship between people and the ecosystem and how they affect each other. The point of departure (so-called 'well-being assessment')

16 D.M. Haybron, *The Pursuit of Unhappiness: The Elusive Psychology of Well-Being* (Oxford University Press, Oxford 2008), pp. 28–39.

17 M. McGillivray and M. Clarke (eds), *Understanding Human Well-Being* (United Nations University Press, Tokyo, New York, Paris 2006), pp. 3–17.

18 W. Glatzer, 'Quality of Life in the European Union and the United States of America: Evidence from Comprehensive Indices', 1:169–188 *Applied Research in Quality of Life* (2006), pp. 170–175.

19 R. Prescott-Allen, *The Wellbeing of Nations. A country by Country-by-Country Index of Quality of Life and the Environment* (International Development Research Centre and Island Press, Washington, Covelo, London 2001), p. 5.

is the assumption that both people and the ecosystem are covered and given equal weight. According to Prescott-Allen there are two major kinds of well-being: (1) the well-being of the human and (2) the well-being of the ecosystem.[20] Human well-being is a condition in which all members of society are able to determine and meet their needs and have a large range of choices to meet their potential. The well-being of the ecosystem is a condition in which the ecosystem maintains its diversity and quality – and thus its capacity to support people – and its potential to adapt to change and provide a wide range of choices and opportunities for the future. A high level of human well-being is essential because no one wants to sustain a low standard of living. A high level of ecosystem well-being is just as essential because the ecosystem supports life and makes possible any standard of living. The necessity of both is illustrated by Prescott-Allen as the metaphor of the Egg of Wellbeing.[21] The ecosystem surrounds and supports people much as the white of an egg surrounds and supports the yolk. Just as an egg is good only if both the yolk and the white are good, a society can only be well and sustainable if both people and the ecosystem are well.

The Reflectivity Paradigm

Society is not a static, constant and 'existing' being, but a reality that is happening and keeps 'becoming' over and over again. It follows from the fact that everything that exists in a society comes down to social events: fluid, always changing, fluctuating configurations of culture-moulded people's actions related to other people's actions. For society undergoes constant transformation and reproduction – in a word: it develops. It is connected with a belief in the power and creativity of the human mind and knowledge, which means that man can understand not only nature but also the mechanics of the social world and therefore man can act consciously.[22] Today sociologists attach the feature of 'reflectivity' to the postmodern, contemporary society. The reflective characteristics consist in creating movements capable of collective learning and shaping new man who can think both creatively and critically and – most importantly – is capable of human cooperation.[23] 'Reflectivity' is a form of social consciousness and one of its principal goals is to reverse unfavourable trends in society. It might be perceived

20 *Ibidem*, p. 5.

21 *Ibidem*, p. 5.

22 Z. Brodecki and A.M. Nawrot, *Świątynia w cyberkulturze. Technologie cyfrowe i prawo w społeczeństwie wiedzy* [*Temple in Cyberculture. Digital Technologies in Information Society*] (Wydawnictwo Uniwersytetu Gdanskiego 2007), pp. 82–83. See also K. Bolestuta-Kukulka, *Sociologia Ogólna* [*General Sociology*] (Oficyna Wydawnicza ASPRA-JR, Warszawa, 2003), p. 318.

23 A. Giddens, *Stanowienie Społeczeństwa* [*The Constitution of Society*] (Wydawnictwo Zysk i S-ka, Poznan 2003), pp. 216–217.

as a new, important competence of our present society. It is frequently manifested in activities of social movements, often taken up in spite of economic interests in a broad sense.[24] 'Reflectivity' is comprehended as an ability to use the mechanisms of self-correction. The mechanism can be seen as a 'motor of post modernity'. It results from the fact that a society is able to overcome any problems by activating self-correction mechanisms or forming antibodies, which fight dangerous effects of its own development.[25] Environmentalism 30 years ago and the access to knowledge (A2K) movement at present are important examples.

Today thinking of reflective society in the global context is a must.[26] Therefore we must first consider the kind of occurrences which transgress the limits of traditional objects of analysis (countries and regions).[27] One of the most important occurrences of this type is 'knowledge'. The era of late modernity we are entering into has the opportunity to be characterized by knowledge as the basis for the most important solutions. Together with the entrance of the era of digital technologies, knowledge becomes a central commodity for the economy and the utmost good of a society. In this way a specific trend is outlined which can be defined as a postanalogue society. The kind of work that may be referred to as productive is, basically, a work that uses visions and ideas and therefore one that is based on the power of the human mind and not the strength of arms. The development of society begins to be determined by the intellectual resources of the members, i.e., their knowledge.[28] The postmodern society is characterized by the replacement of material values with postmaterial values. In this way, new values are established, supported by newly-emerged social movements like for example A2K movement.[29]

---

24 cf. R. Towse, *Creativity, Incentive and Reward* (Edward Elgar, Cheltenham, UK 2001), pp. 1–24 and 131–157.

25 cf. D. Matthews, *Intellectual Property, Human Rights and Development. The Role of NGOs and Social Movements* (Edward Elgar, Cheltenham, UK 2011), pp. 221–257. cf. P. Sztompka, *Socjologia. Analiza Społeczeństwa* [*Sociology. An Analysis of Society*] (Wydawnictwo Znak, Krakow 2004), p. 573.

26 cf. R. Deazley, *Rethinking Copyright …* , pp. 1–9.

27 R. Robertson, 'Globality, Global Culture and Images of World Order', in: H. Haferkamp and N.J. Smelser (eds), *Social Change and Modernity* (California University Press, Berkeley 1992), pp. 395–411.

28 P. Drucker, *Post-Capitalist Society* (Harper, New York 1993), p. 12.

29 L. Shaver, 'Intellectual Property, Innovation and Development: The Access to Knolwedge Approach', in: L. Shaver (ed.), *Access to Knolwedge in Brazil* (Bloomsbury Academic, London, New York 2010), pp. 1–8; P. Nicoletti Mizukami and Ronaldo Lemos, 'From Free Software to Free Culture: The Emergence of Open Business', in: L. Shaver (ed.), *Access to Knolwedge in Brazil* (Bloomsbury Academic, London, New York 2010), p. 13–40. See also M. Chon, 'A Rough Guide to Global Intellectual Property Pluralism', in: R.C. Dreyfuss, H. First and D.L. Zimmerman, *Working Within the Boundaries of Intellectual Property. Innovation Policy for the Knowledge Society* (Oxford University Press, Oxford 2010), pp. 448–446. M. Chon introduces an interesting theory of global intellectual property pluralism.

A characteristic feature of these new values is the gradual decrease of the significance of the economic dimension as a totality in social and cultural life.[30]

The Commons Paradigm

Thank to digital technologies, property (also referred to as 'digital') can be freely reproduced and distributed to an infinite number of addresses and locations, even behind its author's back.[31] The mere possibility to distribute intellectual property in such an easy way is provided by the characteristics of the Internet itself, being global, decentralized, multi-juridical and deprived of digital regulations of law.[32] Globalism makes the Internet the most popular and largest public computer network in the world. The decentralization of the Internet is achieved by a great number of different networks communicating with one another. The web of the networks functions on the basis of packet switching. Messages containing such data as music, film or regular electronic mail are broken into transmittable packets, each of which is then sent along a number of network paths to be put back together at the destination. This kind of transmission is recognized by different computer systems because it is based on defined standards, which makes it possible to connect a lot of different computer networks to form such a powerful communication medium as the Internet. From the point of view of intellectual property rights, the most prominent feature of the Internet is its digitality.[33] Unlike traditional analogue methods used to record output, digitization converts all words, sounds, images and graphics into the binary format (a sequence of zeros and ones). Consequently, the digitally recorded output has no physical form and thus it is more difficult

---

30 R. Inglehart, *Modernization and Postmodernization. Cultural, Economic and Political Change in 43 Societies* (Princeton University Press, Princeton 1997), p. 76.

31 The history of the Internet starts in 1969 when the first ARPANET link was established at the University of California in Los Angeles (USA), as part of a military experiment. ARPANET can be considered as a direct predecessor of the contemporary World Wide Web. Initially, the network was designed to serve strategic and defensive purposes. However, it soon became evident that it was a perfect tool for scientists to make remote calculations on mainframe computers. Today, the popularity and the variety of uses for the network have gone far beyond the expectations of its creators.

32 L. Jones, 'An Artist's Entry Into Cyberspace: Intellectual Property On The Internet', 22(2) *EIPR* (2000), pp. 80–83.

33 See also D. Rowland, U. Kohl and A. Charlesworth, *Information Technology Law* (Fourth Edition, Routledge, London, New York), pp. 319–354; H.L. Macqueen, 'Appropriate for the Digital Age? Copyright and the Internet: 1. Scope of Copyright', in: L. Edwards and Ch. Waelde (eds), *Law and the Internet* (Hart Publishing, Oxford and Portland, Oregon 2009), pp. 181–203; A. Guadamuz, 'Free and Open-Source Software', in: L. Edwards and Ch. Waelde (eds), *Law and the Internet* (Hart Publishing, Oxford and Portland, Oregon 2009), pp. 361–395.

to protect. Furthermore, the protection does not apply to the piece of work itself (e.g. a film or book), but to its digital representation.[34]

We are all witnesses of historic developments in the digital technology era because we are beginning to be more dependent on (and addicted to) computer and network systems.[35] Internet technologies offer quick and easy access to products of intellectual work, the result of which is, among other things, the possibility of copying them.[36] The latest technological developments, such as computer software and the Internet in a broad sense, compel us to introduce a modern way to exercise intellectual property rights since pieces of work have been freed from their physical *beings*.[37]

As Edwin Bendyk stresses in his Foreword to the Polish edition of 'Free Culture', Lessig is a proponent of 'commonism' creation. He explores this idea in his famous – powerfully argued and important – book *The Future of Ideas* (2001). Lessig refers in it to an institution of common good that enjoyed popularity in pre-modern societies. The word 'Commons' in Great Britain was used to denote communal pastures, on which the cattle of villagers grazed. But in the sixteenth century a privatization of common pastures began – known as the process of enclosure. It was one of the most significant factors which enabled the subsequent fast development of British capitalism and the success of the industrial revolution.[38] In the twentieth century 'Commons' became famous again owing to the work of a scientist, biologist Garett Hardin. In 1967 he published in 'Science' journal an article 'Tragedy of the Commons'. The article set out to prove that common good (the communal pasture) has to disappear, sooner or later.[39]

Commons as a subject matter returns in cyberspace in a new perspective. The source of the greatest accumulation of capital is not industrial production any more, but the processing of symbols, knowledge and ideas. Castells, a distinguished sociologist from the University of California in Berkeley, posits that on the ruins of industrial society (whose main organizational principle was industrialism) a network society arose whose principle is 'informationalism'. Drucker writes about the birth of a knowledge society and a knowledge-based economy. This raises the

---

34 cf. P. Pedley, *Digital Copyright* (Facet Publishing, London 2007), pp. 2–44; S. Stokes, *Digital Copyright. Law and Practice* (Hart Publishing, Oxford and Portland 2009), pp. 10–15.

35 cf. from earlier works F. Pollaud-Dulian (eds), *Perspectives on Intellectual Property. The Internet and Authors' Rights* (Sweet & Maxwell, London 1999), pp. 105–119.

36 A. Benczek, 'EU: Intellectual property – recent initiatives at EU level against counterfeiting and piracy', 25(8) *EIPR* (2003), pp. 342–350.

37 A.M. Nawrot, 'The Meaning of Intellectual Property Rights in the Knowledge Society – EU Perspective', in: S.M. Mercado Kierkegaard (ed.), *Legal, Privacy and Security Issues in Information Technology. Vol. 2.* The First International Conference on Legal, Privacy and Security Issues in IT, Hamburg, Germany, 30 April – 2 May 2006, COMPLEX 4/06 (Institutt for rettsinformatikk, Oslo), pp. 11–27.

38 L. Lessig, *Wolna Kultura* [*Free Culture*] … , pp. 13–14.

39 *Ibidem*, p. 14.

question of a common denominator of the above discussion? These are knowledge and money.

A fundamental means of conveying values are presently symbols – the most essential substance of the present world.[40] They attract, more and more, the interest of customers and capital. What is valuable should be protected more and more carefully. What rules, however, guide the life of symbols, the life of culture and science? The most important resources for society are symbols and creativity as well as specific commons, a common good – culture. The resources are at stake because of the *enclosure* process, privatization by means of a broader and broader application of rights protecting intellectual property.[41] On the other hand, a technological progress makes the rights less and less effective and an attempt at their execution is taken to absurd levels. Institutions whose purpose was to protect intellectual property were established to protect authors and inventors, which in turn was to serve the promotion of creativity.[42] Lessig points out that, intellectual property rights, instead of stimulating creativity and inventiveness, are increasingly effective in hampering it.[43]

Some rights reserved within the Creative Commons (CC) licence developed by Lessig, which extends the notion of copyright application, Bendyk calls a Copernican turn. The essence of this innovation is the restoration of the original character of the institutions granting copyright protection. These rights are therefore supposed to stimulate creativity by granting protection to creators (and

---

40 *Ibidem*, pp. 14–15.

41 J. Boyle, *The Public Domain. Enclosing the Commons of the Mind* (Yale University Press, New Haven, London, 2008), pp. 43–53. Boyle on the second enclosure movement:

> Like most criticisms of the enclosure movement, … a conversion into private property of something that had formely been common property or perhaps had been outside the property system altogether. … we are in the middle of a second enclosure movement. While it sounds grandiloquent to call it 'the enclosure of the intangible commons of the mind', in a very real sense that is just what it is. True, the new state-created property rights may be 'intellectual' rather than 'real', but once again things that were formerly thought of as common property, or as 'uncommodifiable', or outside the market altogether, are being covered with new, or newly extended, property rights.

42 *Ibidem*, pp. 179–205 (on creative commons), pp. 230–249 (on environmentalism for information), p. 238:

> We need a political debate about intellectual property that recognizes these trade-offs; that does not impose simplistic, one-sided solutions; that looks to evidence. We need to understand the delicate and subtle balance between property and the opposite of property, the role of rights, but also of the public domain and the commons. Building a theory, let alone a movement, around such an issue is hard. Doing so when we lack some of the basic theoretical tools and vocabularies is daunting. We do not even have a robust conception of the public domain. If they think of it as a legal issue at all, people simply think of it as whatever is left over after an endless series of rights have been carved out.

43 L. Lessig, *Wolna Kultura* [*Free Culture*] … , pp. 13–14, p. 16.

not mainly to publishing houses, phonographic or film companies). Lessig states that at the heart of creativity has always been a combination of copying and imitating of already existing works with acts of original expression.[44] Thus, if creativity (also if humanity) is supposed to flourish, it must be able to legally use the works of other creators.[45] As Bendyk notices, such argumentation may seem too subtle for companies. Consequently, let creators decide by themselves how their works are to be explored. Creative Commons (CC) licence is to become a tool for achieving this goal. 'Copernicanism' of the idea derives from the fact that, instead of defining to what extent the work is to be protected by licence, it transfers these rights to the author – it is the author who is to decide to what extent the work is to be free and available to other creators – that is, practically for everyone.[46]

It was already Richard Stallman – the creator of the Free Software Foundation (that will be developed in the subsequent part of the book) – who had invented the ideas of 'copyleft' and of GPL licence.[47] They delineate the rules of software use, the rules of free copying and sharing the effects of work.[48] Cultural creativity has considerably more shades and needs subtler tools; hence the system of CC licences is multilevel. Importantly, Lessig not only makes specific proposals but also provides a critique of the system, which is of immense value in itself. It is aimed at the protection of creativity, access to knowledge, freedom of expression and autonomy of a broadly understood culture (culture autonomy!). What does it entail? How to create the Constitution of a new, digital society? – Bendyk asks.[49]

With regard to the commons as an important paradigm at stake Hess and Ostrom summarize its recent developments in the following, enumerative way:[50]

1. The rapidly expanding world of distributed digital information has infinite possibilities as well as incalculable threats and pitfalls. The parallel, yet contradictory trends, where, on the one hand, there is unprecedented access to information through the Internet but where, on the other, there are ever-greater restrictions on access through intellectual property legislation, overpatenting, licensing, overpricing, withdrawal and lack of preservation, indicate the deep and perplexing characteristics of this resource.

44 *Ibidem*, p. 17.

45 R. Albritton, 'A Practical Utopia for the Twenty-First Century', in: P. Vieira and M. Marder (eds), *Existential Utopia. New Perspectives on Utopian Thought* (Continuum International Publishing Group, London 2012), pp. 141–156.

46 L. Lessig, *Wolna Kultura* [*Free Culture*] … , p. 17.

47 L. Rosen, *Open Source Licensing. Software Freedom and Intellectual Property Law* (Prentice Hall Books, New Jersey 2004), pp. 2–39.

48 A.M. St. Laurent, *Understanding Open Source & Free Software Licensing* (O'Reilly Media, Sebastopol 2004), pp. 4–8.

49 L. Lessig, *Wolna Kultura* [*Free Culture*] … , pp. 17–18.

50 C. Hess and E. Ostrom (eds), 'Introduction: An Overview of the Knowledge Commons', in: *Understanding Knowledge as a Commons. From Theory to Practice* (The MIT Press, Cambridge), pp. 14–15.

2. Knowledge, which can seem so ubiquitous in digital form, is, in reality, more vulnerable than ever before. When hard-copy journals, for instance, were sold to libraries and individuals, the decentralization of multiple copies made the works robust. When journals are in digital form and licenced to libraries or individuals, the works are centralized and vulnerable to the whims or happenstance of the publisher.
3. Users who rely on certain journals being indexed in LexisNexis or other large indexing services, are frustrated to find one day that those journals were dropped and will no longer be indexed.
4. Collective-action initiatives, such as open access and Free/Libre and Open Source Software development, are ensuring much greater accessibility and robustness of digital resources. Many questions exist as to how to develop future initiatives that will increase the security of digital knowledge while not blocking access to those who would benefit greatly from its use.

As we comprehend the pasture open to all is a type of common pool resource, because it would be hard and costly to exclude someone from it and the use of it by one individual would abstract from the benefits available to the other. Of course, these are the resources for which the regime of commons work very well for. However, knowledge differs.[51] The Commons is a general term that refers to a resource shared by a group of people. It can exist at the global level, like the Internet, deep seas, scientific knowledge, or at the local group level, like a library or a playground. It may have boundaries or it may not.[52] Knowledge is an example

---

51 cf. A. Lukoseviciene, 'Beyond the Creative Commons Framework for production and dissemination of information'. Master's thesis, Faculty of Law, Lund University, Sweden (Master's Programme in International Human Rights Law and Intellectual Property 2011, supervisor: Anna Maria Andersen Nawrot), p. 17.

52 J. Boyle, *The Public Domain. Enclosing the Commons of the Mind* (Yale University Press, New Haven, London, 2008), p. 183:

> From one perspective, Creative Commons looks like a simple device for enabling exercise of authorial control, remarkable only for the extremely large number of authors making that choice and the simplicity with which they can do so. From another, it can be seen as re-creating, by private choice and automated licences, the world of creativity before law had permeated to the finest, most atomic level of science and culture – the world of folk music or 1950s jazz, of jokes and slang and recipes, of Ray Charles's 'rewordking' of gospel songs, or of Isaac Newton describing himself as 'standing on the shoulders of giants' (and not having to pay them royalties). Remember, that is not a world *without* intellectual property. The cookbook might be copyrighted even if the recipe was not. Folk music makes it to the popular scene and is sold as a copyrighted product. The jazz musician 'freezes' a particular version of the improvisation on a communally shared set of musical motifs, records it and sometimes even claims ownership of it. Newton himself was famously touchy about precedence and attribution, even if not about legal ownership of his ideas. But it is a world in which creativity and

of a commons without clear boundaries.[53] The commons celebrate the community and not the heroic individual, the self-made man.[54] The knowledge commons is the new shared territory of globally distributed knowledge.[55] It is based on the idea that the more people that share useful knowledge, the greater is the common good.[56] According to Hess and Ostrom, knowledge commons shall be perceived broadly and can consist of many different goods and regimes and still have the characteristics of a commons.[57] The study of traditional commons and knowledge as precious resources by Ostrom and Hess brings me to the development of the following crucial points of their thesis that shall be introduced for the broader comprehension of its reason:[58]

1. The analysis of knowledge as a commons has its roots in the broad, interdisciplinary study of shared natural resources, such as water resources, forests, fisheries and wildlife. *Commons* is a general term that refers to a resource shared by a group of people. In a commons, the resource can be small and serve a tiny group (the family refrigerator], it can be community-level [sidewalks], playgrounds, libraries and so on], or it may extend to international and global

---

> innovation proceed on the basis of an extremely large 'commons' of material into which it was never imagined that property rights could permeate.

53 C. Hess and E. Ostrom, *Understanding Knowledge as a Commons. From Theory to Practice* (The MIT Press, Cambridge/London/Massachusetts 2007), pp. 4–5:

> Commons is a general term that refers to a resource shared by a group of people. In a commons, the resource can be small and serve a tiny group (the family refrigerator), it can be community-level (sidewalks, playgrounds, libraries and so on), or it can extend to international and global levels (deep seas, the atmosphere, the Internet and scientific knowledge). The commons can be well bounded (a community park or library); transboundary … ; or without clear boundaries (knowledge, the ozone layer).

54 D. Bollier, 'The Growth of the Commons Paradigm', in: C. Hess and E. Ostrom (eds), *Understanding Knowledge as a Commons. From Theory to Practice* (The MIT Press, Cambridge), p. 27.

55 C. Hess and E. Ostrom (eds), 'Introduction: An Overview of the Knowledge Commons', in: *Understanding Knowledge as a Commons. From Theory to Practice* (The MIT Press, Cambridge), p. 4.

56 See further on the origin and meaning of the commons concept M.W.S. Wong, 'Toward an Alternative Normative Framework for Copyright. From Private Property to Human Rights', 26:775 *Cardozo Arts and Entertainment* (2009), pp. 795–798. According to M.W.S. Wong, '… the concept of a commons is traceable to the development, in early English law, of certain customary or traditional rights of access to and use of, land (e.g. for grazing by cattle, for use as pasture, to collect wood or to fish) by persons other than the landowner'.

57 C. Hess and E. Ostrom (eds), *Introduction: An Overview of the Knowledge …* , p. 5.

58 The following points based on: C. Hess and E. Ostrom (eds), *Introduction: An Overview of the Knowledge …* , pp. 4–8.

levels [deep seas, the atmosphere, the Internet and scientific knowledge]. The commons can be well bounded [a community park or library]; transboundary [migrating wildlife, the Internet]; or without clear boundaries [knowledge, the ozone layer].

2. Commons analysts have often found it necessary to differentiate between a commons as a resource system and a commons as a property-rights regime. Shared resource systems – called common-pool resources – are types of economic goods, independent of particular property rights. *Common property* on the other hand is a legal regime – a jointly owned legal set of rights … . Throughout this book, the more general term *commons* is preferred in order to describe the complexity and variability of knowledge and information as resources. Knowledge commons can consist of multiple types of goods and regimes and still have many characteristics of a commons.
3. In fact, the more people who share useful knowledge, the greater the common good. Consideration of knowledge as a commons, therefore, suggests that the unifying thread in all commons resources is that they are jointly used, managed by groups of varying sizes and interests.[59]
4. Another important aspect of collective-action is that it is voluntary on the part of each individual. *Self-governance* requires collective action combined with knowledge and will on the one hand and supporting and consistent institutional arrangements on the other hand.
5. Social capital refers to the aggregate value of social networks [i.e. who people know], and the inclinations that arise from these networks for people to do things for each other [i.e. the norms of reciprocity]. Throughout this book we will see these three elements – collective action, self-governance and social capital – frequently in play.
6. Knowledge also includes creative works, such as music and the visual and theatrical arts. Some view knowledge as polemical, in that it has 'dual functions' – as a commodity and as a constitutive force of society … . This dual functionality as a human need and an economic good immediately suggests the complex nature of this resource. Acquiring and discovering knowledge is both a social process and a deeply personal process.
7. Knowledge is cumulative. With ideas the cumulative effect is a public good, so long as people have access to the vast storehouse, but access and preservation were serious problems long before the advent of digital technologies. An infinite amount of knowledge is waiting to be unearthed. The discovery of future knowledge is a common good and a treasure we owe to future generations. The challenge of today's generation is to keep the pathways to discovery open.
8. Ensuring access to knowledge is made easier by examining the nature of knowledge and identifying the ways in which it is a commons. This approach is in contrast to the standard economics literature. In that literature, knowledge has often been used as the classic example of a pure public good –

59 *Ibidem*, p. 4.

> a good available to all and where one person's use does not subtract from another's use. In the classic treatment of public goods Paul A. Samuelson ... classified all of the goods that might be used by humans as either pure private or pure public.[60]

According to Hess and Ostrom the focus on traditional or new, however, the essential questions for any commons analysis are inevitably about equity, efficiency and sustainability:[61] *Equity* refers to issues of just or equal appropriation from and contribution to, the maintenance of a resource. *Efficiency* deals with optimal production, management and use of the resource. *Sustainability* looks at outcomes over the long term. Many studies hone in on issues of property-rights regimes and the various challenges of common property. Indeed, the important distinctions between the terms 'common *property*' and 'common-*pool resource*' grew out of this scholarship. Moreover, the identification of design principles of robust, long-enduring, common-pool resource institutions are as follows:[62] clearly defined boundaries should be in place, rules in use are well matched to local needs and conditions, individuals affected by these rules can usually participate in modifying the rules, the right of community members to devise their own rules is respected by external authorities, a system for self-monitoring members' behaviour has been established, a graduated system of sanctions is available, community members have access to low-cost conflict-resolution mechanisms and finally nested enterprises – that is, appropriation, provision, monitoring and sanctioning, conflict resolution and other governance activities – are organized in a nested structure with multiple layers of activities.[63]

---

60 *Ibidem*, p. 4.

61 C. Hess and E. Ostrom (eds), 'Introduction: An Overview of the Knowledge Commons', in: *Understanding Knowledge* ... , pp. 6–7.

62 *Ibidem*, pp. 6–7.

63 According to Hess and Ostrom:

> These principles were discovered after conducting a large set of empirical studies on common-pool resource governance. One of the central findings was that an extremely rich variety of specific rules were used in systems sustainable over a long time period. No single set of specific rules, on the other hand, had a clear association with success. Only after grappling with this wide diversity of robust systems was it possible to identify general principles that tended to underline the robust institutions. The eight factors identified were those found to exist in most robust institutions – but they were absent in failed systems. These principles have inspired hundreds of studies. And they are, indeed, helpful as a possible place to start an investigation. But they are in no way prescriptive-nor are they models. Rather, they are insightful findings in the analysis of small, homogenous systems. Whether they apply to the study of large and complex systems like the knowledge commons is a question for further research.

'Many people see the commons as a useful template for making sense of the new social and market dynamics driving so much creativity and knowledge creation' – writes Bollier.[64] According to him the commons is a new (i.e. newly recognized) cultural form that is unfolding in front of us. The discourse of the commons is at once descriptive, constitutive and expressive:[65] 1) Descriptive since it identifies models of community governance that would otherwise go unexamined. 2) Constitutive because, by giving us a new language, it helps us to build new communities based on principles of the commons. 3) Expressive since the language of the commons is a way for people to assert a personal connection to a set of resources and a social solidarity with each other. Bollier creates the commons' perspective for the postmodern society. The commons as a school of thought that can help us begin to articulate certain concerns and provide a public vernacular for talking about the politics of creativity and knowledge:[66] One may suggest it is summarized in the following crucial statements that for the purposes of this work one may name according to Bollier's 'Nine Commons Statements of *Reason*':[67]

1. The commons is traditionally associated with plots of land – and the supposed tragedy that results from its overexploitation by free riders. However according to them there are significant difference between natural-resource commons like land, which are depletable and 'rivalrous' (many people wish to use the resource to the exclusion of others), and commons that manage nondepletable, nonrivalrous resources such as information and creative works.
2. What makes the term *commons* useful, nonetheless, is its ability to help us identify problems that affect both types of commons (e.g., congestion, overharvesting, pollution, inequities, other degradation) and to propose effective alternatives (e.g., social rules, appropriate property rights and management structures). To talk about the commons is to assume a more holistic vantage point for assessing how a resource may be best managed.
3. Librarians, scholars, scientists, environmentalists, software programmers, Internet users, biotech researchers, fisheries scholars and many others share a dissatisfaction with the standard market narrative. They are skeptical that strict property rights and market exchange are the only way to manage a resource

C. Hess and E. Ostrom (eds), 'Introduction: An Overview of the Knowledge Commons', in: *Understanding Knowledge as a Commons: From Theory to Practice* (The MIT Press, Cambridge), p. 7.

64 D. Bollier, 'The Growth of the Commons Paradigm', in: C. Hess and E. Ostrom (eds), *Understanding Knowledge as a Commons: From Theory to Practice* (The MIT Press, Cambridge), p. 30.

65 *Ibidem*, p. 29.

66 *Ibidem*, p. 31.

67 The following statements based on D. Bollier, 'The Growth of the Commons … ', pp. 28–38.

well, particularly in the context of the Internet, where it is supremely inexpensive and easy to copy and share information. 'The great virtue of the commons as a school of thought is its ability to talk about the social organization of life that has some large measure of creative autonomy from the market or the state'.

4. 'Economists tend to regard market activity and growth as inherently good, when in fact it is often a force for eroding valuable nonmarket resources such as family time, social life and ecosystems.'
5. 'In this climate, the language of the commons serves a valuable purpose. It provides a coherent alternative model for bringing economic, social and ethical concerns into greater alignment. It is able to talk about the inalienability of certain resources and the value of protecting community interests. The commons fills a theoretical void by explaining how significant value can be created and sustained outside of the market system'.
6. 'The commons paradigm does not look primarily to a system of property, contracts and markets, but to social norms and rules and to legal mechanisms that enable people to share ownership and control of resources.'
7. 'The matrix of evaluating the public good is not a narrow index like gross domestic product or a company's bottom line, but instead looks to a richer, more qualitative and humanistic set of criteria that are not easily measured, such as moral legitimacy, social consensus and equity, transparency in decision making and ecological sustainability, among other concerns.'
8. 'The spread of the commons discourse in recent years has had a double effect: it has helped *identify* new commons and, in providing a new public discourse, it has helped *develop* these commons by enabling people to see them as commons.'
9. 'The commons reclaims the sovereignty of this cultural activity. It names it as a separate economy that works in tandem with the market, performing its own significant work … . The commons is not a manifesto, ideology, or a buzzword, but rather a flexible template for talking about the rich productivity of social communities and the market enclosures that threaten them.'

Bollier describes the future of the commons in the following way:

> I believe the future of the commons will depend a great deal on a dialectic conversation between practitioners who are inventing new legal and institutional mechanisms to protect the commons, and scholars and thinkers who are developing the intellectual tools to foster better understanding, strategic innovation and public education. If the past decade is any indication, this dialogue is likely to produce many salutary results.[68]

68 *Ibidem*, p. 38.

The development of a paradigm presented thoroughly above became a prototype for Creative Commons and Open Source which will be discussed in detail in the following pages.

The Pooling Paradigm

Usually, when a number of companies work out a specific common standard they remain holders of the patents for the inventions that are required to establish the standard. As a result, each of the companies may block the outsiders (i.e. the companies that are out of the network where the relevant standard is applied), hindering them from manufacturing products to that standard. In practice, the companies which developed a standard frequently try to control the patents for the inventions used to work out the standard. In this way, any company from outside of the standard system wishing to produce a standard-compliant device is forced to obtain a licence from each authorised holder of the relevant rights. This makes the situation of the company very uncomfortable because if one of the licensors introduces restrictive licence terms, e.g. by specifying exorbitant fees, the access to the invention will be denied. The purpose of such institutions as patent-pools (and the related cross-licensing) is to prevent situations where companies block access to inventions, becoming monopolists of a given standard.[69]

A patent-pool is an agreement concluded by authorised patent holders in order to aggregate all patents they hold individually. In a typical pool all the patents collected by the group become available to each member of the group. Patent-pools often make it possible to grant standard licences to organizations which are not members of the particular patent-pool. Moreover, in a typical patent-pool each member of the group pays some licence fees according to an agreed procedure. The main reason that companies form patent-pools is the need to establish a consistent form of regulation as regards any vertical relationships, such as between a company/patent-pool member and a company/non-member and any horizontal relationships, such as between a company/member and other company/member of the same patent-pool. It seems that another reason that patent-pools are formed is the wish to develop a competitive 'package' which, being a product featuring a variety of inherent patents (which allows e.g. the development of equipment that will be compatible with the specific standard set by patent-pool members), will have strong selling points on the competitive market of digital technologies.

The principal goal of patent-pools is the regulation of agreements. This chiefly applies to information technology industry agreements. The economic rationale in such agreements is simple: they largely reduce the costs of the whole

69 See also D.A. Crane, 'Patent Pools, RAND Commitments and the Problematics of Price Discrimination', in: R.C. Dreyfuss, H. First and D.L. Zimmerman, *Working within the Boundaries of Intellectual Property. Innovation Policy for the Knowledge Society* (Oxford University Press, Oxford 2010), pp. 371–394.

transaction. Indisputably, signing a single collective agreement is considerably cheaper than a series of individual licence agreements concluded by each member of a patent-pool separately. Furthermore, thanks to collective agreements the whole system of patent protection has the possibility to work in a more efficient way. In this way a formalized and, so to speak, repeatable collective agreement pattern is established, substantially facilitating the refining of details between the parties. Companies that decided to join a patent-pool usually are obliged to licence all their patents which comprise the technology applied by patent-pool members in the common pool. In return, each patent-pool member is free to use the technology of all other members, applying the so-called cross-licensing principle. This kind of cross-licensing is usually free of charge. In practice, a cross-licensing agreement eliminates the monopolistic position of an inventor (here understood as an information technology company). In this context, one could aptly note that obtaining a licence is more important to the public interest than using the invention by an authorized party enjoying its monopolistic position. Cross-licensing allows all companies that belong to the patent-pool to use the invention. However, a special body, appointed by the specific patent-pool group, determines the licence fee to be charged by the company that granted the licence. In this case we can talk about a particular, unofficial evaluation of the invention by the specifically-formed regulating body of the patent-pool. Summing up, all patent-pools have a single common feature: they introduce a uniform, simplified (collective) mechanism of contracting, which contributes to the provision of technology. It is worth underlining that the mechanism was developed by the society of right-holders both to their advantage and for the benefit of the society of users.[70] Therefore, it is a mechanism whose formation resulted from behaviours and needs of the knowledge society rather than of legislative or judicial interpretation bodies. At the moment we are facing the development of MPEG technology.

Recent years have witnessed increased recognition of patent-pools as a viable instrument. An example of positive reception of this instrument is the Guidelines on the application of Article 81 of the EC Treaty to technology transfer agreements, which state that technology pools are capable of influencing economies in a pro-competitive way.[71] Particularly, the pro-competitive effect is visible in the reduction of transaction costs. Moreover, a positive property of a patent-pool is the creation of one-stop licensing (which means covering of 'all technology' contained in a pool by a single licence agreement). What follows is that a behaviour that quite recently could be seen as violating the freedom of competition within the Community today is actually regarded as a normal activity and which has become an inseparable component of the essential innovation development process, as

70 See also D.A. Crane, *Patent Pools, RAND Commitments and the Problematics of Price …* , pp. 371–394.

71 See *Guidelines on the application of Article 81 EC Treaty to technology transfer agreements* (2004/C 101/02).

well as the process of increasing the level of invention in the knowledge society.[72] A proof of the change in perception of pooling is also evident in the application of competition law. For example, the European Commission agreed to forming patent-pools for patents that include the application of DVD technology and the approval clearly underlines the role of pooling of rights as a phenomenon which promotes technological progress, contributes to acquisition of a single licence comprising all patents included in a pool within a short time and on identical (non-discriminating) conditions.[73] The Commission further stressed that the lower costs of licensing are not to be underestimated either. The positive characteristics of the instrument constitute a benefit to the knowledge society, thanks to its pro-competitive influence.[74]

When analysing the pooling of rights, one can conclude that in the future it should be more a phenomenon that contributes to the improvement of the whole patent system than an anti-competitive instrument. The improvement would consist mainly in simplification of licensing procedures, thus facilitating access to the latest technology of the rest of the right-holding society (i.e. competitors), and therefore to the society of users, who – in turn – would obtain products of a higher level of innovation. In its present form pooling of rights not only aspires to supplement the system of intellectual property rights, but is also getting ready to set a new trend in the realization of the rights.[75] In this context, J. Vuorinen seems to be right in his view when he 'persuades' the authorities that apply and promote intellectual property rights (more specifically, the patent rights) to try to find and maintain a balance between the practices of licensors from patent-pools, which should give pro-competitive effects and to minimize potential anti-competitive effects, which always act to the detriment of the society of users and the rest of the society of right-holders, in other words, those outside of a given patent-pool. The key to reach such a balance might be collaboration between companies both from inside and outside a pool system. This kind of collaboration should produce a pro-competitive effect. The instrument of patent-pools is an example showing that the 'society of right-holders' learns successfully to create mechanisms that facilitate access to intellectual property rights. Such notions as standards or patent-pools have a growing importance for strategies of the companies operating on the market of information technology.

---

72 A. Endeshaw, 'Reconfiguring intellectual property for the information age – towards information property?', 5(2) *JWIP* (2004), pp. 328–330.

73 See *Commission approves a patent licensing programme to implement the DVD standard*, 9 October 2000 (IP/00/1135).

74 J. Davidow, 'Liberalization of antitrust rules for IP licensing. Global trends and unresolved issues', 5(7) *JWIP* (2004), pp. 496–500.

75 H. Hietanen and M. Valimaki, 'Challenges of open content licensing in Europe', an article presented at the conference: Intellectual Property beyond Rights, 25–26 October 2004, Hanasaari, the Swedish-Finnish Cultural Centre, Espoo, Finland, pp. 10–11.

The IT industry and medical industry has experienced an expansion of the market of technology/medical licences. The expansion has substantially affected the behaviour of computer businesses in relation to their patent portfolios. Large computer enterprises, in particular, started to block the activities of competitive companies or to impose licence fees through the policy of so-called 'patent mining'.[76] The mechanism of the policy consists in a careful review of a company's collection of patents, or a patent portfolio, in order to find any patents that are unlawfully applied by other companies to develop and launch their products on the information technology market. This kind of behaviour has resulted in so-called 'patent thickets' (a phenomenon of patent multiplication), which is nothing more than an opportunity to start numerous patent infringement claims against other computer businesses. The existence of patent thickets contributes to two fundamental problems. The first one is the so-called 'complements problem', which arises when there are a number of patent holders whose patents work together to develop a standard and, from a technical point of view, are indispensable for the use of a specific technological solution. In a situation like this problems arise when each of the patentees (whose patents constitute a whole from the technological point of view and are to develop a new, specific product for the information technology market) blocks the use of its patent, for example by raising licence fees or refusing to cooperate.

The second problem is the so-called 'hold-up problem', which is an extension of the complements problem, occurring when companies, creating and developing a standard, are often unaware of the fact that the standard comprises a patent which can eventually contribute to a situation where the market launch of the standard is blocked. Unfortunately, it is commonplace that patentees emerge with their claims only after the standard is announced and demand a share of profits. The reason for such practices is that it is more profitable (although unfair) for the patentees. In this context, a patent has a higher value once the standard is adopted than at the stage of its development. A solution to the two problems described above may be the application of legal mechanisms that will effectively prevent situations where companies unjustly increase licence fees for the application of patents, both in the European Union and internationally.

While looking for such mechanisms it would be useful to consider the element of negotiation. This would mean the development of a new generation of rights and a transformation from declaring intellectual property rights to negotiating, or discussing the rights (here in the context of patents).[77] It seems that negotiating business terms and conditions of a licence before adoption of a common standard (*ex ante*) would be an effective approach to solving the problems discussed above. Such negotiations could be accompanied by disclosure of all patents participating

76 G. Ohana, M. Hansen and O. Shah, 'Disclosure and negotiations of licensing terms prior to adoption of industry standards: preventing another patent ambush', 24(12) *ECLR* (2003), p. 645.

77 *Ibidem*, p. 645.

in the standard setting effort. It is worth underlining that businesses (usually being the biggest companies on the market of digital technology products), which actually take an active part in the development and – subsequently – implementation of standards (i.e. making products to the specific standards), are not interested in restricting their realization or evolution. Their goal is to get the benefits they expected from the standard when they began to work on it in cooperation with the other patentees. For this reason, it is the companies which co-develop a standard that are mainly interested in the introduction of a compatible product to the market, so that it could start bringing the companies specific material benefits or profits. Therefore, when an external party turns up pointing out its patents used in the given standard after it has been announced (*ex post*) and offering the companies which implement the standard a high licence fee, it is perceived as unfavourable for all companies which jointly worked out the standard, both from a financial and marketing point of view.[78]

The Paradigm of Open Source

One of the cornerstones of the Free Software Foundation, briefly mentioned earlier in the book, is, first of all, the idea of sharing software with users and recognizing computer programmes as common goods. The consequence of the ideology presented in this way is a rejection of all principles on which programmes are made available so far, based on property rights and a criticism of the privileges resulting from intellectual property rights (i.e. disapproval of both the copyright law, whose objective is to protect computer software and of the patentability of computer-implemented inventions), as they are not capable of providing 'the society of users' with a free exchange of knowledge.[79] The foundations for Open Source software were provided by Stallman, a computer programmer (the 'openness' does not imply that it is free software, but that its source code is open to free modifications).[80] According to Stallman, intellectual property rights (here in the form of copyright and patents) should not control (or restrict) software because

78 See also D.A. Crane, 'Patent Pools, RAND Commitments and the Problematics of Price Discrimination … ', pp. 371–394.

79 L. Rosen, *Open Source Licensing …* , pp. 2–102. cf. also A.M. St. Laurent, *Understanding Open Source & Free Software Licensing* (O'Reilly Media, Sebastopol 2004), pp. 34–159. Supporters of the Open Source movement wish to manifest that payment is not an indispensable or primary stimulating factor for creative work. The mere joy of creation, the wish to meet intellectual challenges, gain respect of fellow programmers and achieve fame can be motivation enough.

80 J. Gay (ed.), *Free Software, Free Society: Selected Essays of Richard M. Stallman* (Free Software Foundation, GNU Press Boston 2002), pp. 13–55. According to Stallman '… a computer program should be free like air' and 'everybody should have the freedom to use a computer program and the possibility to modify it, on condition that the modified program will be further made available to everybody for unlimited use and adaptation'.

this deprives it of the benefits offered by digital technologies, such as flexibility, the ease of copying and the possibility of sharing.[81] Early in the 1980s R. Stallman started the Free Software Foundation, whose goal was to promote the development of free software around the world.[82]

On the basis of the above-presented ideology the Free Software Foundation worked out the Free Software Definition, according to which:

> through a licence, everyone should be granted freedom to: (1) run the computer program for any purpose, (2) study how the program works and adapt it to the needs, (3) redistribute its copies, (4) licence free programs [with an open source code] integrated with the programs that are made available on standard principles.[83]

The definition above is only a set of 'general premises of free software' and as such cannot be equated with a licence agreement.[84] Open Source software is believed to be any programme whose use principally consists of the following terms of licence: (a) the programme may be duplicated and redistributed (distributed) freely and in an unlimited way on the basis of the original licence (which e.g. excludes the licensor's liability); (b) no licence fees may be charged for using the programme; the right to use is granted for free; however fees may apply to the acts of reproduction and distribution, including payment for the transfer of ownership to a copy of the programme; (c) the source code of the programme must be offered with the programme itself or made otherwise available; the source code (Quelltext) must be handed over with the programme or available through a publicly accessible publication; the source programme may be further distributed; (d) everybody may develop, modify or adapt the programme and further distribute in its altered form, provided that the new incarnation of the programme is subject to Open Source licence terms; it may be necessary to indicate the modifications in the source code

81 P. Wayner, *Free for all. How Linux and the Free Software Movement Undercut the High-Tech Titans* (2000) www.devlib.org/Free-for-All_L141708, visited on 26 March 2010.

82 D. Bollier, 'The power of openness; why citizens, education, government and business should care about the coming revolution in open source code software', The Berkman Centre for Internet & Society at Harvard Law School, research publication Nos. 1999–02 (1999) pp. 4–6 www.cyber.law.harvard.edu, visited on 3 February 2010.

83 The term 'Open Source' has different meanings: (1) to describe software with an Open Source code, used according to specific principles; (2) as a mental shortcut to refer to a particular licensing pattern for certain known programs (Linux, Netscape Navigator); to avoid ambiguity, in legal texts the straightforward term of Open Source licence is used; (3) as a high-level term that encompasses putting various forms of cultural and scientific achievements, such as tests, music, pictures, and so on, in the public domain; however, in this respect we more often meet the more neutral term 'open content'; here Open Source software is a subcategory of open content.

84 L. Rosen, *Open Source Licensing* … , pp. 2–39. cf. also A.M. St. Laurent, *Understanding Open Source* … , pp. 4–8.

and to give them different designation than the one used in the original version of the programme; (e) the licences may not introduce any limitation or restrictions (i.e. discrimination in any form) as regards specific persons, groups, fields of use, private or commercial application; no restrictions may be placed on the methods of distribution, which cannot be in any way conditional; (f) the licence may not affect the use of other programmes distributed together with the licenced programme and particularly it is not permitted to demand that any programme distributed on the same data carrier be regarded as free software.[85]

To enable distribution of Open Source software certain criteria must be met.[86] First of all, the Open Source software must be subject to so-called 'free redistribution', which consists of a lack of any fees. Secondly, the source code must be available to everyone. If the distribution does not allow direct transfer of the source code the licensor is obliged to provide the address where the source code can be found. This kind of behaviour supports development of the source code and research carried out on it. Getting acquainted with the source code enables other users to develop programmes and allows an evolution of the code itself. Moreover, in order to make the distribution of Open Source software practicable, the licence should admit making modifications, which are then included in the redistributed code. The purpose of Open Source software is to maintain the integrity of the author's source code. The licence may require that any new programmes derived from the original one are distinguishable from the original. This happens when a company offers Open Source support services (e.g. Red Hat Inc.). The preservation of the author's source code integrity is a form of protection both for the user and the company, as servicing is only limited to the original version of the Open Source software. The licence may not introduce any discriminating conditions against any entities. No person or entity may be denied the possibility of using the Open Source. Only when each person and entity is allowed to use Open Source software under the same terms and conditions will the total benefit of the process for the society of users be achieved. Furthermore, the licence may not restrict any entity in its application of the programme for specific purposes, e.g. in business or for genetic research. In this way, the Open Source community encourages the use of this specific form of software also for commercial purposes.[87]

---

85 The *Free Software Definition* was subsequently included in the *Debian Free Software Guidelines*, www.debian.org, visited 23 May 2010. The Debian Free Software Guidelines became a basis for the development of the Open Source Definition, www.opensource.org/osd.html, visited on 9 February 2010.

86 B. Perens, 'The Debian Free Software Guidelines' www.opensource.org, visited on 18 January 2012.

87 cf. with regard to Open Source, H. Yamane, *Interpreting TRIPS. Globalisation of Intellectual Property Rights and Access to Medicines* (Hart Publishing, Oxford, Portland, Oregon 2011), pp. 14–16.

Another criterion, which must be satisfied to enable the distribution of Open Source software is the attachment of the licence to the source code regardless of the form of its distribution or provision (whether it is through the agency of such companies as Red Hat or directly by an Internet user – although then the programme is not supported). Also, the distribution of Open Source software may be accompanied by the distribution of non-Open Source programmes, e.g. by Red Hat. The open source licence does not extend to cover the other programmes distributed along with the Open Source software (even though non-Open Source software may become Open Source software in combined distribution). The licence may not impose the form of approval to consider the licence agreement as concluded (technology-neutral licence). An Open Source licence is an agreement which shows that cooperation is possible even on a market that is competitive to the bone. The best example to illustrate this statement is Linux, being ever-increasing competition to such information technology giants as Microsoft.

The next step taken by Stallman to promote the idea of free software was to start the GNU Project in 1983 (GNU is an acronym for 'GNU's Not Unix').[88] Initially, the GNU Project was to be an alternative to the operating system that was popular in the 1970s with government and academic organizations (and which still function there as such).[89] The primary motive to the development of GNU was to start and encourage others to jointly create software and – by cooperation with users – build an operating system on similar principles to Unix. The prominent feature of this cooperation was the intended lack of barriers put up by such software owners as Microsoft. In 1991 the first version of the Linux operating system was released on the Internet. The programme was designed by Linus Torvalds, but thanks to the opportunities offered by the Internet it was later co-developed by volunteer users and programmers from all over the world.[90] As a result, Linux was linked with the system developed thanks to the GNU Project (GNU/Linux).

When the Linux operating system was developed and publicized the Free Software Foundation identified a threat to the freedom brought with the system. The threat was that practically any Linux user, having introduced the tiniest changes possible in the software, could restrict its use by establishing intellectual property rights on it and thus converting it into a product with ownership rights and therefore into something contrary to the ideas of the Free Software Foundation. To avoid situations like this, the Foundation developed the GNU GPL, short for

88 J. Gay (ed.), *Free Software, Free Society: Selected Essays …* , p. 44.

89 Unix is a multitask and multi-user, interactive operating system with a wide range of applications. The first version of Unix operating system was developed at the end of the 1960s at Bell Telephone Laboratories (Bell Labs), being a subsidiary of AT&T. The 1970s marked the boom time for Unix in numerous universities and labs. The system has gained wide recognition at universities, where it is often used for research on operating systems and as a resource of examples.

90 L. Torvalds was at that time the Finnish student who originated the now-popular Linux system. See www.wired.com and www.li.org, visited 16 December 2011.

GNU General Public Licence.[91] The GPL is the most important legal basis on which free software may be made available in the copyleft system.[92] Therefore, the GPL is considered to be a classic copyleft licence, 'left for copying', a licence for programmes with Open Source codes. The characteristic property of copyleft is that the source code is available to all interested users (freedom of software use).[93] Thanks to free access to source code users are not only able to use the programme, but also to modify it, learn its design principles and – most importantly – improve, upgrade and modernize it, i.e. develop it and improve its quality. On the other hand, the users are not permitted to burden the software with licence fees or any other restrictions. In this way the rights to such free software as e.g. Linux become inalienable. Therefore, each user of free software, or everyone with a copy of it, has a guarantee that their rights to the copy cannot be taken away.[94]

One of the characteristic premises of the GPL is that in order to be able to release some software on the Internet for reproduction (copyleft), it must be first protected by means of intellectual property rights and pertinent terms of its distribution must be provided.[95] In this way it is a legal instrument which gives any Internet user the right to use Linux, modify it (including studying the source code and improving it, in the first place) and redistribute it (popularize).[96] This is possible when the terms of licence are not altered. Then the source code and the freedom promoted by R. Stallman become, in his opinion, inseparable from the point of view of law.[97] It is difficult to argue with Stallman, who claims that software developers, whose programmes are copyrighted, use intellectual property rights to take the freedom away from the users, while the supporters of the Open Source movement use the same rights to an opposite end – namely, to guarantee the freedom to the users in the best possible way. Therefore, the goal of the GPL is to secure users the freedom to use software, in its broad sense.[98] The tool to

91 See www.gnu.org/copyleft/gpl.html, visited 23 May 2012.

92 Open Source licences are divided into copyleft and non-copyleft licences. The GPL is considered a classic copyleft licence and therefore it is discussed herein in more detail. Non-copyleft licences (cf. BSD or Berkley Software Distribution) by leaving the computer programmer 'the freedom to decide whether or not the modifications should be proprietary and used under ownership scheme'. See www.fsf.org/copyleft/gpl.html, visited 25 February 2012.

93 J. Gay (ed.), *Free Software, Free Society: Selected Essays of Richard M. Stallman* (Free Software Foundation, GNU Press Boston 2002), p. 44.

94 P. Lambert, 'Copyleft, copyright and software IPRS: is contract still king', 23:4 *EIPR* (2001), pp. 165–166.

95 L. Rosen, *Open Source Licensing* … , pp. 1–13.

96 See www.linux.org/info/gnu/htm, visited 2 February 2010.

97 D. Bollier, 'The power of openness; why citizens, education, government and business should care about the coming revolution in open source code software', Nos. 1999–02, The Berkman Centre for Internet & Society at Harvard Law School (1999), p. 5.

98 J. Gay (ed.), *Free Software, Free Society* … , p. 44.

guarantee the freedom is intellectual property rights. On the other hand, the goal of other, typically commercial, licences is to deprive (or restrict) the freedom of software use. At the same time, intellectual property rights are another tool used to restrict the freedom. In this respect, we face a specific situation where the same intellectual property rights serve two different, contradicting purposes. On the one hand, it is the guarantee of preserving freedom and, on the other, of taking it away (or restricting). In this context, the view of Barta and Markiewicz that the Open Source movement (mainly as regards copyleft) aims at an emphasis on extra-pecuniary interests related to ownership (the idea of sharing) rather than at exposing the idea of ownership, being a distinctive feature of intellectual property rights.[99] The focus on extra-pecuniary interests related to ownership seems to be likely thanks to copyright. At first glance it sounds a little contrary, but Barta and Markiewicz refer to a peculiar instrumentalization of copyright, where it is used as a means to attain ends which have not been found within the scope of this field of law before, such as promoting the ideas of free software and sharing 'non-valuable' (in this context) knowledge with the society at large.[100] Lambert also is right in stating that intellectual property rights exist in copyleft works and their existence is established (granted and acknowledged) in public licences.[101]

The most fundamental goal of public licences, such as the GPL, is to guarantee the right to share software (which is made available to all interested users) and to

99 Programs distributed under the Open Source scheme are not excluded from the scope of copyright; it is just by referring to the rights of use provided in copyright law that the freedom of adaptation of a program can be ensured and – what is important – it is possible to oblige the users engaged in modification of the program to disclose and share the source code (also in its modified form), free of charge.

100 M. Valimaki and V. Oksanen, 'How to manage IPR infringement risks in open source development?', an article presented at the conference 'Intellectual Property beyond Rights', 25–26 October 2004, Hanasaari, the Swedish-Finnish Cultural Centre, Espoo, Finland, p. 3. They indicate three basic types of entities which develop the Open Source system. These are large IT businesses, so-called Open Source companies and joint projects. Examples of large businesses engaged in Open Source activities include Hewlett-Packard, IBM and Apple, i.e. companies with a minor status on the market of software development and – primarily – operating systems. The companies, by virtue of their core activities, are interested and engaged in the development of Open Source software. This in large part is due to the necessity to popularise their software products or hardware platforms. Open Source companies, on the other hand, are small-to medium enterprises, whose activities consist in manufacturing and selling Open Source-based products (Open Source components). One of the pioneers, which started to develop software on the basis of Open Source, is Red Hat Inc., the creators of Red Hat Linux (being simply a distribution of Linux where technical support for the software is included). An example of a non-commercial project of a large importance is Apache, an Internet server established to host websites. Another example can be Linux itself (but only in its original version, available to everyone on the net; however deprived of technical support from Red Hat Linux).

101 P. Lambert, 'Copyleft, copyright and software IPRS: is contract still king', 23(4) *EIPR* (2001), p. 57.

contribute to it, while the object of this sharing and contributing are intellectual property rights. The rights, however, have a specific character because their holders have not monopolized them, i.e. have not applied for patents – in the case of an invention, or do not use their copyright entitlements against other users of the software. On the contrary, the intellectual property right holders decided to share them and make them a common good in the name and for the benefit of the whole community gathered around and taking advantage of copyleft (today, the community has achieved a global scope).

Considering the above, a conclusion can be drawn that the terms of a public licence (GPL) for Open Source software are in complete opposition to the elementary purpose of any regular licence, which is to take away the right (freedom) to share, contribute to and modify the software covered by the licence.[102] Freedom, not price, is fundamental to a public licence for free software. The goal of a public licence is to provide the freedom of distribution of copies, of acquisition of the source code and of modification or application of any part of the free programme to other Open Source software. Nobody has the right to deprive users of free software of the above-listed rights to the open source. Every Open Source user who decides to distribute copies of free software, whether for a fee or free of charge, is obliged to transfer all the rights held in the free software onto the recipient. The party transferring Open Source software must provide its source code, as well. The licence does not include any warranty for the software.[103]

Summing up, the GPL is the most liberal Open Source licence, in which the source code is open and available in the public domain and the licence itself is free of charge. If a software developer/user decides to use even the smallest part of the licenced content, he or she is inevitably obliged to make the whole modified code freely available on the same principles. Therefore, the idea of Open Source popularizes software designed for a specific, supported platform and contributes to its dissemination and popularity. It is worth mentioning that this type of 'popularization' is not required by large companies operating on the market of software development. For example, Intel and Microsoft have recently jointly developed their own Wintel platform. For that reason, neither Intel nor Microsoft is interested in cooperating with other companies and endorsing their software, as it sells well without it. Besides, making their software Open Source would mean disclosing the source code developed by Intel and Microsoft, a situation that neither company would be happy with. Therefore, such companies as Hewlett-Packard, Apple or IBM promote Open Source to popularize their own hardware platforms (being useless without compatible software). Open Source is also a way to challenge companies with market dominance. Companies like IBM or Apple and their operating systems are no threat to Microsoft, a tycoon on the market, because they do not have comparable financial resources and an Open Source

102 L. Rosen, *Open Source Licensing …* , pp. 2–102. cf. also A.M. St. Laurent, *Understanding Open Source …* , pp. 34–159.

103 See www.gnu.org, visited 18 April 2012.

licence allows them to develop a product to be used on an IBM or Apple system. After all, software developers/users of Open Source sill adapt any programme to their needs.[104]

Just like in the case of reverse engineering, the application of Open Source is an unquestionable benefit to the society of knowledge, because it supports a widespread dissemination of knowledge and creation of new software products, i.e. new computer programmes. Nevertheless, a question can be brought up whether the use of Open Source is safe for its subsequent developers or users? Do they not infringe intellectual property rights (namely copyright and patents, if applicable)? In practice, it is not unlikely that an Open Source developer, acting in good faith, violates copyright or infringes a patent by copying, modifying or selling a product containing a portion of the code (copyright), or by creating, marketing or selling patented inventions contained in the product created by the developer with the use of such inventions. An infringement of intellectual property rights by the first developer is carried over on the successors, i.e. subsequent Open Source developers. It is difficult to find a perfect solution to prevent this kind of situation. M. Valimaki and V. Oksanen put forward some propositions that may lead to reduction of the risk of infringement of intellectual property rights for future developers.[105] Three of the propositions seem capable of providing an efficient solution to the problem. The first one consists in the possibility to sell a liability guarantee for Open Source, the second one resorts to taking out a relevant liability insurance and the third proposition concerns only large information technology business and consists of the establishment of a strong patent portfolio.

The first of the above-named methods is already to a great extent applied in practice. In this method big companies and Open Source organizations sell liability guarantees for their developers/users. This kind of guarantee usually covers the violation of specific intellectual property rights contained in the source code. It would seem ideal if the guarantee also covered faults in programmes (self-evident problems) or the so-called software bugs (problems which appear in programmes

104 The most important features of the GPL are that all users of a free programme are committed to give its adaptations, in which they acquire copyright, the status of free software (of the Open Source type) as well as approving its further reproduction, distribution and adaptation by third parties, yet providing the redistributed copies with a relevant copyright reservation and a disclaimer of any liability under warranty or in tort related to the use of the programme. The principal purpose of GPL regulations is to prevent transformation of GPL software into proprietary software. Therefore, the GPL is a specific kind of licence, as its objective is to prevent situation where the licence can be reserved by law under intellectual property rights. The licence is not a measure to privatization of software, but to an 'unlimited' preservation of software as a common good for the good of all. Thus, the same function is attributable to intellectual property rights.

105 M. Valimaki and V. Oksanen, 'How to manage IPR infringement risks in open source development?', an article presented at the conference 'Intellectual Property beyond Rights', 25–26 October 2004, Hanasaari, the Swedish-Finnish Cultural Centre, Espoo, Finland, p. 63.

in specific circumstances). Unfortunately, situations like this hardly ever happen in real life, because this kind of liability is carried over from the first developer/user onto subsequent developers/users with the end user being the last.

The second method that contributes to the reduction of the liability of subsequent developers/users of Open Source is to cover them with intellectual property rights infringement insurance, applicable to the property contained in the processed source code. Perhaps, an ideal solution would be to introduce a public insurance scheme, similar to the motor insurance system. Naturally, this would involve higher costs of administration, but the benefits would really outweigh the costs because, as a result, the problem of the passing of liability onto subsequent developers/users would be practically eliminated and not only as far as infringement of intellectual property rights is concerned but even as regards faults in the software.

The last of the suggested methods is mainly applicable to global computer companies, as it is connected with patent portfolios held by large information technology businesses. These portfolios are simply collections of thousands, as it is often the case, of patents obtained by employees of those companies over the last decade. Most of the patents often have a note that they are illegally (thus violating the patent law) used by other companies to develop new products. Patent portfolios are essentially used for protection against the Open Source environment. The companies make an effort to ensure that their solutions are not found in the Open Source and if it happens anyway Open Source companies abandon the problematic solutions. Open Source communities are also considering the application of patents to their solutions. When a commercial company attempts to prove that their patent is used in an Open Source programme, the Open Source company may counterclaim that the commercial company is in possession of an Open Source patent. Where both patents are of a similar value the companies negotiate, which is usually successful.

As the discussion above shows, none of the methods seems efficient enough to ensure a maximum reduction of the liability of future developers/users of a source code. The most optimal solution to minimize this kind of risk may be a combination of the three methods with due consideration to individual circumstances. The amount of software developed according to the principles of Open Source is constantly increasing. Linux is proof of the success achieved and is enjoyed daily as free software. Today, Open Source software is a viable alternative to and in competition with commercial products, such as Microsoft Windows. In view of the popularity of Open Source companies such as Microsoft either fight to maintain their dominance on the market, at any cost, using their portfolios of intellectual property rights, or decide to join the concept of Open Source. In the latter case, it could entail 'freeing' some of their intellectual property rights (patents) and starting a promotional campaign for the Open Source software as being friendly to the knowledge society of users and right-holders. Encouraging as many other companies as possible to begin to free their intellectual property rights to the advantage of Open Source would be a key element of this kind of campaign.

Making patents freely available considerably facilitates the work of software engineers and developers of other companies and has a big influence on the development of free software (including Linux). To 'make available' means here to share their intellectual property (in this case valuable software patents). This contributes to the growth of the level of innovation in the society because on the basis of shared patents other companies, operating and competing on the digital technology market, will be given an opportunity to develop and manufacture new and possibly better and more innovative products. Also, the growing popularity of Linux among users is a result of its lower costs of installation, as compared to MS Windows, but – primarily – from the fact that Linux provides its users with the possibility of learning about how it was designed and how it operates. More and more computer programmers work together to develop Linux software. This is undoubtedly a phenomenon of global scale and proof that making profits is not always the motive behind creative work. Simple satisfaction from contributing to the creation of a common good (here: software) that will provide benefits to users worldwide can often be reward enough. Linux exemplifies that progress and creativity of knowledge at the highest level is possible without the need to have a monopoly on this knowledge.[106]

The Paradigm of the Rule of Balancing

This paradigm means finding out how this 'first situation of balancing' works out on the example of American Supreme Court case *Eldred* v. *Ashcroft*.[107] The case will be re-examined here (as the 'hard case') with the application of Alexy's 'Structure of Balancing'[108] as the means of applying access to the knowledge principle. Since balancing is based on the assumption that principles will never establish exactly what should be done or what must not be done ('optimization requirements'), it is necessary that the principle of access to knowledge should be carried out to 'the greatest extent possible'. In order for this to take place, it is necessary to contrast it with an opposing principle such as protection of knowledge. In the *Eldred* case open access to books in the cyberspace library was dependent on the non-extension of the term of copyright protection by the US Congress. When the US Congress passed the Sony Bono Copyright Term Extension Act (CTEA), all copyrighted works were given an additional 20 years of protection before they would enter the public domain. As the result, works that had been ready to enter the public domain in cyberspace were no longer available for publication and valuable literary and digital resources were taken out of public control. Eldred argued that continued congressional expansion of copyright interfered with the

---

106 cf. with regard to Open Source, H. Yamane, *Interpreting TRIPS* … , pp. 14–16.

107 L. Lessig, *Free Culture* … , pp. 213–221.

108 R. Alexy, *A Theory of Constitutional Rights* (Oxford University Press, Oxford 2004), pp. 29–73.

constitutional mandate that copyrighted works only be protected for a limited time (according to *Public Clause* Congress is obliged to promote the development of science through the assurance of copyright for a definite period of time). This implies a conflict between two principles: access to knowledge and protection of knowledge. In order to discuss the conflict according to 'Structure of Balancing' three elements ought to be analysed: Rule of Balancing, Weight Formula, Burden of Argumentation.

According to the Rule of Balancing the establishment of the 'importance', 'abstract weight' and 'reliability' of the access to knowledge principle and the protection of knowledge principle are required. While focusing on the 'importance' of each principle, it is relevant to establish whether the 'importance' of the access to knowledge principle justifies the detriment to, or non-satisfaction of, the protection of knowledge principle. In this way a commensurability can be established with the use of the following triadic scale: 'light' is 1, 'moderate' is 2, 'serious' is 4. The range of the importance of these principles depends on normative and factual premises. The normative premise concerns the 'meaning' of the relevant positions of the access to knowledge principle and protection of knowledge principle from the 'concept of person' viewpoint that the legal and political system must presuppose.[109] Thus, protection of knowledge should be given more weight in a liberal society. If an act of public power interferes with intellectual property rights, this results in a serious violation of the principle underlying them. However, while considering the concept of a person from the commons society perspective, the access to knowledge principle is perceived as the most required.

As for the empirical premises, they concern what the measure in question means for the importance of both principles. From this point of view, the importance of the access to knowledge principle depends on the efficiency, speed, probability, reach and duration of the CTEA in failing to satisfy this principle at stake. The more efficient, fast, probable, powerful and long the CTEA is in failing to satisfy the access to knowledge principle the greater the importance of this principle (4 for 'serious'). The importance of the protection of knowledge principle depends on the efficiency, speed, probability, reach and duration of the CTEA in satisfying this principle at stake. The more efficient, fast, probable, powerful and long the CTEA is satisfying the protection of knowledge principle the greater the importance of this principle (4 for 'serious'). Therefore, in the *Eldred* case a hypothetical court could consider that the degree of detriment to the protection of knowledge principle (principle 1) is 'serious' (4) as is the 'importance' of the access to knowledge principle (principle 2).

The second element of the Rule of Balancing is 'abstract weight'. This means finding out the 'greater abstract weight'. Abstract weight is derived not only from the different legal hierarchies of the legal sources but also from the social values using the same triadic scale as previously. Thus, the measurement of the 'abstract weight' of the principle of access to knowledge as well as the

109 C.B. Pulido, 'The Rationality of Balancing', 92 *ARSP* (2007), pp. 195–208.

principle of protection of knowledge depends on the search for the best substantial theory of the constitution that the judge is to undertake. The judge will give the highest abstract weight to protection of knowledge and liberty if this theory is an individualistic one. However, if the theory is a communitarian one, the judge might give the highest weight to access to knowledge and to the common good. The hypothetical court could consider that in the *Eldred* case the 'abstract weight' of protection of knowledge is 'moderate' (2) and that the access to knowledge principle is 'serious' (4).

The third element of the Rule of Balancing is 'reliability'. It concerns the reliability of empirical assumptions. It answers the question what the measure means for the non-realization of protection of knowledge principle (principle 1) and the realization of the access to knowledge principle (principle 2) in the *Eldred* case. This ought to be established with the help of the following scale: 'reliable' is 1, 'plausible' is ½, 'not evidently false' is ¼. The hypothetical court could state that the 'reliability' is reliable in both principles.

In order to have a balancing outcome for the *Eldred* case, 'importance', 'abstract weight' and 'reliability' should be assessed. The tool for this is called the Weight Formula. According to this formula, the concrete weight, in the *Eldred* case, of protection of knowledge principle (principle 1) in relation to the access to knowledge principle (principle 2) results from the quotient between, on the one hand, the outcome of the 'importance' of protection of knowledge principle (principle 1) (4 for 'serious'), the 'abstract weight' for this (2 for 'moderate'), and the 'reliability' of the empirical assumptions regarding that importance (1 for 'reliable'), on the other hand, the outcome of the importance of access to knowledge principle (principle 2) (4 for 'serious'), the 'abstract weight' of this (4 for 'serious'), and the 'reliability' of the empirical assumptions relating to that importance (1 for 'reliable').[110] The concrete weight of principle 2 in relation to principle 1 is greater than the concrete weight of principle 1 to principle 2; thus, the *Eldred* case should be decided in accordance with principle 2, namely access to knowledge. Thereby the meaning of the well-being would be discovered.

110 The third element of Alexy's Structure of Balancing is the Burden of Argumentation. It refers to the situation when the weight of both principles is identical, which is not the case. See also J. Habermas, *Between Facts and Norms* (The MIT Press, Cambridge, MA 1996), pp. 414–415.

Chapter 5
Thinking from Within the Metaphor: The Right to Science and Culture

Cathedral and Bazaar

Metaphors are circulating around the context of both *Myth* and *Reason*: Cathedral and Bazaar.[1] The Cathedral serves as a metaphor for intellectual property and it projects static and long-lasting protection. Copyrights and patents are the main pillars of this projection. It is based on the belief that a strong intellectual property protection serves as an incentive to create new knowledge and to foster industrial and economic development.[2] There is a belief that more rights automatically equals more innovation and that creativity and innovation often means expansion of intellectual property protection standards at the expense of different human rights and the interests of licencees, users and consumers.[3] In this vision of the future, industries and interest groups that rely upon intellectual property would invoke the authors' rights and property rights provisions in human rights treaties to expand existing standards of protection.[4] Humanity is subjected to the intellectual property regime.[5] Music, painting and poetry are creations of the right side of the

1 E.S. Raymond, *The Cathedral and the Bazaar: Musings on Linux and Open Source by an Accidental Revolutionary* (O'Reilly Media, Sebastopol 2001), pp. 19–64.

2 R. Dreyfuss, D.L. Zimmerman and H. First (eds), *Expanding the Boundaries of Intellectual Property. Innovation Policy for the Knowledge Society* (Oxford University Press, Oxford 2001), pp. 4–29. cf. D. Matthews, *Intellectual Property, Human Rights and Development. The Role of NGO's and Social Movements* (Edward Elgar, Cheltenham, UK 2011), pp. 221–257. cf. also M. de Cock Buning, 'Expansion and convergence in copyright law', in: W. Grosheide (ed.), *Intellectual Property and Human Rights. A Paradox* (Edward Elgar, Cheltenham, UK 2010), pp. 47–72.

3 cf. H. Yamane, Interpreting TRIPS … , pp. 9–14. See also T. Murphy, 'Repetition, Revolution and Resonance: An Introduction to New Technologies and Human Rights', in: *New Technologies and Human Rights* (Oxford University Press, Oxford 2009), pp. 7–84.

4 R. Deazley, Rethinking Copyright … , pp. 135–139. See also C. Colston and K. Middleton, *Modern Intellectual Property* (Cavendish Publishing, London, Sydney, Portland, Oregon), pp. 295–321.

5 A.M. Nawrot and Z. Brodecki, 'In Search for Common Sense in Cyberspace', 2 *Masaryk University Journal of Law and Technology* (2008), pp. 47–61. The primary aim of this paper is to introduce some thoughts and insights about the application of the law of balancing in cyberspace, the concept of identity … , the code of legal culture structure and the 'lex-net' and 'ius-net' programs.

brain and are in the nature of 'expressions'. The creations of the left side of the brain are in the nature of 'ideas', which are found in scientific and technical innovations. Expressions are subject to copyright law; ideas are subject to patent law.[6] We are, however, at the same time obliged to acknowledge that 'the boundary line between expression and idea is in general fuzzy. This is particularly the case with regard to computer software. There may be two hemispheres, but there is one brain, and ultimately the software products of our creative intellect are simultaneously art and science, simultaneously expression and idea'.[7] The human right to benefit from the moral and material interest of the Author is, when applying the metaphor of the Cathedral, reduced to intellectual property regime.[8] Contrasting, Bazaars are free, dynamic, evolving and with alternatives. The Bazaar is a metaphor for the access to knowledge movement. Open Source software (OSS) and Creative Commons (CC) licensing are its main representatives. The goal of access to knowledge is premised on a few simple beliefs about human beings, taken as a whole. Firstly, the people of the world are enormously creative. Secondly, their creativity will emerge naturally when they are allowed to express it without suppression or hindrance.[9] Thirdly, that the world is better off when we allow ordinary people to be free to learn, innovate, make and build new things and share their work and their knowledge with others. Access to knowledge is perceived as a central human development issue of our time.[10] It is based on the assumption that there is a need to reconsider the idea that the answer to an increased need of creativity is to create more intellectual property.[11]

The Commons – analysed before as one of the crucial paradigms for the postanalogue society – serves of course as a foundation for access to knowledge. Open Source is a significant example of commons in the digital technologies era that still uses the intellectual property regime as a tool. Some of the authors do not want the full set of intellectual property rights to be their only tool to protect their

6 cf. L. Zemer, *The Idea of Authorship in Copyright, Applied Legal Philosophy* (Ashgate, Hampshire 2007), pp. 2–73.

7 L. Rosen, *Open Source Licensing …* , pp. 15–16.

8 cf. G. Davies, *Copyright and the Public Interest* (Thomson Sweet & Maxwell, London 2002), pp. 305–367. cf. also M.A. Ress 'Open-Access Publishing: From Principles to Practice', in: G. Krikorian and A. Kapczyński (eds), *Access to Knowledge in the Age of Intellectual Property* (Zone Books, New York 2010), pp. 475–497.

9 G. Krikorian, 'Access to Knowledge as a Field of Activism', in: G. Krikorian and A. Kapczynski (eds), *Access to Knowledge in the Age of Intellectual Property* (Zone Books, New York 2010), pp. 57–99. cf. also A. Kapczyński, 'Access to Knowledge: A Conceptual Genealogy', in: G. Krikorian and A. Kapczyński (eds), *Access to Knowledge in the Age of Intellectual Property* (Zone Books, New York 2010), pp. 17–57.

10 C. Hess and E. Ostrom (eds), *Understanding Knowledge as a Commons. From Theory to Practice* (The MIT Press, Cambridge/London/Massachusetts 2007), pp. 28–36.

11 D.A. Posey and G. Dutfield, *Beyond Intellectual Property. Toward Traditional Resource Rights for Indigenous Peoples and Local Communities* (International Development Research Centre, Ottawa 1996), pp. 1–3.

intellectual productions and creations.[12] They are searching for other options that are suggested by the reflective society – a tool that is easy to use and that licences back to the public some of the power to control the work that the public gave to the authors through copyright law. The Creative Commons movement is a modern example of such a tool, which has been introduced in the digital era. [13] The general licences developed by this movement replace the 'all rights reserved' with a more modest 'some rights reserved' approach. Owing to such licences, the authors are able to extend the range of usage of their creations without at the same time losing their copyrights.[14] A Creative Commons licence is a form of a copyright licence that can be linked via the Web.[15] Carroll is calling Creative Commons a work in progress, an ongoing natural experiment, suggesting that much of the creativity that digital technology enables is 'conversational' in nature. From the user's perspective, for example, this kind of licence answers the following question: 'What can I do with this work?' The user can copy, distribute, display, perform and make a public digital performance of the work. A Creative Commons Attribution Share Alike Licence is an example of a very frequently chosen licence where 'attribution' means that the creator requires 'attribution' as a condition for using his or her work (you can use the work in whatever way you like as long as you give the creator of it attribution and licence any derivative of it under a Share Alike licence).[16] Since the 'attribution' requirement became so popular, Creative Commons made 'attribution' a required condition of all licences.[17]

As Lessig notices, Creative Commons is characterized as a system, which provides for an easy creation on the basis of others' works. Such a system will facilitate creators stating freedoms which will allow others to take their works and build on them.[18] Lessig explains that this is possible thanks to simple tags combined with descriptions which are easy for people to understand that, in turn, are bound by bullet-proof licences. As a result of such a simple set of licences, which creators can attach to the content by themselves, Creative Commons intends to establish a collection of content on whose basis one can easily create further.[19] Moreover, tags are also combined with licences which are machine-

12 S. Vaidhyanathan, *Copyrights and Copywrongs: The Rise of Intellectual Property and How it Threatens Creativity* (New York University Press, New York 2001), p. 116.

13 See www.creativecommons.org, visited on 12 April 2012.

14 L. Lessig, *Wolna Kultura* [*Free Culture*] … , p. 367.

15 See Creative Commons, Choose a Licence, www.creativecommons.org, visited on 12 April 2012.

16 See Creative Commons, Licences Explained, www.creativecommons.org/about/licences, visited on 12 April 2012.

17 M.W. Carroll is introducing the development of the project known as Creative Commons International (CCI). The aim is to develop versions of Creative Commons licences that would take into account legal features specific to a country's copyright law. Electronic copy available at www.ssrn.com/abstract=978195, visited on 3 June 2012.

18 L. Lessig, *Free Culture* … , p. 311.

19 *Ibidem*, p. 311.

readable and therefore enable an automatic identification of content and facilitate their use. Lessig distinguishes three modes of expression constituting Creative Commons licence, which guarantees everyone who will read it the following rights:[20] 1) legal licence; 2) human-readable description; 3) machine-readable tags. Lessig concurrently emphasizes that what is crucial for the practicality of the scheme is that it constitutes an expression of faith of a person bound by a licence in something different (in something other) from encountered extremes of: 'all rights' or 'no rights' (as in the case of intellectual property rights – with subtle exceptions). In this way, attributing a CC mark to the content does not involve waiving of copyright, but granting some freedoms. However, there is a provision that the freedoms exceed freedoms guaranteed by the rule of permitted use. Their final form depends on the creator's decision. The creator has the following options within creative commons system[21]: 1) selection of a licence, which permits any use, if the work will be marked with the name of the author (moral rights secured); 2) selection of a licence, which permits only non-commercial use of the work; 3) selection of a licence, which permits every use provided that the same freedoms are granted for subsequent use ('share and share alike'); 4) selection of a licence, which permits the use of the work if no derivative works are created; 5) selection of a sampling licence, on condition that no copies of a full work are produced; 6) selection of a licence for any use for educational purposes. As we can see, the scope of creator's freedom contained in the above options is very broad and definitely exceeds the standard copyright model.[22]

In this context, it is worthwhile to note that Wikipedia – which is the world's largest encyclopedia – in 2009 made the transition to a dual-licensing model. Wikipedia was originally licenced under a GNU Free Documentation Licence. Today content previously written for Wikipedia, as well as all future articles, is licenced under the more flexible Creative Commons Attribution Share Alike Licence. In this way content will be more easily shared between Wikipedia and other similar Creative Commons licenced publications. Proposals made by the founders of Creative Commons are regarded as most interesting, as they foster the idea of a shortened period of copyright validity and a return to the formal requirements which would make the *conditio sine qua non* for the protection provided by the copyright. 'Information and communication technologies allow people, anywhere in the world, to access information and knowledge almost instantaneously. Individuals, organizations and communities should benefit from access to knowledge'. This was declared in 2003 as the direct result of the World Summit of the Information Society (WSIS).[23] Since then, further declarations and other texts on access to knowledge

---

20 *Ibidem*, p. 311.

21 L. Lessig, *Free Culture …* , pp. 311–312.

22 cf. V. Franz, 'Back to Balance: Limitations and Exceptions to Copyright', in: G. Krikorian and A. Kapczyński (eds), *Access to Knowledge in the Age of Intellectual Property* (Zone Books, New York 2010), pp. 517–531.

23 Electronic copy available at www.itu.int/wsis/index.html, visited on 2 June 2012.

have been drafted by a variety of civil society and private sector coalitions. These include: the Geneva Declaration on the Future of the World Intellectual Property Organization (WIPO); the Adelphi Charter on Creativity, Innovation and Intellectual Property; the Paris Accord; the Munich Declaration on Copyright Limitations and Exceptions; the Treaty on Access to Knowledge; the Berlin Declaration on Open Access to Knowledge in the Sciences and Humanities; the Bethesda Statement on Open Access; and the Budapest Open Access Initiative.[24]

One of the major international statements that refers to access to digital knowledge is the draft Treaty on Access to Knowledge.[25] It emerged in 2004 after a call from Brazil and Argentina at the Development Agenda for the World Intellectual Property Organization.[26] There are several significant factors for access to digital knowledge that could be recognized within the Treaty on Access to Knowledge. The first one is the need for global action to protect and enhance access to knowledge resources. The Treaty parties are determined to protect, preserve and enhance the public domain (which is essential for creativity and sustainable innovation) and create the broadest opportunities to participate in the development of knowledge resources. Secondly, the importance of knowledge resources in supporting innovation, development and social progress and of the opportunities arising from technological progress, particularly the Internet, is of particular concern.[27] Thirdly, there is the need for greater transparency and disclosure of knowledge resources and technologies and for new incentives to create and share knowledge resources without restrictions on access.[28] Here the success and potential of new methods of creating and sharing knowledge should be recognized, for example Open Source software (OSS). Finally, the importance of knowledge resources that are created for the benefit of all and the need to protect and expand the knowledge commons are also recognized.[29]

'A Manifesto on WIPO and the Future of Intellectual Property', presented by J. Boyle in 2004, is an example of a crucial statement claiming that there are systematic errors in contemporary intellectual property policy that influence

24 Links available at www.earlham.edu/-peters/fos/overview.html, visited on 3 June 2012.

25 Electronic copy available at www.cptech.org/a2k/a2k_treaty_may9.pdf, visited on 29 May 2012.

26 WO/GA/31/1, 27 August 2004, WIPO Geneva, WIPO General Assembly, 31st (15th Extraordinary) session, Geneva, 27 September – 5 October 2004, Proposal by Argentina and Brazil for the Establishment of a Development Agenda for WIPO.

27 cf. L. Lessig, *Code 2.0 …* , p. 1–8. (note of interest: L. Lessig uses CC Attribution-ShareAlike Licence for this book and many others he wrote).

28 cf. T. Murphy (ed.), 'Repetition, Revolution and Resonance: An Introduction to New Technologies and Human Rights', in: *New Technologies and Human Rights* (Oxford University Press, Oxford 2009), pp. 2–18.

29 A. Kapczyński, 'Access to Knowledge: A Conceptual Genealogy', in: G. Krikorian and A. Kapczyński, *Access to Knowledge in the Age of Intellectual Property* (Zone Books, New York 2010), pp. 17–57.

access to knowledge.[30] According to Boyle it is time for the promotion of innovation in science, technology and culture for the benefit of the peoples of the world and WIPO has a significant role to play in building this kind of approach. Openness to alternatives, participation and transparency and balancing public and private interest, among others, are seen as priority issues for WIPO to resolve. A crucial follow-up step in this process was the adoption, in September 2007, of a Development Agenda for WIPO. The Development Agenda includes 45 recommendations.[31] The recommendations contain groundbreaking language on intellectual property, development and public policy concerns. They include the promotion of a development-oriented intellectual property culture, the preservation of the public domain and the exchange of experiences on open collaborative projects and the undertaking of new studies to assess the economic, social and cultural impact of the use of intellectual property systems.[32] Discussions of new minimum copyright limitations and exceptions by WIPO's Standing Committee on Copyright and Related Rights (SCCR) is so far the most significant outcome of WIPO's Development Agenda. The limitations and exceptions to be studied by the SCCR include those for education, libraries, archives, innovative services and persons with disabilities.[33]

Access to knowledge is starting to be the objective of a collective pattern of thinking in Europe. This is best reflected in the turn in European law policies towards greater acceptance of access to knowledge in general. In July 2006, the European Parliament adopted the 'Resolution on the execution of the Commonwealth Lisbon programmer: research and innovation as investment for the sake of increase and employment – a common concept'. The Parliament is in the said Resolution drawing attention to the necessity of a European Union (EU) system of intellectual property protection which would be friendly for all users and will not coincide with access to knowledge.[34] The Resolution chose as its main concern

30 J. Boyle, 'A Manifesto on WIPO and the Future of Intellectual Property', 0009 *Duke Law and Technology Review* (2009), pp. 17–20. Electronic copy available at www.law.duke.edu/journals/dltr/articles/2004dltr0009.html, visited on 21 April 2012.

31 Electronic copy available at www.wipo.int/ip-development/en/agenda, visited on 3 May 2012.

32 To date, three meetings of WIPO's Committee on Development and Intellectual Property (CDIP) have been held and at the latest such meeting in April and May 2009, the WIPO Secretariat presented a progress report on the steps taken towards the implementation of 19 of the recommendations.

33 Treaty for Blind, Visually Impaired and Other Reading Disabled Persons as the first concrete proposal (May 2009). cf. Lida Ayoubi, 'Human Rights Perspectives on Access of Blind, Visually Impaired and Other Reading Disabled Persons to Copyrighted Material', Master's Thesis (Master's Programme in International Human Rights Law and Intellectual Property Law, Faculty of Law, Lund University, supervisor: Anna Maria Andersen Nawrot), p. 20 *et seq.*

34 Building the Knowledge Society: Social and Human Capital Interactions, Brussels, 28.05.2003, SEC (2003) 652.

the promotion of a society based on knowledge as well as the propagation and support of the General Public Licence (GPL) charge free and open software. The Resolution is unquestionably an unprecedented document in terms of European integration as the European Union with the adoption of this resolution for the first time fully backs up free licences in Europe. Of final crucial importance is the fact that in 2007, in its review of the Single Market, the European Commission highlighted the need to promote free movement of knowledge and innovation as the 'Fifth Freedom' in the Single Market.[35]

The Berlin Declaration on Open Access to Knowledge in the Sciences and Humanities, the Bethesda Statement on Open Access and the Budapest Open Access Initiative introduced three major public definitions of 'open access' (OA). Even though these three definitions to a smaller degree differ from one another, they agree on the essentials. One can also refer to them collectively, or to their common ground, as the Budapest-Bethesda-Berlin (or 'BBB') definition of open access.[36] According to this definition OA content must be free of charge for all users with an Internet connection. OA removes both price and permission barriers. By OA to literature we mean its free availability on the public Internet, permitting any users to read, download, copy, distribute, print, search, or link to the full text of these articles, crawl them for indexing, pass them as data to software, or use them for any other lawful purpose, without financial, legal, or technical barriers other than those inseparable from gaining access to the Internet itself. The only constraint on reproduction and distribution and the only role for copyright in this domain, should be to give authors control over the integrity of their work and the right to be properly acknowledged and cited. The Bethesda and Berlin statements are as follows: for a work to be OA, the copyright holder must consent in advance to let users copy, use, distribute, transmit and display the work publicly and to make and distribute derivative works in any digital medium for any responsible purpose, subject to proper attribution of authorship.

The Long-Marginalized Normative Content of the Human Right to Science and Culture – Art 15 of the International Covenant on Economic, Social and Cultural Rights (ICESCR)

In order to give grounds to the long-marginalized normative content of the human right to science and culture (that opens up for the theories that carry a promise of the adventure of utopia) one needs to focus on the relation between human rights and the intellectual property at stake, followed by the deconstructed meaning of the normative content of Article 15 of the International Covenant on Economic, Social and Cultural Rights (ICESCR) that primarily encompasses the right to

35 COM 2007 724 final of 20.11.2007 – A Single Market for 21st Century Europe.

36 Electronic copy available at www.earlham.edu/-peters/fos/overview.html, visited on 3 June 2012.

benefit from the protection of the moral and material interests resulting from any scientific, literary or artistic production of which she or he is the author and the right to take part in cultural life.[37]

Human rights and intellectual property rights have been isolated for a long time.[38] There is only one explicit reference to intellectual property in the 'Charter of the Fundamental Rights of the European Union' that says that intellectual property shall be protected.[39] There are no references to human rights in the major intellectual property treaties.[40] One can distinguish four approaches while debating the interaction between human rights law and intellectual property law.[41] According to the first there is no conflict between human rights norms and the expansion of intellectual property protection. A second view suggests that there is a conflict between human rights and intellectual property in special areas such as, for example, the right to science and culture, the right to education or the right

---

37 See also W.A. Schabas, 'Study of the Right to Enjoy the Benefits of Scientific and Technological progess and Its Applications', in: Y. Donders and V. Volodin (eds), *Human Rights in Education, Science and Culture. Legal Developments and Challenges* (Ashgate, Unesco Publishing 2007), pp. 273–303; see also Y. Donders, 'The Legal Framework of the Right to Take Part in Cultural Life', in: Y. Donders and V. Volodin (eds), *Human Rights in Education, Science and Culture. Legal Developments and Challenges* (Ashgate, Unesco Publishing 2007), pp. 231–261; F. Coomans, 'Content and Scope of the Right to Education as a Human Right and Obstacles to Its Realization', in: Y. Donders and V. Volodin (eds), *Human Rights in Education, Science and Culture. Legal Developments and Challenges* (Ashgate, Unesco Publishing 2007), pp. 183–221.

38 W. Grosheide (ed.), *Intellectual Property and Human Rights A Paradox* (Edward Elgar, Northampton 2010), pp. 3–37; L.R. Helfer and G. Austin, *Human Rights and Intellectual Property. Mapping the Global Interface* (Cambridge University Press, Cambridge 2011), pp. 64–81. See also A. Eide, 'Interdependence and Indivisibility of Human Rights', in: Y. Donders and V. Volodin (eds), *Human Rights in Education, Science and Culture. Legal Developments and Challenges* (Ashgate, Unesco Publishing 2007), pp. 11–49. See also Alfredsson, G., 'UNESCO and a Common Framework for Ethics. Human Rights Concerns', in: Bexell, G. and D.-E. Andersson (eds), *Universal Ethics. Perspectives and Proposals from Scandinavian Scholars* (Martinus Nijhoff Publishers, Kluwer Law International, The Hague/London/New York 2002), p. 59. Alfredsson writes: 'The primary responsibility for respecting and implementing the international human rights standards rests with States'.

39 Article 17(2) of the Charter of the Fundamental Rights of the European Union. See also R. Deazley, Rethinking Copyright … , pp. 135–139.

40 See Agreement on Trade-Related Aspects on Intellectual Property (TRIPS Agreement) (1994) (The TRIPS Agreement is recognizing intellectual property rights as private rights); Paris Convention for the Protection of Industrial Property (1883); Berne Convention for the Protection of Literary and Artistic Works (1886). See also L.R. Helfer, 'Human Rights and Intellectual Property: Conflict or Coexistence?', 5 *Minn. Intell. Prop. Rev.* (2003) p. 50. Electronic copy available at mipr.umn.edu/archive/v5n1/Helfer.pdf, visited on 28 May 2012.

41 See for all of the approaches Helfer, *Ibidem*.

to health (copyrights in digital, educational and other materials, access to patented medicines).[42] A third approach focuses on the right to development, stating that this right is threatened by international intellectual property rules and that special limits and exceptions should be permitted for developing countries. According to Lea Shaver, who is representing the fourth approach, international intellectual property law is in tension with human rights norms not only in certain narrow instances but systematically.[43] Laurence Helfer presented three possible human rights frameworks for intellectual property.[44] One of them, called 'Achieving Human Rights Ends Through Intellectual Property Means' is the concluding remark of this chapter. In L.R. Helfer's opinion, in order to build an effective human rights framework for IPRs, it is crucial to specify first the minimum outcomes – in terms of, for example, education, health, sustainable development, the right of everyone to benefit from the protection of the moral and material interests resulting from any scientific, literary or artistic production of which he or she is the author, the right to take part in cultural life – that human rights law requires of states.[45] As L.R. Helfer points out ' … intellectual property plays only a secondary role in this version of the framework. Where intellectual property laws help to achieve human rights outcomes, governments should embrace it. Where it hinders those outcomes, its rules should be modified. But the focus remains on

42 cf. also T. Pogge, M. Rimmer and K. Rubenstein (eds), *Incentives for Global Public Health. Patent Law and Access to Essential Medicines* (Cambridge University Press, Cambridge 2010), pp. 101–133. cf. also V. Muzaka, *The Politics of Intellectual Property Rights and Access to Medicines, International Political Economy Series* (Palgrave Macmillan, New York 2011), pp. 109–137. cf. also H. Hestermeyer, *Human Rights and the WTO. The Case of Patents and Access to Medicines* (Oxford University Press, Oxford 2007), pp. 76–136. cf. also D. Hodgson, *The Human Right to Education* (Ashgate, Dartmouth 1998), pp. 133–153. cf. also L.O. Gostin and Z. Lazzarini, *Human Rights and Public Health in the AIDS Pandemic* (Oxford University Press, Oxford 1997) see Foreword. cf. also Y. Donders and V. Volodin (eds), *Human Rights in Education Science and Culture. Legal Developments and Challenges* (Ashgate, UNESCO 2007), see Introduction. cf. also F. Coomans, 'Content and Scope of the Right to Education as a Human Right and Obstacles to Its Realization', in: Y. Donders and V. Volodin (eds), *Human Rights in Education, Science and Culture. Legal Developments and Challenges* (Ashgate, UNESCO 2007), pp. 273–309.

43 L. Shaver, 'The Right to Science and Culture', *Wisconsin Law Review* (2010), p. 5. Electronic copy available at ssrn.com/abstract=1354788.

44 L.R. Helfer, 'Toward a Human Rights Framework for Intellectual Property', 40 *U.C. Davis Law Review* (2007) pp. 971, 1014–1020. Electronic copy available at ssrn.com/abstract=891303, visited on 10 March 2011. cf. also M. Sinjela (ed.), *Human Rights and Intellectual Property Rights, Tensions and Convergences* (Martinus Nijhoff Publishers, Leiden, Boston 2007), see Introduction.

45 L.R. Helfer and G.W. Austin, *Human Rights and Intellectual Property. Mapping the Global Interface* (Cambridge University Press, Cambridge 2011), pp. 503–522.

the minimum levels of human well-being that states must provide, using either appropriate intellectual property rules or other means'.[46]

Different international organizations have not developed one common approach.[47] Both the World Trade Organization (WTO) as well as the High Commissioner of Human Rights share the coexistence approach.[48] However, the United Nations Sub-Commission on the Promotion and Protection of Human Rights has emphasized the conflict approach.[49] The Committee on Economic, Social and Cultural Rights for the first time interpreted the relationship between intellectual property provisions and economic, social and cultural rights in 2001, when presenting a 'Statement on Human Rights and Intellectual Property'.[50] In this statement, intellectual property is perceived as a social product having a social function and intellectual property protection is introduced as the one that should serve the objective of human well-being, to which international human rights instruments give expression.[51] The Committee also points out that intellectual property regimes must both promote and protect all human rights, which means also cultural rights. What is crucial for the Committee is the fact that Article 15 of the International Covenant on Economic, Social and Cultural Rights (ICESCR) adopts the requirement to balance the protection of private and public interest in knowledge. Therefore, the private interest should never be unduly advantaged. According to the Committee the public interest in enjoying broad access to new knowledge (including digital knowledge) should be given due consideration. In

46 L.R. Helfer, 'Toward a Human Rights Framework for Intellectual Property', 40 *U.C. Davis Law Review* (2007), pp. 971, 1014–1020.

47 P.K. Yu, 'Ten Common Questions about Intellectual Property and Human Rights', 23(4) *Georgia State University Law Review* (2007), p. 710.

48 World Trade Organization, Protection of Intellectual property Under the TRIPS Agreement, 9, UN Doc. E/C12/2000/18, 27 November 2000. Electronic copy available at www.unhchr.ch/tbs/doc.nsf/0/292864197888d603c12569ba00543291?Opendocument.

UN Economic and Social Council (ECOSOC), Sub-Commission on the Promotion and Protection of Human Rights, The Impact of the Agreement on Trade-Related Aspects of Intellectual Property Rights on Human Rights: Report of the High Commissioner, 11, UN Doc. E/CN.4/Sub.2/2001/13, 27 June 2001. Electronic copy available at www.unhchr.ch/Huridocda/Huridoca.nsf/e06a5300f90fa0238025668700518ca4/590516104e92e87bc1256aa8004a8191/.

49 Intellectual Property Rights and Human Rights, Sub-Commission on Human Rights Resolutions 2000/7, UN Doc. E/CN.4/Sub.2/RES/2000/7. Electronic copy available at www.unhchr.ch/Huridocda/Huridoca.nsf/0/c462b62cf8a07b13c12569700046704e?Opendocument.

50 UN Economic and Social Council (ECOSOC), Comm. on Economic, Social and Cultural Rights, Substantive Issues Arising in the Implementation of the International Covenant on Economic, Social and Cultural Rights, UN Doc. E/C12/2001/15, 14 December 2001. Electronic copy available at www.unhchr.ch/tbs/doc.nsf/0/lelf4514f8512432c1256ba6003b2cc6.

51 L.R. Helfer, 'Toward a Human Rights Framework for Intellectual Property' … , pp. 971, 1014–1020.

this Statement the Committee introduced an agenda to draft General Comments on each of the CESCR's intellectual property clauses.

The Privilege of the Interpretations of The Committee on Economic, Social and Cultural Rights (General Comment Nos. 17 and 21)

So far two General Comments have been issued. They both address cultural human rights, such as: 1) the right to benefit from the protection of the moral and material interests resulting from any scientific, literary or artistic production of which she or he is the author and 2) the right to take part in cultural life. The Committee on Economic, Social and Cultural Rights interpreted both rights in 2005 and 2009 (General Comment Nos. 17 and 21).[52] Both will have a very strong impact on the future development of legal norms and morality related to access to knowledge since the rights provisions of CESCR have the same status as the domestic constitutional laws of its state parties. Cultural rights are universal, indivisible and interdependent – just like other human rights. They are an integral part of human rights; however, they had been neglected for a long time.[53]

In General Comment No. 17 (the right to benefit from the protection of the moral and material interests resulting from any scientific, literary or artistic production of which he or she is the author) to the CESCR firmly distinguishes between intellectual property rights and human rights, putting them in contrast and pointing out that intellectual property rights are only means by which states parties seek to provide incentives for creativity and inventiveness, encouraging dissemination of creative and innovative intellectual productions and preserving the integrity of such productions for the benefit of society as a whole.[54] The Committee is confirming that intellectual property rights are of a temporary nature and may be limited in time and scope, traded, amended, revoked, licenced and assigned to someone else. Intellectual property regimes protect business interests – and overprotection may be more detrimental than beneficial to society.[55] To the contrary human rights are fundamental as they are inherent to the human person as such. Human rights are

52 General Comment No. 17 on the right to benefit from the protection of the moral and material interests resulting from any scientific, literary or artistic production of which he is the author, adopted on 21 November 2005 by the Committee on Economic, Social and Cultural Rights, 35th session, 7–25 November 2005. cf. W.A. Schabas, 'Study of the Right to Enjoy the Benefits of Scientific and Technological Progress and Its Applications', in: Y. Donders and V. Volodin (eds), *Human Rights in Education, Science and Culture. Legal Developments and Challenges* (Ashgate, UNESCO 2007), pp. 273–309.

53 L.R. Helfer, 'Toward a Human Rights Framework for Intellectual Property' … , pp. 971, 1014–1020.

54 L. Zemer, 'The Idea of Authorship … , pp. 43–49.

55 T. Kongolo, *Unsettled International Intellectual Property Issues* (Wolters Kluwer, New York 2008), p. 5.

timeless expressions of fundamental entitlements of the human person.[56] According to the provisions of General Comment No. 17 it is particularly important not to equate intellectual property with the human right to benefit from the protection of the moral and material interests resulting from any scientific, literary or artistic production of which he or she is the author.[57] This is ground-breaking language confirming that intellectual property rights are not themselves human rights. It means that the intellectual property rights regime is just an available tool to safeguard the material interests of authors, which is necessary in order to enable them to enjoy an adequate standard of living. This certainly weakens the position of the advocates of the vision that intellectual property rights (particularly copyrights and patents) as human rights that shall expand more within the digital environment and hence passive use of digital technology is to be the standard for users (in comparison to the active one like Creative Commons or Open Source Software). In this context intellectual property rights will always have to be adjusted whenever they are in conflict with fundamental norms of human rights law.[58]

In the view of Wong this clear distinction between intellectual property rights and human rights presented by the Committee constitutes proof of the view that intellectual property rights and human rights are in conflict. Therefore human rights considerations shall prevail over economic policy and primacy shall be given to human rights norms and principles.[59] On the other hand Yu suggests that instead of inquiring whether human rights and intellectual property conflict or coexist with each other, it is more relevant to identify the human rights attributes of intellectual property rights as a first step and then secondly distinguish them from the non-human rights aspects of intellectual property protection.[60]

Article 27(2) of the Universal Declaration on Human Rights (UDHR) and Article 15(1) (c) of the ICESCR put forth the right of everyone to benefit from the protection of the moral and material interests resulting from any scientific, literary or artistic production of which he or she is the author.[61] In 2005 the Committee on Economic, Social and Cultural Rights introduced the General Comment on this right – General Comment No. 17. Following General Comment No. 17, there are

56 General Comment No. 17, supra note 10, p. 1.

57 *Ibidem*, p. 2.

58 cf. P.L.C. Torremans (ed.), *Intellectual Property and Human Rights. Enhanced Edition of Copyright and Human Rights* (Wolters Kluwer, The Netherlands 2007), pp. 3–23.

59 M.W.S. Wong, 'Toward an Alternative Normative Framework for Copyright. From Private Property to Human Rights', 26(775) *Cardozo Arts and Entertainment* (2009), p. 812.

60 P.K. Yu, 'Ten Common Questions about Intellectual Property and Human Rights', 23(4) *Georgia State University Law Review* (2007), p. 710.

61 This right is also recognized in regional human rights instruments, such as Article 13(2) of the American Declaration of the Rights and Duties of Man of 1948, Article 14(1)(c) of the Additional Protocol of the American Convention on Human Rights in the Area of Economic, Social and Cultural Rights of 1988 ('Protocol of San Salvador') and in Article 1 of Protocol No. 1 to the European Convention for the Protection of Human Rights and Fundamental Freedoms of 1952.

three main purposes behind the right to benefit from the protection of the moral and material interests resulting from any scientific, literary or artistic production of which he or she is the author.[62] Safeguarding the personal link between authors and their creations is the first one. The second one is to protect the link between peoples, communities and their collective cultural heritage. To safeguard the material interests of the authors, which is necessary in order to enable them to enjoy an adequate standard of living, is the third purpose. The Comment leaves room for alternative tools of benefiting from the protection of works or inventions, such as Open Source and Creative Commons licensing. They are safeguarding the personal link between authors and their creations as well as the link between peoples, communities and their collective cultural heritage (namely the digital culture heritage). This might be perceived as a perfect choice for those authors who produce royalty free literature – however, it is not limited to them. In this context one can suggest that alternative forms are often using the copyright regime for the purpose of making knowledge available to users – active use of digital technology.[63] In this light it is important to note that according to the Committee, one of the functions of the right to benefit from the protection of the moral and material interests resulting from any scientific, literary or artistic production of which he or she is the author is also to encourage the active contribution of creators to the arts and sciences and to the progress of society as a whole.[64] In this regard it is linked to the other right, to take part in cultural life. The Committee explicitly confirms that the public interest in enjoying broad access to authors' creations should always be given consideration and the private interest of authors must not be unduly advantaged.[65] The protection under the right to benefit from the protection of the moral and material interests resulting from any scientific, literary or artistic production of which he or she is the author does not have to reflect the level of protection that is present in the intellectual property regime.[66] To the contrary, the level might be even lower or different as long as the protection available is suited to secure the moral and material interests of the authors.[67] Therefore, all the alternatives are welcomed as long as they are suited to secure these interests which according to the Committee includes: 1) 'moral interest' – the right of authors to be recognized as the creators of their productions as well as the right to object to any distortion, mutilation or other modification in relation to their productions which would be prejudicial to their reputation and honour[68] and 2) 'material interest' –

62 General Comment No. 17, pp. 1–2.

63 L. Rosen, *Open Source Licensing …* , pp. 1–11.

64 General Comment No. 17, p. 2.

65 *Ibidem*, p. 9.

66 *Ibidem*, p. 4.

67 *Ibidem*, pp. 4–5.

68 See about the historical perspective on 'moral interest' F.W. Grosheide, 'In search of the public domain during the prehistory of copyright', in Ch. Waelde and H. MacQueen (eds), *Intellectual Property, The Many Faces of the Public Domain* (Edward Elgar Publishing, Northampton 2007), pp. 10–14.

needs to enable authors to enjoy an adequate standard of living, which means that it does not have to extend over the entire lifespan of an author (i.e. can be achieved via Creative Commons, Open Source software or simple one-time payments).[69] Thus, understanding 'material interest' in the cultural human rights framework means that it is not tied to objectives of market efficiency and utilitarianism. In this light, Wong suggests that 'by recognizing a narrower scope for authors economic rights, a better balance can be achieved as between authors' rights and the public's interest in acquiring access to information …',[70] and accordingly knowledge.

The right of everyone to take part in cultural life is one of the most important aspects of cultural rights that are based on Article 27 of the UDHR and Article 15 of the ICESCR. 'The right to take part in cultural life' has been little interpreted and not clearly defined.[71] Particularly in the era of digital technologies the right of everyone to take part in cultural life is seeking a clear interpretation – going towards a static or dynamic approach, putting emphasis on the culture as a process.[72] Finally, in December 2009, after many years of public debate, the Committee on Economic, Social and Cultural Rights interpreted this right in its General Comment No. 21. In the Committee's view, cultures have no fixed borders and 'the right to take part in cultural life' can be characterized as a freedom and as a cultural choice and, as such, should be protected recognized and respected on the basis of equality.[73] The Committee perceives culture as an inclusive concept encompassing all manifestations of human existence. According to the General Comment, culture is a living, dynamic, evolving and interactive process with its past, present and a future, never seen as an isolated manifestation.[74] The Committee in particular considers the interactive component of culture stating that via this process both individuals and communities give expression to the culture of humanity.[75] Culture is understood as the creation and product of society where both

---

69 General Comment No. 17, p. 5.

70 M.W.S. Wong, 'Toward an Alternative Normative Framework for Copyright. From Private Property to Human Rights', 26:775 *Cardozo Arts and Entertainment* (2009), p. 812.

71 Y. Donders, 'The Legal Framework of the Right to Take Part in Cultural Life', in: Y. Donders and V. Volodin (eds), *Human Rights in Education, Science and Culture. Legal Developments and Challenges* (Ashgate, UNESCO 2007), pp. 231–273. cf. also W.A. Schabas, 'Study of the Right to Enjoy the Benefits of Scientific and Technological Progress and Its Application' … , pp. 273–309.

72 P. Thornberry, 'Cultural rights and universality of human rights', paper submitted for Day of General Discussion on Right to take part in cultural life (article 15(1)(a) of the Covenant), Friday, 9 May 2008, UN Economic and Social Council, Distr. General, E/C.12/40/15, Committee on Economic, Social and Cultural Rights, 40th session, Geneva, 28 April–16 May 2008.

73 General Comment No. 21 on the right of everyone to take part in cultural life adopted on 2–20 November 2009 by the Committee on Economic, Social and Cultural Rights, 43rd session, 2–20 November 2009.

74 *Ibidem*, p. 2.

75 *Ibidem*, p. 3.

individuality and otherness are highlighted.[76] Broadly understood, cultural life, for the purposes of implementing Article 15 (1) (a), encompasses, *inter alia*, different ways of life and technology.[77] Therefore one may enumerate different forms of cultural life and digital cultural life will be one of them. Thus the revolution is that one can speak about an access to digital culture within the right to take part in cultural life. According to General Comment No. 21, 'cultural life' is dynamic and it constantly develops. Saying that it is dynamic and vibrant we are also saying that it is open.[78] Different 'commons' are examples of digital 'cultural life' of the contemporary society. Following the wording from General Comment No. 21, the Committee recognized that the term 'everyone' may denote both the individual and the collective. Therefore, the right to take part in cultural life may be exercised by a person (a) as an individual, (b) by a person in association with others, or (c) within a community or group.

The Committee presents three major components of the right to take part in cultural life ('to participate' has the same meaning as 'to take part'): (1) 'participation' in cultural life; (2) 'access' to cultural life; and (3) 'contribution' to cultural life.[79] To act freely, to choose his or her own identity, to act creatively and to take part in creative activity, to seek and develop cultural knowledge and to share it with others are only some of the examples of the meaning of 'participation'.[80] 'Access' refers in particular to the right to know and understand his or her own culture, the right to learn, to follow a certain way of life and the right to benefit from the cultural heritage and the creation of other individuals and communities. 'Contribution' covers the right of everyone to be involved in creating the intellectual expressions of the community.[81] Participation in the digital cultural life is about creating opportunities where users can engage in creative

76 *Ibidem*, pp. 3–4.

77 Ch. Groni, 'The right to take part in cultural life', paper submitted for Day of General Discussion on Right to take part in cultural life (article 15(1)(a) of the Covenant), Friday, 9 May 2008, UN Economic and Social Council, Distr. General, E/C.12/40/15, Committee on Economic, Social and Cultural Rights, 40th session, Geneva, 28 April–16 May 2008, pp. 13–15.

78 L. Shaver and C. Sganga, 'The right to take part in Cultural Life: On Copyright and Human Rights', electronic copy available at ssrn.com/abstract=1437319, visited on 29 May 2012.

79 General Comment No. 21, p. 4.

80 See on the 'limits on participation' M.B. Land, 'Intellectual Property Rights and the Right to Participate in Cultural Life', paper submitted for Day of General Discussion on Right to take part in cultural life (article 15(1)(a) of the Covenant), Friday, 9 May 2008, UN Economic and Social Council, Distr. General, E/C.12/40/15, Committee on Economic, Social and Cultural Rights, 40th session, Geneva, 28 April–16 May 2008, pp. 3–5.

81 Following General Comment No. 21, '... this is supported by the right to take part in the development of the community to which a person belongs and in the definition, elaboration and implementation of policies and decisions that have an impact on the exercise of a person's cultural rights'.

activities such as for example use of Open Source software, which then can be adapted, modified and redistributed in its original or modified form for further use, modification and redistribution. Thereby users are obtaining knowledge and a better understanding of the particular Open Source software. On the one hand individuals develop their personal digital knowledge skills and on the other hand progress of the society in digital technologies is possible.

General Comment No. 21 recognizes certain conditions for the full realization of the right to take part in cultural life on the basis of equality and non-discrimination. Four of them are especially relevant with regard to the empowerment of the access to digital culture. The first condition is the presence of cultural goods and services that are open for everyone to enjoy and benefit from. This condition is called 'availability' and includes, *inter alia*, knowledge, literature, arts in all forms and libraries. Following the broad definition of 'cultural life' presented in General Comment No. 21, digital knowledge, digital libraries as well as literature and art stored in a digital manner shall be included (e.g. as knowledge commons). The second crucial condition is termed 'accessibility'. It refers to both effective and concrete opportunities for individuals and communities to fully enjoy culture. This is a fundamental requirement for the full realization of the right to take part in the digital cultural life. To fully enjoy culture would mean to include not only passive but also active use of digital knowledge.[82] The third condition calls for consultations that should be held with the individuals and communities concerned in order to ensure that the measures to protect cultural diversity (digital culture) are acceptable to all. This condition is called 'acceptability'. 'Adaptability' is the last condition to be introduced and it refers to the flexibility and relevance of strategies, policies, programmes and measures adopted by governments. There are three levels of obligations that the right of everyone to take part in cultural life imposes on state parties. They are the obligations to respect, protect and fulfil. The fact that state parties are obliged to respect human rights means that they have to refrain from acting in ways that inappropriately limit the enjoyment of the right. Therefore both laws and polices shall incorporate access to knowledge and expand access to knowledge in their legislation. To take part in cultural life requires freedom from overly restrictive laws but also different ways of realizing intellectual property rights in the digital technologies era as pre-steps for the full recognition of access to knowledge arguments. As analysed and suggested, states, while focusing on efforts to eliminate discriminatory barriers, shall pay

82 J. Smiers, 'Is Copyright fit for the 21st century? No!', in: W. Grosheide (ed.), *Intellectual Property and Human Rights. A Paradox* (Edward Elgar, Cheltenham, UK), pp. 105–118. cf. also: J. Smiers, 'No copyright and no domination of cultural markets – two conditions for realizing active participation in cultural life', paper submitted for Day of General Discussion on Right to take part in cultural life (article 15(1)(a) of the Covenant), Friday, 9 May 2008, UN Economic and Social Council, Distr. General, E/C.12/40/6, Committee on Economic, Social and Cultural Rights, 40th session, Geneva, 28 April–16 May 2008.

more attention to the fact that an imbalanced intellectual property regime may negatively impact cultural participation across the entire society. For example, developing a global approach to limitations and exceptions to copyright law is one of the solutions.[83] The obligation to respect requires governments to take appropriate steps to prevent third parties from interfering with the right to take part in cultural life. One of the crucial issues here is how the state parties address anti-competitive practices since they influence cultural participation as well as misleading copyright claims.

It is important to note that states parties are, *inter alia*, obliged to respect and protect cultural heritage in all its forms – including digital forms. 'Cultural heritage must be preserved, developed, enriched and transmitted to future generations as a record of human experience and aspirations, in order to encourage creativity in all its diversity'.[84] With regard to the obligation to respect and protect cultural heritage, 'particular attention should be paid to the adverse consequences of globalization, undue privatization of goods and services and deregulation on the right to participate in cultural life'.[85] The obligation to fulfil the right to take part in cultural life can be subdivided into the obligations to 'facilitate', 'promote' and 'provide'. To 'facilitate' the right of everyone to take part in cultural life includes taking a wide range of positive measures, including legislative, judicial, financial, promotional and other measures that would contribute to the full realization of this right. For example, under the obligation to facilitate, state parties are obliged to adopt policies for the protection and promotion of cultural diversity and to facilitate access to a rich and diversified range of cultural expressions. For digital culture that would entail the promotion of the term 'digital culture' in general as well as the promotion and protection of the different kinds of commons. Another example is the obligation to promote that requires governments to take effective steps to ensure that there is appropriate education and public awareness concerning the right to take part in cultural life. This would particularly include awareness-raising and education about access to digital knowledge on different levels. Under the obligation to provide, states parties must provide programmes aimed at preserving and restoring cultural heritage. Therefore, programmes aimed at the preservation of the digital cultural heritage shall be included.

Finally, it is important to point out that according to General Comment No. 21 states parties are obliged to adopt measures to protect and promote the diversity of cultural expressions and enable all cultures to express themselves and make them known. In this respect, digital culture with its growing commons is supported since the need to protect the free flow of ideas by word and image is underlined.

83 L. Shaver and C. Sganga, 'The right to take part in cultural life: on copyright and human rights', electronic copy available at ssrn.com/abstract=1437319, visited on 29 May 2012.

84 General Comment No. 21, p. 13 (citation from the Universal Declaration on Cultural Diversity).

85 *Ibidem*, pp. 13–14.

Also the right to information and expression is relevant. This is the responsibility of the state – compliance with the ICESCR. However, the Committee notes that international organizations, such as, *inter alia*, the World Intellectual Property Organization, should intensify their efforts to take into account human rights principles and obligations in their work concerning the right of everyone to take part in cultural life, in cooperation with the Office of the United Nations High Commissioner for Human Rights.[86] Within the normative content of General Comment No. 21, there are statements that are not only supporting access to knowledge but are also opening up new perspectives. One of them is referring to the protection of cultural diversity as an ethical imperative, inseparable from the respect for human dignity and requiring a commitment to human rights. The other one is suggesting that states parties should acknowledge that there are two dimensions of cultural activities, goods and services – an economic one and a cultural one. Thus, they must not be treated as having solely a commercial value. States parties are obliged to advance progressively towards the full realization of the right to take part in cultural life, in order to ensure that everyone has effective access to cultural life.[87] However, in implementing this right governments should go beyond the material aspects of the culture and also promote effective access to all intangible cultural goods such as, for example, knowledge, also in its digital form.

86 General Comment No. 21, p. 18.

87 See also G. Alfredsson, 'UNESCO and a Common Framework for Ethics. Human Rights Concerns', in: Bexell G. and D.-E. Andersson (eds), *Universal Ethics. Perspectives and Proposals from Scandinavian Scholars* (Martinus Nijhoff Publishers, Kluwer Law International, The Hague/London/New York 2002), p. 59.

PART III
The Myth and the Reason

Chapter 6
An Introduction to a Far-Sighted Morality in the Thought of Bauman

'Now Just Step Back for a Moment'[1]

'Now just step back for a moment', writes Lessig, professor of law at Stanford University, in his work 'Free Culture'.

> There will be a time thirty years from now when our children look back at us and ask, how could we have let this happen? How could we allow a policy to be pursued whose direct cost would be to speed the death of 15 to 30 million Africans and whose only real benefit would be to uphold the 'sanctity' of an idea? What possible justification could there ever be for a policy that results in so many deaths? What exactly is the insanity that would allow so many to die for such an abstraction? Some blame the drug companies. I don't. They are corporations. Their managers are ordered by law to make money for the corporation. They push a certain patent policy not because of ideals, but because it is the policy that makes them the most money. And it only makes them the most money because of a certain corruption within our political system – a corruption the drug companies are certainly not responsible for.
>
> The corruption is our own politicians' failure of integrity. For the drug companies would love – they say and I believe them – to sell their drugs as cheaply as they can to countries in Africa and elsewhere. There are issues they'd have to resolve to make sure the drugs didn't get back into the United States, but those are mere problems of technology. They could be overcome.
>
> A different problem, however, could not be overcome. This is the fear of the grandstanding politician who would call the presidents of the drug companies before a Senate or House hearing and ask, 'How is it you can sell this HIV drug in Africa for only $1 a pill, but the same drug would cost an American $1,500?' Because there is no 'sound bite' answer to that question, its effect would be to induce regulation of prices in America. The drug companies thus avoid this spiral by avoiding the first step. They reinforce the idea that property should be sacred. They adopt a rational strategy in an irrational context, with the unintended

1 Excerpts in this section come from L. Lessig, *Free Culture. The Nature and Future of Creativity* (Penguin Books, New York 2004). See also the Polish version of the book: L. Lessig, *Wolna Kultura* [*Free Culture*] (Wydawnictwa Szkolne i Pedagogiczne, Warszawa 2005), pp. 289–290, 313–515.

consequence that perhaps millions die. And that rational strategy thus becomes framed in terms of this ideal – the sanctity of an idea called 'intellectual property'.

So when the common sense of your child confronts you, what will you say? When the common sense of a generation finally revolts against what we have done, how will we justify what we have done? What is the argument?

***

Why would creators participate in giving up total control? Some participate to better spread their content. Cory Doctorow, for example, is a science fiction author. His first novel, *Down and Out in the Magic Kingdom*, was released on-line and for free, under a Creative Commons licence, on the same day that it went on sale in bookstores.

Why would a publisher ever agree to this? I suspect his publisher reasoned like this: There are two groups of people out there: (1) those who will buy Cory's book whether or not it's on the Internet and (2) those who may never hear of Cory's book, if it isn't made available for free on the Internet. Some part of (1) will download Cory's book instead of buying it. Call them bad-(1)s. Some part of (2) will download Cory's book, like it and then decide to buy it. Call them (2)-goods. If there are more (2)-goods than bad-(1)s, the strategy of releasing Cory's book free on-line will probably increase sales of Cory's book. Indeed, the experience of his publisher clearly supports that conclusion. The book's first printing was exhausted months before the publisher had expected. This first novel of a science fiction author was a total success.

The idea that free content might increase the value of non-free content was confirmed by the experience of another author. Peter Wayner, who wrote a book about the free software movement titled *Free for All* and made an electronic version of his book free on-line under a Creative Commons licence after the book went out of print. He then monitored used book shop prices for the book. As predicted, as the number of downloads increased, the used book price for his book increased, as well.

These are examples of using the Commons to better spread proprietary content. I believe that is a wonderful and common use of the Commons. There are others who use Creative Commons licences for other reasons. Many who use the 'sampling licence'. …

These are first steps to rebuilding a public domain. They are not mere arguments; they are action.

Morality in Close-up: Morality of Feudalism

One will not be far from the truth stating that, in contemporary times, it is common practice to maximize intellectual property rights as well as use them in the most radical and restrictive possible manner. As Lessig describes in an interesting manner, in the past there already existed such a system of ownership well-known to the whole world, and it was feudalism. It not only involved the fact that rights protecting the ownership were powerful and vast. Lessig continues that the feudal system was based on the creation of protections against a situation in which people who enjoyed such ownership right, pursuant to the system, would weaken it by letting people or things under their control enter the free market. What follows is that feudalism was based on a maximal control and concentration as well as fighting freedoms which could stand in the way of such a control.[2] The fact that we have a postanalogue society and a postmodern era is without doubt. Nonetheless, it is still doubtful whether a postanalogue society will be free or will it be feudal? Therefore, will such a community be a community of either a feudal morality character or of any other character? And if so, what other?

The Lost Difference between Truth and Extremes within Patent and Copyright Law

Our contemporary acceptance of the idea of ownership is completely uncritical. We fail to notice how short-sighted it is denying people access to ideas, people who need them to live or to create.[3] For this purpose one may illustrate the issue with an example from Lessig, who posits a sensible patent policy which could be based on acceptance and a dynamic implementation of a patent system which would not be binding for everyone and everywhere in the same manner. A patent policy could entail the acceptance and support of the system, which would not

2 L. Lessig, *Wolna Kultura* [*Free Culture*] … , pp. 296–297.

3 J. Boyle, *The Public Domain* … , pp. 245–246:

> Is it not silly to equate the protection of the environment with the protection of the public domain? After all, one is the struggle to save a planetary ecology and the other is just some silly argument about legal rules and culture and science. I would be the first to yield primacy to the environmental challenges we are facing. Mass extinction events are to be avoided, particularly if they involve you personally. Yet my willingness to minimize the importance of the rules that determine who owns science and culture goes only so far. A better intellectual property system will not save the planet. On the other hand, one of the most promising sets of tools for building biofuels comes from synthetic biology. Ask some of the leading scientists in that field why they devoted their precious time to trying to work out a system that would offer the valuable incentives that patents provide while leaving a commons of 'biobricks' open to all for future development. I worry about these rules naturally; they were forced to do so. A better intellectual property system certainly will not end world hunger. Still it is interesting to read about the lengthy struggles to clear the multiple, overlapping patents on Golden*Rice* trade mark – a rice grain genetically engineered to cure vitamin deficiencies that nearly perished in a thicket of blurrily overlapping rights.

generate obstacles to distribution of medicines to less affluent countries. It would restore the idea of balance.[4]

A sensible copyright policy could similarly involve the acceptance and implementation of a copyright system that would not regulate dissemination of cultures in a perfect and lasting way.[5] In Lessig's opinion, this would mean developing a method which would permit taking a middle stance: neither 'all rights reserved', nor 'no rights reserved' but 'some rights reserved'. One could not argue with Lessig that it would be undoubtedly a way of respecting copyright and simultaneously enabling creators to liberate their content according to their wishes.[6] This presupposes building a layer of a sensible copyright law, a law which in a way will go beyond and above two extremes which currently dominate. And here the Creative Commons system – hinted at in the preceding pages of the book – comes into play, which provides for an easy creation on the basis of others' works.[7] *Creative Commons*, that is the right to education and culture (as a human right), should constitute an alternative beside intellectual property law whether or not the author uses it. The right to education and culture in containing such an alternative option constitutes an explicit proof of pursuing the perspective of difference between truth and extremes as discussed by Lessig. The energy of the process is distinctly noticeable from the moment of the publication of both General Comments Nos. 17 and 20 of the Committee on Economic, Social and Cultural Rights, expounded on in the preceding pages of this text. Intellectual property laws as viewed from the traditional perspective, together with solutions based on the concept of commons (such as dynamically developing Open Source Software and Creative Commons), should be seen as tools for achieving a creative compensation. The choice will, however, be given to the creators of works – as the postmodern Individuals.

Creative Commons is, thus, an international alternative, a voluntary effort of creators and other people who intend to reform a set of rights presently regulating the sphere of creativity. As Lessig stresses, the project fails to compete with copyright and even supplements it, since its aim is not fighting with creators' rights, but helping authors and creators to execute their rights in a cheaper and more flexible way. As one cannot forget that (as mentioned before) the Open Source and Creative Commons movement aims at an emphasis on extra-pecuniary interests related to ownership (the idea of sharing) rather than at exposing the

4 L. Lessig, *Wolna Kultura* [*Free Culture*] … , p. 290.

5 Cf. D.G. Post, *In Search of Jefferson's Moose. Notes on the State of Cyberspace* (Oxford University Press, Oxford 2009), pp. 163–187. See also K.E. Knutsson, 'Globalization and the Dimension of Culture and Values', in: G. Bexell and D.-E. Andersson (eds), *Universal Ethics. Perspectives and Proposals from Scandinavian Scholars* (Martinus Nijhoff Publishers, Kluwer Law International, The Hague/London/New York 2002), pp. 184–185.

6 L. Lessig, *Wolna Kultura* [*Free Culture*] … , p. 305.

7 *Ibidem*, p. 311.

idea of ownership, being a distinctive feature of intellectual property rights.[8] The focus on extra-pecuniary interests related to ownership seems to be likely thanks to copyright. Thus we are facing a peculiar instrumentalization of copyright, where it is used as a means to attain ends which have not been found within the scope of this field of law before, such as promoting the ideas of free software and sharing 'non-valuable' (in this context) knowledge with the society at large.[9] Due to this fact, creativity will be disseminated more easily in the postanalogue society. As mentioned by Lessig, a supplementary function in the context of the right to science and culture as a human right can be extended by a balancing function that would respond to Lessig's call for restoration of the *idea of balance*. Owing to both General Comments Nos. 17 and 20 of the Committee on Economic, Social and Cultural Rights, Open Source and Creative Commons have already been in operation within human rights, they achieve their functionality within human rights, and in this manner they confirm a unique role that human rights are to play in general – as 'alternatively open rights'.

One cannot also forget that the call for shorter terms of copyright is a part of an extending function as well, which is the result of the right to science and culture. For natural persons the term of copyright in Europe constitutes the lifetime of the author plus 70 years after his death; in the case of juridical persons the term amounts to 50 or 70 years (for broadcasting producers).[10] It seems justified, in order

8 Programs distributed under the *Open Source scheme* are not excluded from the scope of copyright; it is just by referring to the rights of use provided in copyright law that the freedom of adaptation of a program can be ensured and – what is important – it is possible to oblige the users engaged in modification of the program to disclose and share the source code (also in its modified form), free of charge.

9 M. Valimaki and V. Oksanen, 'How to manage IPR infringement risks in open source development?', an article presented at the conference 'Intellectual Property beyond Rights', 25–26 October 2004, Hanasaari, the Swedish-Finnish Cultural Centre, Espoo, Finland, p. 3. They indicate three basic types of entities which develop the Open Source system. These are large IT businesses, so-called Open Source companies and joint projects. Examples of large businesses engaged in Open Source activities include Hewlett-Packard, IBM and Apple, i.e. companies with a minor status on the market of software development and – primarily – operating systems. The companies, by virtue of their core activities, are interested and engaged in the development of Open Source software. This in large part is due to the necessity to popularise their software products or hardware platforms. Open Source companies, on the other hand, are small-to medium enterprises, whose activities consist in manufacturing and selling Open Source-based products (Open Source components). One of the pioneers, which started to develop software on the basis of Open Source, is Red Hat Inc., the creators of Red Hat Linux (being simply a distribution of Linux where technical support for the software is included). An example of a non-commercial project of a large importance is Apache, an internet server established to host websites. Another example can be Linux itself (but only in its original version, available to everyone on the net; however deprived of technical support from Red Hat Linux).

10 Recently the European Commission proposed this be extended to 95 years and following this suggestion the European Parliament passed legislation to increase the term

to support this functionality, to suggest the following three rules concerning terms of copyright.[11] First of all: they have to be short. This means that the term should be long enough to provide the incentive to create. Second of all: they have to be clear. The dividing line between a public domain and the reserved content has to be clearly delineated. In other words, a clear division would exist between 'protected' and 'unprotected' content. In doing so, one will eliminate the complexity of the 'permitted use' term. Third of all: they have to be alive. Copyright thus should be renewed, for example every five or ten years.

The Lost Difference between Truth and Extremes within Morality

In the postmodern era we have lost this important sense of balance.[12] We have lost a critical insight which allowed us to discern differences between truth and extremes. As Lessig aptly argues, in our culture dominates a fundamentalism of ownership rights, which *de facto* has nothing in common with our tradition but has effect on dissemination of ideas and culture more orientated to fundamentalism than any political decision which we can take democratically.[13]

Taking into account the above assertions, it seems that at issue is the sense of balance between responsibility for things, people and issues related to us since involving our neighbourhood, and responsibility for things, people and issues distant from us in spatial (as in another continent, in another country) or temporal (as it may happen in 50 or 100 years) terms. Our responsibility is a kind of a 'short-distance' premodern responsibility, a responsibility mature only in a temporally and spatially limited perspective (or, to put it differently, Levinasian bourgeois 'localness').[14] Additionally, we have lost an important morality to a morality of a

---

to 70 years. See also R. Kuhlen, 'Knowledge and Information – Private Property or Common Good? A Global Perspective', in: Ch. Lenk, N. Hoppe and R. Andorno (eds), *Ethics and Law of Intellectual Property* (Ashgate, Hampshire 2007), pp. 213–230. R. Kuhlen elaborates in an interesting way on who owns knowledge and the tragedy of the commons; the global arenas of WIPO and WTO are also included in the analysis); see also L. Guibault, 'The Limit of Balancing Interests Through Copyright Levies', in: Ch. Lenk, N. Hoppe and R. Andorno (eds), *Ethics and Law of Intellectual Property* (Ashgate, Hampshire 2007), pp. 231–245.

11 L. Lessig, *Wolna Kultura* [*Free Culture*] … , pp. 321–323.

12 See also on culture between state and market and the notion of 'cultural state' Z. Bauman, *Culture in a Liquid Modern World* (Polity Press, Cambridge 2011), pp. 96–117.

13 L. Lessig, *Wolna Kultura* [*Free Culture*] … , p. 290.

14 J. Boyle, *The Public Domain* … , pp. 246–247:

> Good intellectual property policy will not save our culture. But bad policy may lock up our cultural heritage unnecessarily, leave it to molder in libraries, forbide citizens to digitize it, even though the vast majority of it will never be available publicly and no copyright owner can be found. Would you not prefer the world in which your children could look at the library of congress online catalogue and click to get the book or film that otherwise languished as an 'orphan work'?

feudal character. The morality that we have lost (or which, I would rather believe, remains dormant) Hans Jonas calls a 'far-sighted morality'.[15]

An Introduction to a Far-Sighted Morality

The right to science and culture without doubt needs a morality which revolutionizes and simultaneously alleviates tension connected with understanding of norms, as well as politics and economics centred on them. While perceiving potential *Myth* and existing *Reason* concurrently, a question arises of where precisely is one to seek solutions to problems of postmodernity and the postanalogue society? Attempting to answer the question and deploying the influence of Baumanian thought, I suggest the works of Hans Jonas from 1974. Jonas proved the contradiction between the task which morality is to fulfil and what morality is *de facto* able to achieve in conditions of a sudden and profound modernization, as well as technological changes. Technological progress has been surpassing imagination since at least 1903. As the example of the Wright brothers demonstrates, nobody thought that a heavier-than-air mass would lift off the ground. These changes are impulsive and sudden and require sudden changes in our human, humanistic perception of phenomena as well. They require, at first, an increased tolerance and then solidarity. Nowadays, modern technologies and a drama of postanalogue paradigms bring about a situation in which, on the one hand, new moral impulses are not powerful enough to meet newer and newer as well as greater and greater

---

> Good intellectual policy will not necessarily give us great new music. But the policy we have today would make some of the music we most cherish illegal, or at least legally questionable … I do claim that they are facets of a very important problem and one to which we are paying far too little attention … . We should explore ways of compensating artists that are very different from the ones we use now and study the use of distributed creativity and open source in new areas of science and culture. … we need a cultural environmental movement, a politics that enables us first tp see and then to preserve the public domain, to understand its contributions to our art, our technology and our culture.

15 H. Jonas, *Philosophical Essays: from Ancient Creed to Technological Man* (Prentice Hall, Englewood Cliffs 1974), pp. 7–8. cf. revision by Rabbi Louis Jacobs in the *International Journal for Philosophy of Religion*, 7(3) (Fall 1976) p. 454. cf. also L. Vogel and Hans Jonas, *Mortality and Morality. A Search for the Good Auschwitz* (Northwestern University Press, Evanston Illinois 1996), pp. 2–59. From the book:

> Hans Jonas (1903–93) was a German Jew, student of Heidegger and Bultmann, lifelong friend and colleague of Hannah Arendt at the New School for Social Research and one of the most prominent thinkers of his generation. The range of his topics never obscures their unifying thread: that our mortality is at the root of our moral responsibility to safeguard humanity's future. Mortality and Morality both consummate and demonstrate the basic thrust of Jonas's thought: the inseparability of ethics and metaphysics, the reality of values at the centre of being.

requirements. On the other hand, our impulses are unable to give up and do not want to abandon the effort.[16]

Jonas advances a thesis that there exists a kind of morality which each 'I', each Individual received (or which we received as a moral community) as a legacy of premodern times. And it is the only morality we have at our disposal. The modern Individual simply has no other and knows no other morality. By belonging to a moral community we have no other and know no other morality. The ethical world of the past analogue society comprised only neighbours. The situation, in the meantime, underwent a complete change.[17] The morality is characterized by its functionality of an only short-distance character. That is why the morality acts in a limited and short distance.[18] Thus, it has no longer perspective, in other words this is not a far-sighted responsibility. A short-distance responsibility is then of no use in the postanalogue times, when most important actions (above all related to paradigms of the postanalogue society) have distant effects (access to knowledge – a well-educated and autonomous society; access to medicines – a healthy and participating society and so on). As a consequence, we generally feel no responsibility for events distant in time or space – even if they are connected with who we are and what we do.

A short-distance morality of the Individual is focused on his children, family and neighbours. Beyond this it is too far for the postmodern 'I'. Bauman claims that:

> Moral responsibility suffices to protect our children from being cold and hungry, but we would seek its advice in vain when speechless with terror we contemplate a picture of a devastated and wrecked planet which our children and in turn their children will succeed to, in consequence of our conscious or incautious actions or our idleness, intolerance and collective callousness.[19]

The morality which has always guided our actions is in charge of them also today. It has strong hands but short arms. Presently, it needs quite the opposite – very long arms; is it likely that they will grow?[20]

16 See also M. Koskenniemi, *From Apology to Utopia. The Structure of International Legal Argument* (Cambridge University Press, Cambridge 2007), p. 617 (what needs to be articulated outside the law can be so articulated).

17 See also O. Nawrot, 'Na kretych sciezkach bioetyki – "etyka gatunku" Jurgena Habermasa' [On the Bizzare Paths of Bioethics], in: J. Zajadlo (ed.), *Dziedzictwo i przyszlosc. Problemy wspolczesnej niemieckiej filozofii prawa* (Arche, Gdansk 2010), pp. 110–111; see also cited by O. Nawrot and J. Pilikowski, *Podroz w swiat filozofii* [The journey into the world of philosophy] (Krakow 2008), pp. 269–283.

18 Z. Bauman, *Etyka ponowoczesna* [*Postmodern Ethics*] … , p. 336.

19 See also S. Sterckx, 'Lack of Access to Essential Drugs: A Story of Continuing Global Failure, with Particular Attention to the Role of Patents', in: Ch. Lenk, N. Hoppe and R. Andorno (eds), *Ethics and Law of Intellectual Property* (Ashgate, Hampshire 2007), pp. 175–197.

20 Z. Bauman, *Etyka ponowoczesna* [*Postmodern Ethics*] … , p. 338.

But, in the meantime, everything has changed. The ethical scope of our actions has increased in an unprecedented manner when we think of a specific postanalogue 'I' or a postmodern and postanalogue moral community. This is intimately connected with our Levinasian self-sufficiency. We regard our reason as self-sufficient. And, consequently, we have become 'moral impotents'. This also comes as a result of the fact that the moral basis which existed (for instance the faith in God constituted such a basis of a moral education) has almost entirely vanished in the process of an intensive modernization. Furthermore, Bauman talks here not about the lack of any foundations for morality in the postanalogue society living in the postmodern era, but he strongly emphasizes the lack of the very material which could potentially be used to build such foundations.

The Dilemmas of a Far-Sighted Responsibility in the Postanalogue Society

To put it differently, one could ask after Tischner: How to cure such a responsibility (such a thinking) from the narrow-mindedness of a responsibility imposed on us by the postmodern times – when there is nothing to support a responsibility reaching much beyond contractual obligations, obligations based on reciprocity? The proposal of 'being for' presented in this book seems to enable a responsibility to grow in a considerably further direction (extending significantly both in time and in space) than it was assumed by a responsibility characteristic of the premodern 'I'. This raises the question of how to create a far-sighted morality so that we become reasoning and succeeding in our matters' Eldreds here and now; a morality responsible for future generations who, thanks to a wider access to knowledge in the era of digital technologies, are creative and responsive and do not 'die slowly'? How to arouse the Baumanian solidarity discussed in this text, which is a promise of postmodernity continuation?

An explicit need seems to exist to create moral foundations based on not 'being with', but on 'being for' within the right to science and culture in postmodern society. 'Being for' is likely to extend a responsibility in the temporal and spatial sense by identifying paradigms of the postanalogue society. Nonetheless, 'being for' cannot be argued efficiently by us if we deploy categories of a profitable exchange or reciprocity of profits – so characteristic of the postmodern society.[21] What is the character of 'being for' in the postanalogue society and what role is the right to science and culture as a human right to play here? Following the thinking of Jonas and the analysis of Bauman for a bit longer, it seems that the Individual of the postanalogue society should possess a self-evident need of a 'far-sighted morality' (distant in time and space). But how to equip the contemporary, postmodern Individual with a morality of this kind? For this purpose I introduce the notion of Levinasian 'need' and the notion

21 Z. Bauman, *Etyka ponowoczesna* [*Postmodern Ethics*] ... , p. 341.

of responsibility of 'active utopia' character inspired by the thought of Løgstrup and Bauman:

1. The notion of Levinasian 'need' and its description is of significance here:
   - The need turns to something else than us. The something else is at a distance from us. The very need which is felt by 'I' is not exclusively a shortage. In the structure of the need there exists something other than the shortage, much more than the shortage itself. It constitutes an 'insufficiency of our being in the world'. The need conceptualised in this way presses us to seek shelter in something other. The need cannot be defined *a priori* as emptiness in the world.[22]
   - The need is of a dynamic character, not limited to only that which is close to what is local. It is characteristic that the need in Levinasian terms expresses the 'insufficiency of our being in the world'. Accordingly, such a need of excendence is guided by the fact that, although we fail to experience any shortages as 'I' (maybe as a local 'I'), our being in the world is not filled in our opinion in a sufficient manner.
   - The need is of a dynamic character and is orientated to walking away from being toward something else. The need derives from tension, from an ultimate situation of 'one-can-do-nothing-about-it'. The pointlessness of any action shows that it is high time to leave it – to escape, the excendence. The fate of a man without a need will be a grim fate. As Ingarden said, 'I' thanks to the need is given an impulse which goes above man, his temporality (referring to him, his children and his grandchildren) or spatiality (localness or regionality).
2. The concept of responsibility of 'active utopia' character and its description is of significance here:
   - A rejection of treatment of moral behaviour as a contract in compliance with a principle: 'I behave in a moral manner as I rely on the Other (Others) to return my moral behaviour'. This constitutes a falsification of the sense of morality.
   - An adoption of a principle of 'morality as living in uncertainty'.
   - An adoption of the Løgstrupian[23] radical demand paradigm in the following form: a) The demand is of the silent character since nothing is said about how this carrying for the Neighbour (the Other) is to be done; b) The demand brings about moral and cognitive effort on the part of the 'I' since the 'I' assumes responsibility which I refer to, after Bauman, as responsibility of an 'active utopia' character (utopia based on moral behaviour!),[24] which above all comprises responsibility that I call a 'responsibility in pursuit' and therefore one which, in its

22 E. Levinas, *O Uciekaniu* [*On Escape*] … , pp. 18–19.

23 K.E. Løgstrup, *The Ethical Demand* … , p. 22.

24 Z. Bauman, *Etyka ponowoczesna* [*Postmodern Ethics*] … , p. 116.

> deep care, desires to design what the demand requires. I would like to emphasize: what the demand requires according to the 'I' unique in his responsibility; responsibility of an 'active utopia' character and consequently uncertainty (which in a sense is modelled by responsibility) are marked with utopian thought. I would seek it here. It is even a responsibility of a utopian character, since I take responsibility for something distant, generally of a utopian character for me here and now.

Derived from Levinasian philosophy, the concept of 'need' and the notion of responsibility of an 'active utopia' character inspired by the thought of Løgstrup and Bauman seem to have jointly a preliminary potential to delineate future directions for the presence of a 'far-sighted morality' in the postanalogue society, in the society of self-sufficient Individuals, Speech and Text.

Chapter 7
An Introduction to Dignity, Solidarity and *Verbum Interius* in Postmodernity[1]

From Levinas's Thought to Habermasian Dignity

Yet, how to translate the intuitive need of a 'far-sighted morality' into a language of material social interests and therefore real political powers in the case of the right to science and culture? In other words, how to enter a universal level in one's argumentation from a local level? Now, returning to the background of the *Myth* as well as the densely worded trends and law (the *Reason*) that has just been analysed, we must answer the question of how to introduce the myth of the right to science and culture and link it with the law and trends. In other words how do we link it with the reason that belongs to the human right to science and culture that I have tried to unlock so far; and how do we make use of the argument of utopia in this context?

Levinas and his philosophy will be the starting point. As analysed in the part concerned with *Myth* Levinas introduces a concept of personal responsibility we owe to Others which has been placed upon us without our consent.[2] It opens up for discussion, as Bouchetoux and Jones noticed, the notion of interestedness that might be confronted by disinterestedness, that is, by the 'goodness of giving' – both as attachment and concern for the other person.[3] Levinas explains that the most basic mode of responsibility is the approach to the face. At the same time the face of the Other is nothing but verticality and uprightness. What is vivid in this view is that the face is not situated in front of me/us but above me/us. The face is the sign of the Other and it qualifies to no-category. It can neither be domesticated nor consumed. It is just there, waiting for our response. Waiting for us to be reflective. It is me that the Other is calling. The Other will always come first and will become the condition of the existence of everything: of law, of language, of self.[4] Levinas emphasizes the necessity of our response to the Others

1 That '*Myth*' would never be vocal without the constant inspiration that I systematically receive from Professor and Judge Bartosz Wojciechowski.

2 D. Manderson, 'Emanuel Levinas and the Philosophy of Negligence', 14 *Tort Law Review* (2006), pp. 1–2.

3 F. Bouchetoux, C. Jones, 'Sociality and Money, Business Ethics', 16(3) *A European Review* (2007) pp. 1–2.

4 C. Douzinas, *The End of Human Rights* (Hart Publishing, Oxford, Portland, Oregon 2000), p. 348.

and the unique circumstances of each such response.[5] This type of unavoidable responsibility to the Other Levinas exhorts as 'first philosophy'.[6] The essence of the ethics of alterity is the request of the Other from one side and my/our obligation to respond from the other side.[7] Who is calling and who is requesting I cannot see. I comprehend that the Other is never cynical, it is yet vulnerable and its request is fundamentally emergent. I have been chosen to respond. It is a sign of trust in the name of the respect of the autonomy of the Other. My duty is to respond to that concern (and my freedom to respond perceived as the freedom of responsibility and fraternity).[8]

This type of the humanization of the law and in particular the right to science and culture is much needed as reflected in the part about the *Reason*. Applying the 'first philosophy' would mean making an attempt of applying humanism to the Other. As a result of this process certain aporetic concerns (humanism) have been recognized. For example the individual concern regarding access to computer source code or a medicine. I received a source code from the Other because the Other is simply concerned, or I received access to medicine because the Other is concerned, or I got access to formats for the visually impaired for the reason of concern. However, the recognition of these concerns leads to a better applicability on the individual or local level and does not have such a strong impact on the universality of concerns. And that is what is required in the case of the human right to science and culture. A question emerges of how Levinasian thinking orientated towards excendence could cause such an impact? I think that of key importance will be combining it with a recent assertion of Habermas presented in the article 'The Concept of Human Dignity and the Realistic Utopia of Human Rights'.[9] In his view, 'The transition from morality to law calls for a shift from symmetrically intertwined perspectives of respect and esteem for the autonomy of the other, to raising claims to recognition for one's own autonomy by the other. The morally enjoined concern for the vulnerable other is replaced by the self-confident *demand* for legal recognition as a self-determined subject'.[10]

It seems that Habermas's statement opens up the possibility of referring to the right to science and culture as a specification of human dignity – dignity as the moral source from which human rights to science and culture derives its meaning. According to Habermas, what explains the explosive political force of concrete

5 D. Manderson, 'Emmanuel Levinas and the Philosophy of Negligence', 14 *Tort Law Review* (2006) pp. 1–2.

6 *Ibidem*, pp. 1–2.

7 C. Douzinas, *The End of Human Rights …* , pp. 350–351.

8 *Ibidem*, p. 352.

9 J. Habermas, *The Concept of Human Dignity and the Realistic Utopia of Human Rights* (Metaphilosophy LLC and Blackwell Publishing Ltd. 2010), p. 466 *et seq.*

10 *Ibidem*, p. 472.

utopia is the origin of human rights in the moral notion of human dignity.[11] Every single situation of violation of the human dignity creates a space for the creative function[12] (not forgetting the founding function of human dignity in the Universal Declaration of Human Rights).[13] But of course the seismograph of dignity is also linked closely to experiences of the past with its own history of *Myth* and *Reason*.[14] Then the discussion may also lead to human dignity as a part of the catalogue of modern virtues.[15]

In the views of Habermas the idea of human dignity is the conceptual connection that links on one side the *Myth* – which is the morality of equal respect for all of the people and on the other side the reason – which is the law. All of the happenings in between have a potential to give rise to a political order based on human rights.[16] This type of reconciliation of morality and law under the umbrella of dignity will hopefully release the tension between idea and reality in the postanalogue

11 *Ibidem*, p. 466. For a utopian vision of human rights in the context democracy and intercultural society see also B. Wojciechowski, *Philosophical Approach to the Interculturality of Criminal Law* (Peter Lang. International Academic Publishers, Series: Studies in Philosophy and Social Science, Frankfurt am Main – Berlin – Bern – Bruxelles – New York – Oxford – Wien 2010). See also B. Wojciechowski, *Interkulturowe Prawo Karne* [*Intercultural Criminal Law*] … , pp. 106–114. See also D. Luban, *Legal Ethics and Human Dignity* (Cambridge University Press, Cambridge 2008), pp. 88–90 (human dignity as non-humiliation); C. Santiago Nino, *The Ethics of Human Rights* (Clarendon Press, Oxford 1994), pp. 165–185 (the principle of the dignity of the person).

12 *Ibidem*, p. 467.

13 K. Dicke, 'The Founding Function of Human Dignity in The Universal Declaration of Human Rights', in: D. Kretzmer and E. Klein (eds), *The Concept of Human Dignity in Human Rights Discourse* (Kluwer Law International, The Hague, London, New York 2002), pp. 111–123. See also T. Lindholm., 'Ethical Justification of Universal Rights Across Normative Divices', in: Bexell, G. and D.-E. Andersson (eds), *Universal Ethics. Perspectives and Proposals from Scandinavian Scholars* (Martinus Nijhoff Publishers, Kluwer Law International, The Hague/London/New York 2002), pp. 65–68.

14 Y. Arieli, 'On the Necessary and Sufficient Conditions for the Emergence of the Doctrine of Man and His Rights', in: D. Kretzmer and E. Klein (eds), *The Concept of Human Dignity in Human Rights Discourse* (Kluwer Law International, The Hague, London, New York 2002), pp. 1–11.

15 M. Meyer, 'Dignity as a Modern Virtue', in: D. Kretzmer and E. Klein (eds), *The Concept of Human Dignity in Human Rights Discourse* (Kluwer Law International, The Hague, London, New York 2002) pp. 195–207. See also M.J. Meyer, 'Dignity as a (Modern) Virtue', in: D. Kretzmer and E. Klein, (eds), *The Concept of Human Dignity in Human Rights Discourse* (Kluwer Law International, Hague, London, New York 2002), pp. 195–207 (see how the virtue of dignity is a generally modern virtue and how to understand fully the moral fabric of our time and our lives; p. 207 'The present account of the virtue of dignity is therefore, finally, a preliminary attempt to help articulate a catalog of modern virtues').

16 J. Habermas, *The Concept of Human Dignity and the Realistic Utopia of Human Rights* … , p. 466.

society in the postmodern era, if carefully applied. The possibility of the act of specification shows that applied dignity in this sense is a dynamic concept that can always start from a different beginning(s) and act in 'different becoming(s)'.[17] Hence I can start my life from the new beginning in the same way as you can. The beginning is aporetic in character and changes depending on the kind of request of the Other (the diversity and aporetics of beginnings) and then evaluates itself in the process and starts from a new beginning over and over again. In this way, applied dignity has the potential to reverse what we/I thought was/is irreversible; The role of the act of specification would be to construct a new beginnings(s).[18]

It seems that it is important to note that the right to access to knowledge in books online, medicines or accessible formats for the visually impaired on behalf of preserving the quality of our education and our progress as humanity might serve as a functional application of this logic – in terms of our humankind. It is based on the idea that the more people who share useful knowledge, the greater is the common good. It is a request on behalf of humankind. We can also imagine a request from the human being (on the individual level like the Author) or human group level (like the group of Commons, state or postanalogue society). Every specification of dignity will seem unique. However, one can assume that the notion of reversibility accompanied by the process of reflexivity is predominant. This can be merged with the idea of the reflective society at stake.

What is very vocal about the Habermasian idea is that his focus is on the demand and not the concern. Perhaps it makes it more functional on the societal, global level. This invites us to think about 'rights not in terms of having been acquired once and for all by our generation, but in terms of rights that we are borrowing from future generations and that will be our legacy to them'.[19] Hence, there are many areas of possible requests that might be mapped and that emanate directly from (for example) trends and law introduced in this book and that might become the subject(s) of this profound specification such as: the right of everyone to benefit from the protection of the moral and material interests resulting from any scientific, literary or artistic production of which he or she is the author is a human right, which derives from the inherent dignity and worth of persons; the right to science and culture does not equal intellectual property right; the right that progresses for the benefit of society as the whole; the protection under the right to benefit from the protection of the moral and material interests resulting from any scientific, literary or artistic production of which he or she is the author does not have to reflect the level of protection that is present in the intellectual property regime; 'material interest' through lenses of the right to science and culture means that it is not tied to objectives of market efficiency and utilitarianism; culture as an inclusive concept encompassing all manifestations of human existence; cultural

17 C. Dupre, 'Unlocking Human Dignity: Towards a Theory for the 21st Century', 2 *European Human Rights Law Review* (2009), p. 8.

18 *Ibidem*, p. 10.

19 *Ibidem*, p. 10.

life characterized as a freedom and as a cultural choice and, as such, should be protected, recognized and respected on the basis of equality; components of the right to take part in cultural life, namely 'participation' in cultural life, 'access' to cultural life, 'contribution' to cultural life; conditions for the full realization of the right to take part in cultural life such as 'availability' (both traditional and digital formats) 'accessibility' (both effective and concrete opportunities for individuals and communities to fully enjoy culture; to include both passive and active use of technologies); the last one calls for consultations that should be held with the individuals and communities concerned and is called 'acceptability' (call for societal consultations within the society that the measures to protect cultural diversity/digital culture are acceptable to all); 'adaptability' that refers to the flexibility and relevance of strategies, policies, programmes and measures adopted by governments; respect, protect and fulfil.

Bearing in mind the above, it seems justified to quote here a recent thought of Karolina Cern and Bartosz Wojciechowski:

> It should be emphasized that when putting intellectual property rights in question from the human rights perspective, we are talking about human dignity 'taken into action', that is, to put it briefly, the human intrinsic dignity understood as a base for participating in any communicative actions in all three spheres: a) in an individual sphere, where the most important is how we would like to conduct our lives (e.g. if one would like to have as many material benefits as it is possible or maybe the other kind of (social) benefits like knowledge or prestige, or perhaps one would like to conduct modest life of outstanding creator); b) in a social sphere, where we ask how to build our relations with others and what sort of concerns would define them in general (in a given society); c) in an institutional normative dimension, where the question: how do we organize (a)-(b) so that it would be relevant to everybody involved, to everybody … concerned?[20]

Moreover it seems that in this light the demand as such serves as an emancipatory space for the zone of personal autonomy.[21] It also seems justified to quote the statements of two distinguished, international scholars in the field of intellectual property law and its relation to human rights – namely Helfer and Austin:

---

20 B. Wojciechowski and K. Cern – equivalent fragments from B. Wojciechowski and K. Cern, 'The Theory' in (ed. A.M. Nawrot) *Human Rights Based Approach. From Theory to Practice*, Research Project Swedish Institute (SI)2009/2010/RWI, granted by the Swedish Institute and performed in cooperation with the Raoul Wallenberg Institute of Human Rights and Humanitarian Law, Lund University, Sweden and the Institute of Theory and Philosophy of Law, Faculty of Law, Lodz University, Poland, pp. 9–10.

21 A. Barbosa Da Silva, 'Human Rights, Dignity and Autonomy' in *Health Care and Social Services: Nordic Perspectives* (Intersentia, Antwerp, Oxford, Portland 2009), pp. 13–21.

> The more fundamental point, however, is that although creators and innovators do indeed possess a narrow class of inalienable economic and personality rights, they can choose how best to exercise those rights so as to construct a zone of personal autonomy that is both self-empowering and conductive to the broader public values that the human rights framework for intellectual property seeks to achieve.[22]

Toward Communicative Solidarity

The Individual, a human being, decides on the values that make life sensible and on the tools to achieve what is worth pursuing, what is of value.[23] Thus dignity in this context is reflective, rich with historicism perceived as both a peculiar type of social consciousness and a possibility to decide on variability (and it applies to all kinds of society). Historicism means that every variation of society evolves with time and thus has no chance to become a timeless society. The sense of historicism of the world here means not only its overwhelming changeability, but also the enormous capabilities of people at large to set a creative, critical and common direction of change.[24]

This might lead us to the assumption that all of the requests from the Other could also correspond (or connect) to the emerging voices of reflective society (in this case postmodern digital or postanalogue society). Together, rightly collected, merged, recognized and specified under the human right to science and culture they have an extreme potential to become loud and enrich this right with a new language – capable of opening up for a global linguistic communication related to the concrete human right to science and culture. That would include the communication that relates to the specific request of the Other, but also the one that relates to the notion of 'shared commitments' (of the social world related to certain human right). Thus the collection of 'shared commitments' would be the major task. In this context of social worlds, they, the social worlds, would become the analytical concepts used for the study of collective action. Shibutani for instance focuses on the idea of commitment as the basis of social action. With this approach, social worlds are groups with 'shared commitments' to the pursuit of a common human task. They develop ideologies to define their work and they

22 L.R. Helfer and G.W. Austin, *Human Rights and Intellectual Property. Mapping the Global Interface* … , p. 522.

23 J. Bardziej and J. Gockowski, *Rozmyślania o Cywilizacji* [*Reflections on Civilization*] (Wydawnictwo Baran i Suszynski, Krakow 1997), p. 107.

24 A. Giddens claims that the final substratum of social life consists of never-ending social practices, through which a constant reproduction, as well as a transformation of the society, is effected and the totality of society is maintained along with the newly-introduced social change. P. Sztompka, *Encyklopedia Socjologii* [*Encyclopedia of Sociology*] … , pp. 236–241.

accumulate diverse resources required to get the task done. Thus the social world is an interactive unit that arises when a number of individuals strive to act in some collective way.[25] The voice of this type of a world is locked up in T. Shibutani's assumption that any social world needs a core activity to be established in order to exist. In this respect it could be argued that the most present activity for the postanalogue society (as a social world) is the idea of 'communicative justice'.[26] The concept of communicative justice derives from the idea presented by W.J. Burghardt in his book *Justice*.[27] The author concentrates on the comparison of the conception of 'communicative justice' to 'peaceful initiative'. According to him every initiative of this kind has the following features: it is free from aggression, it occurs when there is a dissonance between legislation and public opinion, and finally it is a form of open voice for an appeal for change. In this way trends, law and myth could meet on behalf of the Other (demand) and justice at stake. However, will it in fact be justice in postmodernity in this case?

It seems, taking into consideration the thoughts of Kołakowski and Bauman and attempting to place them in the context of the above discussion, postmodern era and postanalogue society, it turns out that what 'the spirit of the world' expects from the Individual is not justice as a primary foundation.[28] As Kołakowski asserts: 'But what the spirit of the world truly expects from us is not justice at all, but kindness to neighbours, friendship and mercy, so such values which cannot be derived from justice'.[29] Kołakowski's thought can be supplemented with Bauman's

25 A.M. Nawrot, 'Why Do We Need Social Worlds While Talking about D-Knowledge Commons Ecosystem in Cyberspace?' 2 *Masaryk University Journal of Law* (2008), pp. 189–200. This paper is based on the application of the 'Social Worlds' theory created by Shibutani to the worlds of knowledge society, cyberspace, d-Knowledge CommonsEcosystem.1 Knowledge society will be presented as the social world and cyberspace as the sub-social world with the d-Knowledge Commons Ecosystem as the sub-world of cyberspace. This theory will open discussion about activity, boundaries, arenas and values of each social world/sub-worlds. However, the main intention of this paper is an introduction to a discussion about the sub-world of d-KnowledgeCommons Ecosystem as an example of one of the most striking sub-worlds within cyberspace trying to answer the question: why do we need social worlds while talking about d-Knowledge Commons Ecosystem? This paper is to be divided into five parts: 1. Activity, 2. Boundaries, 3. Arena, 4. Values, 5. Conclusion. See also A. Kacperczyk, 'Zastosowanie koncepcji społecznych światów w badaniach empirycznych' [Application of the Social Worlds Concept in Empirical Research], in: E. Hałas and E. Konecki (eds), *Konstruowanie jaźni i społeczeństwa. Europejskie warianty interakcjonizmu symbolicznego* [*Construction of the Self and Society: European Variants of Symbolic Interactionism*] (Wydawnictwo Naukowe Scholar, Warszawa 2006), pp. 178–182.

26 *Ibidem*, pp. 189–200.

27 W.J. Burghardt, *Sprawiedliwość* [*Justice*] (Wydawnictwo WAM, Kraków 2006), pp. 274–279.

28 L. Kołakowski, *Mini wykłady o maxi sprawach* [*Mini-lectures on maxi-issues*] … , p. 266.

29 *Ibidem*, p. 266.

opinion that what is crucial today is solidarity. Moreover, it is solidarity which most staunchly acknowledges dialogism of a situation in the postmodern era. When dialogism becomes a feature of postmodernity, tolerance gives way to solidarity; and solidarity itself can be considered as a continuation of postmodernity.[30] In this respect it could be argued that the most present activity for the postanalogue society (as a social world) is the idea of 'communicative solidarity'.

Gadamerian Text of Law Transformed into Language

How to transform the Text into Language today? How does one recognize the law of today? Human beings are communicative entities that are capable of constructing society by virtue of the force (intersubjective) of mutual understanding. Marek Zirk-Sadowski speaks about a system of orientation points that might be examined on the grounds of varied forms of legal discourse and thus might bring social communication as a basic factor for the building of law.[31] The postanalogue society is constantly searching, re-shaping values, building new domains, abandoning and constructing again toward meta-orientation points. Often new values are established which are supported by newly-emerged social movements like access to knowledge or Pirate Bay, just at the heart of the digital society. A characteristic feature of these new values, new meta-points is the gradual decrease of the significance of the economic dimension as a totality in human social and cultural life.[32] What are the orientation points of our modern, linguistic communication and how do we make the norms discursive, allowing a public debate for both traditional and revisited rights? This has been a concern of elegant and powerful debate of Bartosz Wojciechowski.[33] Hence, how do we act with regard to the human right to science and culture? The language regarding the right to science and culture is exposed to the fundamental challenge that might be explained through the following 'meta-linguistic' as an example in the postanalogue society at stake:

30 Z. Bauman, *Wywiad z Baumanem* [*An interview with Bauman*] … , pp. 19–29.

31 M. Zirk-Sadowski, M. Golecki and B. Wojciechowski (eds), *Multicentrism as an Emerging Paradigm in Legal Theory* (Peter Lang, Frankfurt am Main 2009), p. 66.

32 R. Inglehart, *Modernization and Postmodernization* … , p. 76. For a dialogue as the method to obtain universalism see G. Bexell, 'Universalism in Ethics and Cultural Diversity', in: Bexell, G. and D.-E. Andersson (eds), *Universal Ethics. Perspectives and Proposals from Scandinavian Scholars* (Martinus Nijhoff Publishers, Kluwer Law International, The Hague/London/New York 2002), p. 11. Bexell writes: 'The dialogue itself is an expression of some values, which have to be common, such a respect for the other and respect for rationality'.

33 B. Wojciechowski, *Philosophical Approach to the Interculturality of Criminal Law* (Peter Lang. International Academic Publishers, Series: Studies in Philosophy and Social Science, Frankfurt am Main – Berlin – Bern – Bruxelles – New York – Oxford – Wien 2010). See also B. Wojciechowski, *Interkulturowe Prawo Karne* [*Intercultural Criminal Law*] … , pp. 408–417.

> Moving from 'It is *just* that I have so much. It is *legal* that I have so much. It is *unjust* that I have so little' to 'It is *unjust* that I have so much'. However projecting for postmodernity: 'It is *unsolidaric* that I have so much'.

Taking into account that this book has been inspired by Gadamer, one might propose that the Individual will be able to transform a text into language if he does not view language as a limitation or an impediment – we have an obligation to pursue *verbum interius*. Language is not a copy of meaning or an outer border. Gadamer conceives of language as a medium in which understanding is affected. It is a place in which an all and, thus, unique sense is created. Following the Gadamerian path, the Individual can go beyond language, can leave the space of writing, the space of the Text. One can imagine such a reading of the Text with understanding which notions would speak in the authentic voice of a conversation again. In a conversation, as the Greeks argued, the most intimate closeness would exist between the word and the notion. The essence of Gadamerian conversation is communication. There is no issue which we could not agree upon. It seems that endowing *verbum interius* with a utopian character will bring hope for such a political discourse, in which one can at last be supported by the word liberated from the constraints of the Text and where thinking in terms of excendence will be acknowledged, keeping in mind going beyond the space of the Text. After all, the 'particular something', which refers to what is Other, is present in the word.[34] It is so important to postmodernity that neither the Text, nor the Individual, nor the Speech are and will ever be self-sufficient. And, if interlocutors think so, there is no hope for a utopian impulse in the human right to science and culture. The hope of postmodernity is related to Levinasian and Gadamerian 'non-self-sufficiency' of the Individual, the Speech and the Text *sensu largo*, which refer to what is Other and even utopian.

We have a capacity to grow as humanity and we will bring the human right to science and culture as a common achievement.[35] And I believe that within this capacity we have no right to betray the utopian dimension of our humanity. It is a condition *sine qua non* for us not to perish. Without this utopian dimension we do not communicate to the fullest. We perish on the plane of the Individual and on the planes of the Speech and the Text. However, the search for the *ideal* right to science and culture must continue since this was a humble beginning also on behalf of the digital Other.

34 J. Grondin, *Wprowadzenie do hermeneutyki filozoficznej* [*An Introduction to Philosophical Hermeneutics*], p. 47.

35 cf. G. Alfredsson and A. Eide (eds), *The Universal Declaration of Human Rights. A Common Standard of Achievement* (Kluwer Law International, The Hague 1999), pp. 576–577.

Epilogue
On Happiness, Dignity, that which is Social and that which is Utopian

> There is an element of utopia in what I say – an acceptance of something which cannot be manifest, but still guides moral actions eventually … . There is no moral life without utopia – utopia is for morality what sanctity is for goodness.
>
> E. Levinas, 'The Paradox of Morality'

The Epilogue project sets out to return to three questions, so essential to this book and asked by Levinas himself in his work 'On Escape'. Moreover, I intend to incorporate here a fourth question, not derived from Levinas but closely connected with the thesis of the work and inspired by Habermasian stance on dignity. Thus, the questions are as follows:

1. What is the ideal of happiness which excendence could promise?
2. What is the ideal of human dignity which excendence could promise?
3. How does that which is social emerge through excendence?
4. How does that which is utopian emerge through excendence? What is the ideal of utopia at this point?

I believe that the spirit of my book responds otherwise to these questions (although I obviously assume that the interpretation of this thesis may vary depending on the interpreter and that the interpreter will otherwise try to 'go beyond the constraints of my Text' in Gadamerian spirit). Consequently, I am to present four responses proposed in the form of the following descriptions:

The First Description: On Happiness

It seems that close to the ideal of happiness what excendence could promise is the so-called optimistic stance toward the relation of happiness and moral value, which the Polish philosopher Władysław Tatarkiewicz elaborated on in his famous treatise *On Happiness* first published in Poland in 1962 and, to be more specific, in the last chapter of the work entitled 'An obligation of happiness and the right to happiness'.[1] What kind of thinking leads to the ideal of happiness which will be

---

1 W. Tatarkiewicz, *O szczęściu* [*On Happiness*] (Panstwowe Wydawnictwo Naukowe, Warszawa 1979), pp. 537–567.

discussed here? In other words, what constitutes the inspiration for such a thinking (what other thinking?)? I suggest the following paths of thinking:

A. The right to solitude and the deprivation of the right
B. The sources of happiness according to Protestants
C. The Epicurean school of thought
D. Morality and happiness

Re. A) The right to solitude and the deprivation of the right

Solitude is indeed polysemous and a lonely person is one who is not tied with stronger feelings to people, even though he has a lot of contact with them. The opposites of solitude are, according to Tatarkiewicz, the following four cases: a) associating with people, b) having contact with people, c) emotional attachment to people, d) having solidaric business with people; in the first instance it will be all relationships and in the others, relationships of a special character: social, emotional and metaphysical.[2] Tatarkiewicz says that when people seek solitude, they usually do it in the first two meanings: they want to liberate themselves from superficial relationships with people, from world relationships and social relationships. But they do not want to liberate themselves from deep emotional or metaphysical relationships. Tatarkiewicz states:

> And generally in the two meanings: a) associating with people and b) having contact with people [the Author's note] and solely in these relationships people can decide by themselves whether they will be lonely: they can begin and not begin world and social relationships, but they cannot dispose of emotional [and metaphysical – the Author's note] relationships to the same extent.[3]

Happy people can, therefore, be lonely provided that the solitude omits excluding interpersonal emotional and metaphysical relationships. Without these relationships people have a lower potential to become happy. The Individual will minimize his right to happiness if he begins disposing of his emotional and metaphysical relationships. As it seems, in Tatarkiewicz's opinion the Individual has no right to such disposal (!).

Re. B) The sources of happiness according to Wiśniewski and Hilty

In the chapter entitled 'Sources of Happiness' Tatarkiewicz quotes two, among many others, figures who represent two religions and talk about happiness from the perspective of different times.[4] Antoni Wiśniewski, who lived and created

2 *Ibidem*, pp. 237–238.
3 *Ibidem*, p. 238.
4 *Ibidem*, pp. 312–313.

in the eighteenth century, expounding on the sources of happiness follows the Thomistic schema in his line of thinking: 1) 'true happiness of man is in no respects dependent upon the well-being of the body, i.e. upon pleasures and indulging one's senses', but also 2) 'the goods of fortune, such as wealth and prominent positions of authority do not make man completely happy'; as well as 3) 'the goods of the soul, education and wisdom do not make man completely happy'; 4) friendship also lets down; and 5) the happiness of the homeland is of no use; 6) one therefore cannot think of the accumulation of all goods, since 'the accumulation of all goods is generally a chimera, which is easy to imagine but cannot be achieved'; 7) renouncing goods is of no use, as 'to have nothing and be happy is a contradiction in terms'; 8) eventually,'man is never content with who he is and what he has'. And hence a conclusion: 'There is no perfect happiness for man in the world. Only in the future life does a perfect happiness or a perfect unhappiness await us'.[5]

An argumentation of a similar character is provided by Protestant writers. Tatarkiewicz refers to the book of Hilty who, like Wiśniewski, begins with negative assertions that no goods of a purely worldly nature will lead to happiness in a reliable manner.[6] In Tatarkiewicz's interpretation of Hilty, a mere enjoyment of life fails to lead to happiness (it does not correspond to an active human nature), neither an egoistic satisfaction (human nature is social after all), nor a peaceful and carefree life (only a person who never lived such a life can consider this negative state as happiness, nor love (since it is unreliable), nor work. As a result 'I', according to Hilty, needs something other to be happy. The 'other', in Hilty's view, is first of all a need to 'believe in a moral order of the world'.[7] The happiness of 'I' becomes here synonymous with a need to believe in something greater, in something other than only 'I'. Many find this in religion but Those who do not believe seek ceaselessly.

Re. C) The Epicurean school of thought

This is one of the two (along with the Cyrenaic school) prominent hedonistic schools of the Antiquity. It advanced the idea that everyone can seek pleasure (which was perceived as happiness). However, the practice proves that, in pursuit of happiness, one has to have a priority. And this constitutes a path of virtue. Thus, Epicureans linked virtues with a pleasurable life and a pleasurable life is inseparable from virtues, as Tatarkiewicz describes Epicurus's thoughts. Arisstipus emphasized that in pursuit of pleasure not only prudence of life and its moderation are significant, but he thought that of utmost importance is taking other people's

5 W. Tatarkiewicz citing after: A. Wiśniewski, *Rozmowy w ciekawych y potrzebnych filozoficznych y politycznych materyach* [*Discussions on interesting, necessary, philosophical and political matters*] 1760; W. Tatarkiewicz, *O szczęściu* [*On Happiness*] (Panstwowe Wydawnictwo Naukowe, Warszawa 1979), pp. 312–313.

6 Cited after W. Tatarkiewicz, vide p. 313: C. Hilty, *Gluck*, 1917.

7 W. Tatarkiewicz, *O Szczęściu* [*On Happiness*] … , p. 313.

needs into consideration as well.[8] The Epicurean life of 'I' is primarily dependent upon a moral significance of the life, which originates from taking other people's needs into consideration.

Re. D) Morality and happiness

The Stoics treated morality and happiness as synonyms. This is also the path of thinking of some modern thinkers, such as Spinoza, who regarded happiness as a virtue itself and not as a reward for a virtue. If, as Tatarkiewicz points out, morality is marked with the letter M and happiness with the letter H, this belief may be written as follows: *M and H are identical.*[9] An assertion close to this belief states that although 'morality' and 'happiness' denote something else, they refer to the same phenomenon. In an attempt to explain this, Tatarkiewicz deploys a 'Shakespeare example': the 'author of Hamlet' and the 'author of Macbeth' are expressions which denote something else, but refer to the same Shakespeare. In consequence of the assertion, as Tatarkiewicz writes, 'there is no happy life which would not be moral and there is no moral life which would not be happy'.[10]

Epicurus also associated closely M with H, considering them to be in a permanent relation. Kant concurred with these assumptions as well in asking: 'How could one make man happy without making him moral and wise?' Tatarkiewicz also quotes Huxley, who asks: 'Do you think that one can experience satisfaction, but true satisfaction, without worrying about anything and without putting one's heart in anything? Can one be happy in this way, if I may use this old-fashioned expression?'[11] The questions may be written in the following manner: *M is the cause of H* (or M is an essential or a sufficient condition of H).[12]

Given the paths of thinking presented above and leading to the ideal of happiness inspired by the work *O Szczęściu* (*On Happiness*) of this great Polish philosopher, it seems that an apt suggestion will be one stating that the ideal of happiness, which excendence could promise, is connected with the following 'negative assumptions' – although one can infer one from another (I also suggest that the catalogue of assumptions is of an open character):

- Individual will not dispose happily of his relationships of a metaphysical character with other Persons (or with the Text) – that is Tatarkiewicz's 'having solidaric business with people' (I call it a negative assumption of Tatarkiewicz);
- Individual will not be happy if he has no Hilty's need to 'believe in a moral order of the world' (I call it a negative assumption of Hilty);

8 *Ibidem*, pp. 509–510.
9 *Ibidem*, p. 538.
10 *Ibidem*, p. 538.
11 *Ibidem*, p. 539.
12 *Ibidem*, p. 540.

- Individual will not be happy if he fails to take into account a 'moral significance of life' which derives from taking other people's needs into consideration (I call it a negative Epicurean assumption).

The Second Description: On Dignity

How does what is worthy arise through excendence? I think that in order to attempt an answer to the question one should return to the four philosophers referred to in the book: Socrates, Levinas, Kępiński, Habermas and Gadamer – in the order suggested by the Author.

Socrates expressed an assertion that a speaker who 'knows that he knows nothing' before starting a dialogue, always finishes the dialogic relation being enriched in some way. On finishing communication he simply knows more, irrespective of the fact of whether conclusions or a specific portion of knowledge or achieved consensus is at issue. That is not to say that he was not wise before the relation. He was the one who knew that 'he knows nothing'. Socrates might have been thinking not so much of reaching an agreement, as a classical motif of a dialogue, but rather of a shift in perspective. By stopping at the level of aporia, the Individual is not an 'appropriatory' Individual but, above all, he is committed to listen to and to listen intently to what is preached as the first teaching. Levinas argues that a relation with the Face involves immediately taking responsibility for the Face in the 'ethical' manner. The Individual is therefore expected to be inactive, passively open and to anticipate no reciprocity. Receptivity, discussed by Levinas signifies, apart from openness to the Other, 'passivity more passive than the passivity of experience'. It is a patient passivity, it is a passivity of not anticipating payment, it is a passivity waiting for the orders of the Other. Its sense entails a non-disturbance of listening to the Other and a fulfilment of a mission in relation to him. It is in the mission that the identity of a free, autonomous subject is realized. Thus, it is in the mission of passivity that an identity of an autonomous Individual who refrains from passing judgements is realized.

Autonomy of the Individual, according to Levinas, is based on receptivity and transcendence. The Individual thus fails to expect gratitude, enjoys his non-integrability and continuous opposition to Totality. It may denote Totality as a unification of norms, an agreement based on consensus, universalism and so on. The Individual is an autonomous subject who is lonely but happy in his autonomy. The Levinasian model seems to confirm the fact that the Individual does not reach and does want to reach, an agreement in the meaning of adoption of someone's viewpoint. One should stop at the level of aporia which is, moreover, enhanced by an axiological barrier – the system of values.

At this stage I suggest proceeding to the philosophy of good hope of Kępiński which states that what is most essential is the desire to see in the Other his humanity. The dominant 'technical' approach to man which notices to a lesser and lesser extent human traits in him, while focusing more and more on attributes related to proper functioning of a technical and political and economic machine, may be one of the greatest dangers of a postmodern civilization. Kępiński thinks of something more, that is of accepting freedom in another person. Inspired by the thought of Kępiński, the attitude of the Individual will be characterized by refraining from judgements in moral issues and pursuing by the Individual an acceptance of, above all, humanity in a man and of his freedom. It seems that, owing to creation of such conditions, the Individual will be able to evaluate himself and will be freed from various fears. The Individual thus appears as a free entity who recognizes his place of settlement. This discovered kind of axiological atmosphere, as Tischner reminds us, originates from a general intuition of a man's humanity, his dignity and, above all, from an unclear and yet impossible to conceal premonition of where lies the 'place of settlement' of a man. The Individual feels able to be free. Furthermore, he brings with himself a particular hope. The main discovery, which hope intends to protect, is that the humanity of a man manifests itself and remains in a direct relation to an inner freedom to which he feels able.

Dignity which excendence opens up before us focuses on the worthy Individual (on a worthy man), one who has an intuition of humanity in the Other. The ability to have an intuition of humanity in another man seems to be at the heart of dignity. While the action which leads to the dignity is finding (identifying) a place of the Individual's settlement. Only then will the Individual become a man fully resisting Totality here and now –with dignity. The Dignity responds to the question of why we, as self-sufficient people, are most afraid of taking unconditional responsibility for the Neighbour and his radical, silent demand? A question also arises: Can we talk about the concept of *excendent dignity*, emerging in this way, as a dignity which postmodernity especially needs for the postanalogue society today? Yes, it seems to be the case.

First, I would situate the notion more in morality so that it would stand against the praise of common indifference (and along with tolerance and solidarity in the thoughts of Kołakowski and Bauman). The dignity will be less protected by law and more by consolidation of morality of excendent dignity. According to Levinas, the self cannot arise from withdrawal, a self-alienation, but from connection with the Other, from opening up to the Other. It is thanks to this connection with the Other that 'I' becomes a unique, irreplaceable self.

As Levinas asserts:

> Being a man involves: living as if one was not an entity among entities ... It is me who supports the other, whom I am responsible for ... . My responsibility is irremovable. Nobody could replace me ... it entails the statement of the very sameness of a human 'I', starting with responsibility ... . Responsibility is what exclusively burdens me and which I, as a man, cannot reject. This burden is the greatest dignity ... . I am the irreplaceable 'I' inasmuch as I am responsible. I can replace everyone but no-one can replace me.[13]

13 E. Levinas, *Ethics and Infinity: Conversations with Philippe Nemo ...* , p. 57.

Of key importance to the concept of dignity which is provided by excendence becomes the sense of humanity in other man, which means that the Individual cannot reject responsibility. It is a special kind of responsibility which makes me become a worthy man.

Second, I would situate *excendent dignity* inspired by Habermas within the law. It would be a *dignity* as the moral source from which human rights to science and culture derives its meaning. In Habermas view,

> The transition from morality to law calls for a shift from symmetrically intertwined perspectives of respect and esteem for the autonomy of the other, to raising claims to recognition for one's own autonomy by the other. The morally enjoined concern for the vulnerable other is replaced by the self-confident *demand* for legal recognition as a self-determined subject.[14]

Habermas statement opens up the possibility of referring to the right to science and culture as a specification of human dignity – dignity as the moral source from which human rights to science and culture derives its meaning. According to him, what explains the explosive political force of concrete utopia is the origin of human rights in the moral notion of human dignity.[15]

That creates a common theme for the excendent Individual which could be called 'a copy-Duty'.[16] It has it roots in the problem of 'accessibility' which centres more on copy-RIGHT than on copy-DUTY. While in the postmodern, postanalogue society the problem ought to centre more on copy-DUTY which is the duty of owners of protected property by copyright regime to make that property accessible.[17] This 'copy-DUTY' derives directly from cultural human rights – that open up for alternatives and dynamic perception of cultural life. Both Comments No. 17 and No. 21 are a point of departure for creating a clear 'human-rights-consistent' value to emerge that has the capacity to guide international and domestic law initiatives. This might be just the beginning of better practice.[18] Accordingly, the idea of *excendent dignity* would be the conceptual connection that links on one side the *Myth* – which is the morality of equal respect for all of the people and on the other side the reason – which is the law – the *Reason.*

---

14 J. Habermas, *The Concept of Human Dignity and the Realistic Utopia of Human Rights* … , p. 472.

15 J. Habermas, *The Concept of Human Dignity and the Realistic Utopia of Human Rights* … , p. 466.

16 Lessig, L. *Code Version 2.0* … , p. 93.

17 *Ibidem*, p. 93.

18 cf. A.M. Nawrot, 'The Involvement of Human Rights in Limiting the Adverse Effects on Access to Digital Knowledge – as One Step Towards a Multicentric Principle of Access to Digital Knowledge', in: M. Zirk-Sadowski, M. Golecki and B. Wojciechowski (eds), *Multicentrism as an Emerging Paradigm in Legal Theory* (Peter Lang, Frankfurt am Main 2009), pp. 291–303.

All of the happenings in between have the potential to give rise to a political order based on human rights.[19] This type of reconciliation of morality and law under the umbrella of *excendent dignity* will hopefully release the tension between idea and reality in the postanalogue society if carefully applied.

At this point I would like to refer to the philosophy of Gadamer. The person who interprets a Text should be worthy in an excendent way. To put it differently, I propose that morality should arrive at the interpretation of a legal text through the concept of excendent morality. I would begin the pursuit of dignity of the interpreting excendent Individual with Gadamerian atopism (atopon, i.e. 'that which is deprived of a place'; the Greeks had a very beautiful word denoting a situation in which our understanding is hindered. They called it *atopon.* The term denotes that which is deprived of a place, which cannot be subsumed under schemes of our expectations concerning understanding and that – for this reason – astonishes us). In Gadamer's hermeneutics it is atopism that determines experiencing of what is historical – the impossibility of finding it on a map of our experiences and thereby fitting it into some ready-made conceptual schemes. It is the moment which makes us take the Gadamerian effort of understanding at all. This constitutes a difficult process; one can also talk of a drama of the experience. In an experience of this kind we are always painfully confronted with the limits of our understanding. Since we face precisely and directly that which is – at first sight – foreign (and nonsensical).[20] In Gadamer's view, a cultural past (and the future as well) is dynamic and constant in its essence. Gadamer believes that there is no concept of a 'permanent legacy' which one can dispose as a particular object whose meaning can be identified and defined.[21]

As Paweł Dybel points out in his unique analysis of Gadamerian hermeneutics, the way which is most closely connected with the source, of relating to testimonies of a cultural past, is encountering them as 'partners in a conversation'.[22] These partners say something to us – they always pose a question of what they mean.[23] It is precisely their 'talking' that we encounter in light of a constantly moving horizon of modernity; the talking is also subject to moving, it is always already 'talking in a different manner' on a given subject matter. In this perspective, a cultural past is a part of the process of a historical tradition as the highest form of the world of human life, in which the basic element, the air we breathe, is a never-ending conversation with its testimonies.[24] This conversation with a text

19 J. Habermas, *The Concept of Human Dignity and the Realistic Utopia of Human Rights* … , p. 466.

20 P. Dybel, *Granice rozumienia i interpretacji. O hermeneutyce H.-G. Gadamera* [*The Limits of Understanding and Interpretation. On Hermeneutics of H.-G. Gadamer*] … , pp. 406–407.

21 *Ibidem*, p. 409.

22 *Ibidem*, p. 409.

23 *Ibidem*, p. 409.

24 *Ibidem*, p. 409.

seems to also require dignity from the Individual of an excendent character, as the possibility of atopism itself proves that he has found the place of his settlement.

In addition, dignity which opens before us through excendence concentrates on the Individual (on a worthy man) as the one who has a special intuition by being in relation with a Text. The intuition is characterized by the fact that a cultural product from the past is not a product at all, but a relation between the reality of history and the reality of an interpreter. In Gadamerian hermeneutic interpretation a fusion of horizons takes place – of the past horizon and of our contemporary horizon, which is not motionless but is in constant motion. It is continuously formed, *inter alia* by being with tradition and by interpreting its Texts. By the confronting of our presuppositions with the message from the Text, we can confirm or reject them, thereby broadening our horizons, our understanding of ourselves and of the world. A hermeneutic interpretation, thanks to its characteristic feature of openness, turns out to be a path to broadening our self-awareness – to broadening self-awareness of the excendently worthy 'I' toward a 'limitless horizon of the sense' in Gadamer's terms.

I would like to conclude my attempt at providing a response on the issue of dignity with a passage from Bartosz Wojciechowski's work, who talks about dignity – it may be the case that and otherwise, also about its excendent aspect:

> … this semantically open dignity is called 'the sanctity of the human being' and it constitutes a value which is recognized and confirmed rather than established by the positive law. Human dignity is innate, thus it is an intrinsic, fundamental and universal value. Its source is 'humanity as such'. The innate character of dignity stands for its inalienability. It follows further that every person is vested with it, regardless of the individual characteristics, i.e., without regard to race, religion, nationality, height, weight, aptitude or origin and so on, and therefore it has a non-gradable and inalienable character, because if someone is a man, he is a man to the same extent as any other man.[25]

The Third Description: On that which is Social

How does that which is social arise through excendence? As an introduction I propose seeking suggestions in Levinas himself, but interestingly enough not in his work on excendence but in his other great work, a treatise on totality and infinity quoted in the pages of this book. For this purpose I will utilize a meticulous interpretation of Barbara Skarga.

25 Based on the manuscript version: B. Wojciechowski, *Human rights as an element of mutual recognition and equality of opportunity* (forthcoming in compilation in 2013). The author would like to express her gratitude for letting her access the manuscript version.

'But for intellect itself a thinking which goes beyond intellect is essential', writes Levinas in his 'Totality and Infinity'.[26] It was crucial for Levinas to encounter the other in an ethical relation. He thought not of an epistemological and ontological but of an ethical perspective *sensu stricto*. Since, in this ethical relation in compliance with Levinas's guiding principle, one encounters the other who eludes confinement in the here and now. Skarga stresses that the Levinasian other is always beyond my time and omits to let himself be fitted into what is present. If one tries to run out to the other in one's desire, the other flees in a diachrony that cannot be totalized. The other is not-present always and everywhere. Thus Levinas, as Skarga rightly emphasizes, in order to describe this relation (a challenging relation) with the other, the most significant and fundamental relation (to which Levinas devoted the whole work 'Totality and Infinity') has to use a different language. Levinas held a position that philosophy in its inspirations can be ethics in the same manner as ontology is. Philosophy can be Greek equally well as non-Greek in its inspirations. It is in 'Totality and Infinity' that Levinas criticizes European philosophy and its Greek roots from a different vantage point. Levinas argues that being became (as early as Heraclitus) a pivotal problem for European philosophy. European philosophy related this being to violence and war. It is precisely in war, in power, as Skarga points out, that what is being was to be manifest.[27]

In this way war became an inseparable attribute of being. The attribute of being did not involve annihilating or hurting someone. It entailed forcing someone to play a role for the benefit of a totality demonstrated by the reason, religion or history (*vide* World War I and, subsequently, World War II). Skarga writes:

> The ideal of European philosophy has always been totality and unity. The philosophy is convinced that all thinking and acting make sense only if it is orientated to an all-encompassing and lasting idea, such as the Platonic idea for which one fights and to which everyone should be subordinated. ... It proves the unity of being and the unity of thinking, striving to reduce what is different to what is identical. Nonetheless, where *the same* rules, there is no place for what is different. ... These metaphysical principles are contrasted by Levinas with his own metaphysics based on the concepts of difference and infinity. Infinity is not subject to totalization, it frees us from the constraints of thoughts, actions and desires. Infinity cannot be denoted in concepts, grasped by intuition; it can only be desired. The desire for infinity is an experience of an ethical character, which reveals itself in the moment of the encounter with the other.[28]

However, what is distinctive in Levinasian thought is the possibility of coming into contact with the other. The Levinasian other is someone who cannot be

26 B. Skarga, Introduction to: E. Levinas, *Całość i nieskończoność* [*Totality and Infinity*] ... , p. 12.

27 *Ibidem*, p. 13.

28 *Ibidem*, p. 14.

identified with me. It is someone who is outside me. It is someone transcendent. It is someone whom I cannot (either I, or anyone else) understand or embrace by thought. This contact cannot be described in any logical categories. But it is precisely in this significant contact that the individual (standing before infinity) liberates himself from the rule of an objectified totality and ceases to be an instrument of history. In this manner the individual recovers his independence and the sense of full responsibility.[29]

As Skarga states:

> The task of 'Totality and Infinity' is therefore to present the precedence of the philosophy of infinity over the philosophy of totality by revealing the sense of a relation with others, conditions of this relation, its forms and consequences. … It is to defend subjectivity, but, as Levinas adds, not because of its egoism, of its rebellious attitude to totality … but because of an inalienable desire for infinity existing in it and of a more source character than any reasoning thought.[30]

Levinas, therefore, depicts discovering the sense of intersubjective relations and arising of societies in the sense of a desire for living for others and for the Other. As a result of the above analyses, Levinas asks how that which is social arises (social also denotes all institutions). Does that which is social arise from muzzling individual freedoms and from a proclivity for fighting and violence? Or may it, nevertheless, be that that which is social emerges from experiencing infinity that awakens in the ethical relation?[31] As Skarga concludes regarding Levinasian thought, in the first instance we would deal with the policy of legal regulation orientated to totality, in the second instance with spontaneity of human actions becoming a foundation in the social organization.[32]

Skarga asserts:

> It is self-evident that Levinas stands for the second thesis. However, in order to present and describe an ethical relation, he has to employ new formulas of language. That is why Levinasian works brim with notions such as: the epiphany of the face, other and the other … and so on. These are metaphors which elude capturing in a formal definition and Levinas is fully aware of this fact. Since metaphor, as he writes, refers to what is absent, to an order other than the one which we were given in a popular view of the world treated by empiricists as a foundation of all knowledge. Besides, the meanings of words fail to let themselves be treated as building blocks, defined once and for all, situated in the same places as elements in Euclidean space.[33]

29 *Ibidem*, p. 14.
30 *Ibidem*, p. 14.
31 *Ibidem*, p. 15.
32 *Ibidem*, p. 15.
33 *Ibidem*, p. 15.

A great challenge is posed by the question of social formulated in the introduction of the Epilogue (this is the case with other questions as well). Keeping in mind, however, the analysis of Skarga along with all other issues presented in this book and concerning the Face, it seems that one can suggest a response which *de facto* will be identified only with one word: *anxiety*. That which is social arises in anxiety. It is anxiety about Others which is crucial. It will be both the anxiety about Persons and the anxiety about Tradition situated in the Text. Anxiety will be a significant element against building an adiaphoric society. Levinasian discovering of the sense of intersubjective relations and arising of societies in the sense of the desire for living for others and for the Other is directly related to the first question regarding the ideal of happiness (which excendence could promise). It comes to light in an 'Epicurean negative assumption' in which 'I' will not be happy if he fails to bear in mind a 'moral significance of life' originating from taking others' needs into consideration. The anxiety can, in a way, be noticed in happiness, the more so as Tatarkiewicz quotes the words of Wiśniewski: 'Eventually, man is never content with who he is and what he has'.[34] The excendent Individual is happy in 'non-statics', in 'non-peace'. This is also the case with moral community.

Does the postanalogue society characteristic of our postmodernity and discussed in this book – and which is situated in the context of knowledge commons, access to knowledge – have a preliminary potential to create within itself that which is social through excendence? The response will be rather affirmative provided that the element of reflectivity of the society will be highlighted by the moral collectivity, and reflectivity will be endowed with a Levinasian quality of anxiety. I suggest, concurrently, that access to knowledge and a corresponding concept of knowledge commons are contemporary forms of this anxiety. A Nobel laureate Elinor Ostrom, previously mentioned in this book, is talking about the application of the concept of commons to knowledge commons, in the subject matter actions of an adiaphoric character. Additionally, including commons in the right to science and culture as a human right, as an open alternative (along the alternative of ownership) based on the sixteenth-century idea of pasture division (when, let me remind you, a privatization of common pastures began – known as the enclosure process) is relating to Gadamerian Tradition, to Gadamerian interpretation of the text. It is a great success of human rights – the moment in which under General comments No. 17 and also No. 21 the concept of commons becomes, along with intellectual property rights in the traditional sense, a tool stimulating creators.

What I think is most significant, and what excendence can promise, is that the postanalogue society in the postmodern era fails to have a feudal morality, a morality which is not a far-sighted morality but a short-sighted and premodern morality in its description (so that a far-sighted morality is likely to emerge in anxiety – this is crucial). Thereby, it seems that if we enrich our social world

34 W. Tatarkiewicz citing after: A. Wiśniewski, *Rozmowy w ciekawych y potrzebnych filozoficznych y polityczych materyach* [*Discussions on interesting, necessary, philosophical and political matters*] 1760; W. Tatarkiewicz, *O szczęściu* [*On Happiness*] … , pp. 312–313.

with thinking orientated to excendence, there will exist a chance to create a moral collectivity based on anxiety and non-adiaphorisation.

The Fourth Description: On that which is Utopian: toward an Active Utopia?

Excendence, therefore, promises that which is happy, worthy and social. It seems that a notion in which that which is happy, worthy and social may unite is the notion of an active utopia inspired by Baumanian analyses of ethics of the postmodern society. It is the Levinasian metaphor of the Face which stimulates the individual or society to an 'active utopia', i.e. a utopia capable of awakening moral actions.[35] I will, therefore, call this utopia an excendently and dialogically active utopia, because I aim to look at utopia from the dimension of the excendent Individual and thereby emphasizing the fact that it is exactly the excendent 'I' who is the unique 'I' predestined to looking both 'ahead of' and 'beyond' being. Levinas argues as follows:

> The responsibility for the Other cannot begin with my engagement, my decision. The unlimited responsibility that I experience derives from beyond my freedom, from something preceding all memories, from something succeeding all fulfilment, from something which is not present, which in the full, proper meaning of the word is not source, is anarchical, which lies beyond or above entity.[36]

The metaphor of Levinasian Face refers to what is absent, to an order other than the one which we were given in a popular view of the world treated by empiricists as a foundation of all knowledge.[37] As can be learnt from this book, the excendent Individual is predestined in a utopian manner and his utopia is active in an excendent direction. This means that utopia conceived in this way involves an escape to something other than being, as well as a responsibility of an escape to something other than being. I relate the escape to the element of hope from the works of Kępiński and Tischner. The expression of the Face conveys a heroic order, the first teaching that the Individual has to listen to in peace and quiet. The 'I' is aporetic in every respect. It is precisely in this transformation that I seek something which I call 'the first utopia' (or a primary moment of utopia). That is not to say that one discovers oneself as a self 'other than before', but that one discovers the Other as the Face in the expression of the Face. It is a kind of a miracle. The very miracle of awakening (Levinasian awakening) initiates all morality, without being an ethical event itself. The miracle itself gives rise to a possibility. It can be

35 Z. Bauman, *Etyka ponowoczesna* [*Postmodern Ethics*] … , pp. 115–116.

36 E. Levinas, *Inaczej niż być lub ponad istotą* [*Otherwise than Being or Beyond Essence*] (Fundacja Aletheia, Warszawa 2000), p. 23.

37 *Ibidem*, p. 23.

described as the 'possibility of morality' or as the 'hope of morality'. The miracle of moral awakening which the transcendent Individual undergoes here makes the Individual discover that he is not *for himself* but that he is *for others*. Bauman even refers here to a moral sobering up.[38] And Habermas writes:

> The tension between idea and reality that was imported into reality itself as soon as human rights were translated into positive law confronts us today with the challenge to think and act realistically without betraying the utopian impulse. This ambivalence can lead us all too easily into the temptation either to take an idealistic, but noncommittal, stance in support of the exacting moral requirements or to adopt the cynical pose of the socalled realists.[39]

We have no right to betray the utopian impulse and on the other hand we have to think and act realistically. I believe that pursuing the excendent philosophy will prevent the betrayal and will become a lodestar for reason regarding the right to science and culture in the postmodern, post-analogue society – where 'the explosive fusion of moral contents with coercive law as the medium in which the construction of just political orders must be performed'.[40] While Plato's utopia was constructed around the idea of goodness, the utopia for the postanalogue society with respect to the right to science and culture is constructed around happiness, dignity and that which is social. I have faith, to a certain extent, that this thought will be an impulse for developing in the future foundations of philosophy of a utopian intention to take unconditional responsibility for the Other (in various aspects of the Otherness).

A man without a need is a person who cannot arouse in himself a responsibility of an 'active utopia' character (from the thoughts of Løgstrup and Bauman) and thus a person who can live without utopia and cannot separate himself from being and 'sober up' from insobriety with being. This comes as a result of the fact that the moral conscience of such a man is dormant or dazed (I hope that it is still alive). But, as Bauman claims, it is such a conscience of the moral self in which exists the potential for such Levinasian awakening, of feeling the need for excendence.[41] Obviously, Baumanian thesis that the conscience of the moral self would be the only hope for humanity may seem nonsensical, absurd or pretentious (or even all three combined).[42]

Bauman asks: 'What triumphs may morality count on?' A morality that is discredited by the reason as being 'timid', 'only subjective', 'capricious'.[43]

38 Z. Bauman, *Etyka ponowoczesna* [*Postmodern Ethics*] … , p. 116.

39 J. Habermas, *The Concept of Human Dignity and the Realistic Utopia of Human Rights* … , p. 478.

40 *Ibidem*, p. 479.

41 Z. Bauman, *Etyka ponowoczesna* [*Postmodern Ethics*] … , p. 386.

42 *Ibidem*, p. 386.

43 *Ibidem*, p. 386.

Bauman continues by supporting his thesis with the moral lessons of Hannah Arendt. Whereas I would like to return at this point to the philosophy of good hope of Kępiński dealt with earlier in this text. Kępiński writes about people who were deported to Auschwitz during World War II as follows:

> A biological imperative is extremely strong and one needs plenty of effort of will not to think only of bread when one is hungry, of water when one is thirsty, or of an aching spot if it hurts. Yet the effort is indispensable to keeping inner freedom – an open space in which one could think freely, dream, plan, take a decision or liberate oneself from the horror of the present moment. If in the concentration camp life, in this *anus mundi*, there was so much sacrifice, it was due to inner freedom.[44]

Kępiński talks here of a biological imperative, contrasting it with an even superhuman effort that is free thinking, dreaming about the future, decisions related to these dreams and the future itself. 'Otherwise beautiful and good', as he adds. The effort becomes, for him, the only path to liberation, to an escape from the present being. This need is overwhelming and essential. The effort becomes a *sine qua non* condition to keeping inner freedom – an open space in which one could think freely, dream, plan, take a decision or liberate oneself from the horror of the present moment. It was this effort that gave hope and strength to sacrifices for others, to taking responsibility, an anxious, radical, non-reciprocal responsibility for which we receive no payment. In the context of the philosophy of Kępiński I would like to introduce a new imperative and call it 'an excendent imperative' which concentrates in itself hope, separation from being, happiness, that which is social and above all dignity that is dignity stemming from being a responsible Individual in society.

I have deep faith that morality, the moral self of each Individual, can count on such triumphs. However, the moral conscience has to 'awaken' through an impulse sent by what is Other. That is why the call of the Other is dramatic since this drama is likely to awaken the Individual. Otherwise, he will be dormant to what is distant in terms of time and space. May such awakenings be most numerous. And if someone is still doubtful, then, writing in Baumanian terms, he has to ask his conscience for advice:

> Moral responsibility is the most personal and inalienable of human freedoms and the most valuable of human rights. One cannot deprive a man of it, it cannot be shared with other man, it cannot be transferred, put in a pledge or kept for safe-keeping. Moral responsibility is unconditional and unlimited and reveals itself in a constant anxiety that it reveals itself insufficiently. Moral responsibility fails to seek protection, it does not need assurances that it is right, nor justification for the fact that it is as it is. Moral responsibility *is* – and is before one furnishes

44 A.Kępiński, *Rytm* życia [*The Rhythm of Life*] … , p. 9.

proof of its convictions – and it will be long after producers of excuses will pension it off.[45]

It is exactly the moral responsibility of the excendent Individual which contains an element (impulse) of utopia, it is a responsibility that we should never betray as a postmodern moral collectivity – ever so hurried in its adiaphorization.[46]

In conclusion, following Tischnerian thinking, it seems that one should restore to the word 'politics' the most profound meaning in society, one which would embrace a moral foundation based on not 'being with' but on 'being for' within the human right to science and culture in the postmodern society. Politics is, after all, in the radical meaning of the word, a science of a project, of a sensible project for human sacrifices at the present stage of history. Tischnerian thinking has here both metaphysical and political meaning – it entails discovering a suitable project for these sacrifices to which people of good will are called by our present historical drama.[47] It seems that thinking according to excendence has this metaphysical and political meaning as well.[48]

45 Z. Bauman, *Etyka ponowoczesna* [*Postmodern Ethics*] … , p. 388.

46 'The Paradox of Morality', an interview with Emmanuel Levinas conducted by Tamara Wright, Peter Hayes and Alison Ainley, translated by Andrew Benjamin i Tamara Wright, in: Robert Bernesconi and David Wood (eds), *The Provocation of Levinas: Rethinking the Other* (Routledge, London 1988), p. 169.

47 J. Tischner, *Myślenie według wartości* [*Thinking in Values*] … , pp. 544–545.

48 See also a powerful debate of U. Görman 'Universal Ethics – A Futile Effort? A Contractual Analysis of the Search for Universal Ethics', in: G. Bexell and D.-E. Andersson (eds), *Universal Ethics. Perspectives and Proposals from Scandinavian Scholars* (Martinus Nijhoff Publishers, Kluwer Law International, The Hague/London/New York 2002), p. 31. Görman writes: 'Universal ethics can also be understood in a more weak sense, implying universal involvement, universal openess and respect. In this sense, universal ethics may be possible to realize'.

Annex
The Painting, Or How the Metaphor Functions in the Practice of Response of Others

This book proceeds to make a challenging attempt at moving from *Myth* (morality) represented by various metaphors (e.g. the metaphor of the Other or of the Face) to *Reason* (the law and its trends) represented by the right to science and culture.

This device inspired by Habermas proved to be a challenge for scientists, but it also resulted in a question of a more private and practical nature regarding the reasoning from metaphor to practice within the subject matter of access to knowledge: How do we think from abstract to concrete? What do we pay attention to when we think? What is of primary importance in such thinking? What absorbs us more: *Myth* or *Reason*? It may be that we create our own *Myth* or *Reason* in our thinking; do we connect or separate them?

Therefore I asked different people to answer the question: What is the meaning of access to knowledge? In order to make it more visionary (so they could think from myth to reason) they were requested to give their comments on the painting from 1658 titled 'Blind Orion Searching for the Rising Sun' by Nicolas Poussin (oil on canvas; 46 7/8 × 72 in. (119.1 × 182.9 cm), Metropolitan Museum of Art).

At the very last stage I decided to leave their comments in their original form – without any interpretation on my behalf. The only one comment that I might make is that it appears to me that the journey from the *Myth* (metaphor, morality) to *Reason* is not completed in its sense and a person who sets out on this journey can stop by excendence as well.

This picture is derived from the Greek mythology where the blind giant Orion carried his servant Cedalion – the dwarf – on his shoulders for a tour of the East. There the rays of Helios restored Orion's sight. Dwarfs standing on the shoulders of giants is a metaphor that was used by the 17th century scientist Isaac Newton who famously remarked in a letter to his rival Robert Hooke in 1676 that: 'What Descartes did was a good step. You have added much several ways and especially in taking the colours of thin plates into philosophical consideration. If I have seen a little further it is by standing on the shoulders of Giants'.

> Through her book Anna Maria Andersen Nawrot brings up an essential aspect of human rights: its communicative element. She describes it using the classic metaphor about the Dwarf and the Giant [in Latin, *nanos gigantum humeris insidentes*], which provides us with a symbolic picture of the basic

communicative qualities, which are also the basic social skills. Naturally there are many ways of approaching the issue of human rights and many different levels on which to work with them. In order to create a comprehensive picture of human rights, it is, however, necessary to look at all its basic qualities, its elementary building blocks. This also means that all levels and elements are of equal importance when creating a functioning whole.

As a researcher in culture and art history I am inclined to approach the metaphor from the perspective of semiotics. The metaphor about the Dwarf [Cedalion or Kedalion] and the Giant [Orion] expresses something essential about the future of human rights: For human rights to develop in line with the technology and media driven times we live in, versatile communication between different parties is essential. The communicative element is based on a variety of points of interaction for the exchange of information and on the flow of information. The Dwarf represents access to knowledge. As in the classic metaphor, the Dwarf through his vision underlines the importance of information and understanding. Symbolically, information is the light that enables us to see. In the current era of new technology and new techniques, owners of intellectual property assets that are patented or copyrighted are the providers of knowledge that opens up new avenues for the continuous development of human rights. The Giant represents the vital and massive force of action: Human rights are brought forward through cooperation. The high number of providers and users of knowledge constitutes a massive united force and thereby bears considerable resemblance with the power and physical strength of the giant in the metaphor. We possess the strength to change; we are composed of energy and vitality. Just as the Giant, we are capable of forwarding new ideas rapidly and efficiently.

The metaphor also represents the possibility of rewarding interaction. The Giant Orion was a gigantic warrior. In the context of the right to knowledge the Giant represents the search for knowledge and the eagerness to understand. Without a respectful and trusting relation to the Dwarf, the Giant will not reach far and in the worst case will only cause considerable harm in making use of its force. Without access to information and knowledge, we are blind to the possibilities of development and incapable of greater achievements. Without interaction and relations to each other, we are alone and remain weak. This is also the basic principle of the communicative element: Without interaction, the flow of information will die and new ideas will not be born. For the Dwarf, the lack of the powers of the Giant is a crucial quality that he does not possess – in particular if the aim is to create fast and considerable change and development.

The metaphor is a symbol of communication and therefore also touches on the underlying question about the wish to give. The Dwarf in the metaphor represents a servant that is willing to assist the Giant to regain his eyesight. To provide access to knowledge in the end means the establishment of a communicative relationship where both parties are of equal importance. This is also a basic element in human rights. In the metaphor the two parties stand against each other. This in turn naturally generates an increased interest in gaining access to the strengths and qualities of the other that you yourself lack and need. Cooperation between the Dwarf and the Giant therefore presents a possibility that makes considerable increase in the capacity of both parties possible.

The metaphor provides a symbolic picture of an ideal mode of cooperation that is both productive and leads to both parties reaching their goals. The basic idea behind the philosophy of human rights is that the implementation of human rights will create and provide the possibility to increase the welfare of all humans. The welfare of all humans and the increase in level of human rights enjoyed by all must be achieved through approaching the work at different levels and through using a variety of methods. The structural element of human rights is represented by laws and different regulations, which symbolically constitute the backbone of the development of human rights. The different methods used represent the muscles, or the capacity to generate movement. The communicative element in the language of the metaphor represents the capacity to see, to hear and to speak. The Giant therefore stands for the pragmatic, raw strength and the Dwarf represents the communicative element.

Through the sharp eyesight of the Dwarf and the greatness of the Giant we are given a glimpse of the future. As stated by Johannes of Salisbury in *Metalogicon* [1159], the capacity to see at a great distance was contingent upon the strength of the Giant and not the sharp eyesight of the Dwarf. Knowledge, coupled with substantive cooperation, generates the possibility of a big leap forward in the achievement of the well-being of all humans. '*The bigger we'll allow the giant to grow, faster will the improvements show*'. The knowledge of the Dwarf helps us all to understand the challenges of the future at the same time as the force of the cooperation facilitates the work towards achieving greater welfare of humans in all countries. The same type of change is being seen in the environmental movement: The higher the number of people interacting, the greater the results will be.

The metaphor basically builds on moral and ethics. Common interest and cooperation do not always directly benefit both parties: Within certain areas the benefits increase cumulatively with time. Both environmental questions and issues regarding the well-being of humans are in their entirety of the former type. The metaphor therefore also tells us something about the choice to influence development. To provide the possibility of influencing development and taking action to establish a relation are the first building blocks of communication. The biggest challenge in adopting a communicative method of working with human rights – Culture of Access – is to conquer your fear of changing established ways of thinking. In its essence, communication stands for rapid change; the decisive element is the level of interest in looking at the issue of ownership over all knowledge from a humanistic perspective. The level of interest in increasing our knowledge of how to achieve a higher level of well-being for all humans is generally equal to our actual appreciation of human rights.

The metaphor about the Dwarf and the Giant also tells us something about our historic time. We live in and through the communicative element. The achievement of our physical and material welfare generally is initiated through communication at different levels. Communication and the establishment of relations activate different powers to generate projects at a practical level. Media, culture and educational materials are often available in digital format and therefore easy to distribute and access. Internet, mobile phones and computers are good examples of different tools that reflect the spirit of information and communication of our times. While most of us are guaranteed the right to communicate, this is not the case for all. If the Dwarf is left alone with his information, he will not reach further than his own capacity allows him. At the same time it is important to realize that blocking the access to knowledge may hinder development, which may lead to disastrous consequences – environmentally, for example: if the owner of a patent on a certain type of solar cell decides not to exploit it, this may lead to a lost opportunity to decrease the consumption of fossil fuels. The blindness of the Giant may lead to serious negative consequences. Access to knowledge is therefore also part of our human rights. The right to communicate and the right to access knowledge may be brought forward in various propitious and productive ways in relation to different areas of usage.

Anna Nawrot's project is important because it brings together the vital power, the structure and the communicative element without ignoring the fundamental building blocks of the human rights ideology. The brilliant quality of the communicative work through Culture of Access and Access to Knowledge lies in its simplicity. Change is achieved through the choice to give and to take part. We are all already beforehand taking part in determining the level of implementation of the welfare of all humans: We are influenced by the lives of others – not least seen from the environmental perspective. Knowledge needs to be shaped through discussion and visions of the future must be based on ethical standards.

The metaphor also tells us something about our consciousness of communicative interaction and the use of information and knowledge. The sociologist Robert King Merton (1910–2003) used the same metaphor in his research, where he, using his own method, explored the unforeseen consequences of our social behaviour. Whether as the Giant or the Dwarf, we go about reaching our goals through calculating the deliberate consequences of our acts, but all social interaction also has unforeseen effects, so-called 'self-defeating prophecies'. As Nietzsche wrote in his work *Thus Spoke Zarathustra* (1883), it is possible that the Dwarf does not fully fathom the depth of his own vision. This in my view leads to the conclusion that we must acknowledge the importance of mutual communication based on communicative equality. To understand means to have the will to consult different sources of information in order to comprehend. Through communication based on common interest and awareness raising, it is possible to prevent and eliminate the stumbling blocks in that process. In the classic metaphor, the Giant Orion regained his vision through the Goddess of the Dawn, Eos. He finally saw the light, found his own way and access to knowledge. He was given the possibility of acting through the efforts and helpfulness of the Dwarf. This is one of the aims of the Culture of Access: Results achieved through increasing the implementation of human rights, it is believed, will provide consequential effects with regard to increasing the welfare of all humans (human well-being) (Elina Larsson[1]).

What is the significance of the discussion about the relationship between IP and Human Rights for the implementation of human rights in the developing world?

The classic tale of the Giant Orion and the Dwarf is commonly used as a metaphor to describe the process of intellectual progress. In order to reach further intellectually than those that have gone before us, we need to build on their accumulated knowledge. Access to that knowledge becomes crucial, not only to the intellectual progress of the individual, but indeed also to that of mankind. In my mind and from the point of view of the pursuit of a higher level of welfare for all, this interconnection between the protection of the rights of the individual and those of the others raises a number of questions of interest to the discussion on the evolving relation between intellectual property and human rights. There are no easy answers to these questions, but they need to be posed as they are crucial to the creation of a fairer society in the interest of human kind.

To use the metaphor, from the point of view of the development of a fairer society, one would need to take a closer look at the duties of governments to put in place systems of governance that guarantee the highest possible level of equal access to the shoulders of the Giant by the individual scholars of the world, regardless of the circumstances of their origin. In today's world this is not the case. Much (some would say more and more) of the access to the accumulated knowledge is restricted, mainly for economic reasons, to a select few who are allowed access in order, primarily, to further the interests of the holder of the right to the knowledge in question. This often regards knowledge that is essential to further the development of societies and consequently also a higher level of implementation of human rights, in particular, but not only, in developing countries. In that regard it may be of interest to discuss the obligation of governments to reform laws and practices that are not in accordance with the human rights instruments that the state has ratified, including patent and copyright laws.

From the global development point of view, the negative influence of the current system of intellectual property rights protection is indeed tremendous. The fact that more and more of the essential cutting edge knowledge in the world is available only to the select few that are admitted at relatively few universities and other centres of knowledge and research in the developed world leads to a chain of negative effects that are impossible to ignore. Not only do developing

1 Elina Larsson, Researcher, PhD in Cultural History, Faculty of Cultural History, University of Turku, Finland, Elina.Larsson@utu.fi.

countries lack access to the latest scientific and technological developments that are often quoted as necessary to lead their populations out of their situation of underdevelopment, but in addition the lack of access to that knowledge in their home countries compels the brightest students in developing countries, as well as in fact in a large number of developed countries, to consider leaving their countries to take up scholarships and positions at the few universities and other research centres that have the capacity to offer the access to the knowledge they need in order to excel in their chosen fields. This of course is not a new phenomenon, but it is a phenomenon where considerable negative effects on society have been exacerbated through the rapid developments of today's world, where access to cutting edge knowledge is crucial to meet the more and more acute basic needs of the growing population of this world, to provide health care, to provide housing and not least to ensure that the development of societies on a global scale is environmentally sustainable.

The adverse effects of the current intellectual property rights system is of course not the only reason for the flight of intellectual capacity from developing countries and it is certainly not the only reason for the lesser quality of education and research at universities in developing countries, but it is without doubt an important element in that process.

The unfairness of the intellectual property rights protection system is problematic from the human rights point of view. Although all human rights must be exercised so as not to unduly interfere with the rights of others and to meet the just requirements of morality, public order and general welfare in a democratic society, the traditional interpretation of the right to benefit from the protection of the moral and material interests resulting from any scientific, literary or artistic production of which he/she is the author (Article 15 of the International Covenant on Economic, Social and Cultural Rights [ICESCR]) has generally been seen as reinforcing the current system of strong patent and copyright laws. As the human rights protection regime has developed and the universality and indivisibility of human rights has been recognized, this interpretation has, however, become increasingly awkward, since it does not sufficiently take into account the infringement on the rights of others that the enjoyment of this individual right has lead to. There is today a growing understanding that a better balance needs to be found between the right of the individual intellectual property rights holder and a variety of human rights of others.

Central to the question of the balance between intellectual property rights and human rights is the effect of the application of the current system on the creation of wealth as well as on the distribution of that wealth. Are all of the conditions required for the creation of wealth also justified from a human rights perspective? Certainly the individual accumulation of wealth cannot in itself be a sufficient argument in favour of human rights protection. Equally, I would like to state that the redistribution of wealth in itself cannot be seen as a panacea for the insufficient human rights developments in the world. A balance needs to be struck that takes into account both the interests of the individual rights holder to benefit and to a reasonable extent control the exploitation of his or her achievements and the rights of others. That new balance will have to reconsider the weight given to the economic interests of private individuals and corporations.

Seemingly unrelated to the human rights development, the information technology and Internet revolution during the last 15 to 20 years has lead to additional criticism of the current intellectual property rights protection system as no longer being in sync with modern times. Copyright and patent laws are increasingly flaunted by, in particular, the younger generations that have grown up hooked up to the Internet and that see it as natural to download information as they please, to copy music, films, artwork, photography and virtually any information they can get their hands on, legally or illegally. This behaviour, however, does not only stem from a wish to obtain for free the music and film experiences that older generations paid much more dearly for. Mixed into their self-interest is also a profound sense of the unfairness of the system in place. There is in fact a very low level of popular approval of the restrictions that society through the legal system is imposing on access to knowledge. This is not least true with regard to many of us who believe in the creation of a fairer society, based on democracy legitimized by its adherence to the human rights and freedoms of the individual and it does not only concern access to music and Hollywood movies. It touches on the limitations placed on the implementation of the basic needs of the individual that current restrictions to access to knowledge impose.

It is very important to understand when pursuing this discussion that human rights law, like other systems of norms, is not static. It develops and changes with the times. The traditional interpretation of the right to protection of the moral and material interests resulting from any scientific, literary or artistic production of which an individual is the author is not written in stone. As the global understanding and recognition of human rights is increasing, the minimum level of human rights protection that the international standards provide should also evolve. Perhaps the momentum is there for a sincere discussion on more equal access to (cutting edge) knowledge for scholars worldwide and perhaps a higher degree of recognition of the duties of the rights holders and the duty bearers with regard to the distribution of the benefits derived from their contribution to the accumulated knowledge in their field of work?

There is no doubt that the pursuit of a higher level of welfare for all necessitates the analysis of the imbalance between the protection of the rights and freedoms of the individual and the impact the enjoyment of these rights and freedoms have on those of others. It is not without importance in this regard that the Member States of the United Nations represented at the International Human Rights Conference in Vienna in 1993 unanimously agreed that human rights are universal and indivisible. All rights are of equal value and they are inherent to all individuals, regardless of the circumstances of the individual.

While the negative effects of the restrictions to the access to knowledge thus seem obvious, the solution to the dilemma is perhaps not equally obvious. Nevertheless, and to return to the metaphor of the Giant and the Dwarf, for the above reasons, it is no doubt a justified request to ask lawmakers, as well as the judiciary and other stakeholders in the process of implementing human rights, to reconsider their interpretation of Article 15 of the ICESCR. It is in fact the obligation of governments to take a closer look at who is sitting on the shoulders of the Giant and why, and if the arguments supporting the current situation cannot be justified within the framework of the international human rights system, governments that have ratified the ICESCR have committed themselves to take steps to the maximum of available resources, with a view to achieving progressively the full realization of the rights recognized in the present Covenant by all appropriate means, including in particular the adoption of legislative measures.

If the human rights standards and norms are to be applied to the benefit of all, the possibility of realizing one's intellectual capacity and reaching that vantage point high above that of others on the shoulders of the Giant should not be reserved for the few to the benefit of the few (Henrik Andersen[2]).

My initial reaction to Anna-Maria's invitation to consider this picture was the metaphor 'Standing on the shoulders of giants'. This, I think, must be the most obvious and common association when seeing this picture. However, as a researcher, I cannot resist but doing at least a little research. A Google search on 'Standing on the shoulders of giants' shows a very high number of hits, most of them of little interest to me. Although the metaphor and the ideational first captured my interest, art and the picture as such – the visual appearance – soon dominated my thinking. This painting was made a long time ago, in 1658, which makes the relationship between the present and the past worthy of some brief consideration. It also makes the history of art – in particular the practice of oil painting – and developments from the past to postmodernism worthy of some brief consideration. From time to time I reflect and realize that digitalization and the Internet has affected copyright in ways very similar to the ways postmodernism has affected contemporary philosophy and social theory. Legal theory has also been affected, but perhaps not to the same extent. Since I am not an art historian, John Berger's 'Ways of Seeing' will provide us with some support concerning the history and thinking of art.

Not long ago, the only way to look at this painting was to go to the place where it was physically placed, probably at a museum somewhere. Nowadays anyone who has a computer and Internet access can watch the appearance of it

2 Henrik Andersen, Programme Officer, Programme Department, Raoul Wallenberg Institute of Human Rights and Humanitarian Law, Lund, Sweden, Henrik.Andersen@rwi.lu.se.

on the screen anytime she/he wants. Berger teaches us that the uniqueness of every painting once was part of the uniqueness of the place where it resided. Paintings were often an integral part of the building, such as images on the ceilings of a church. 'Sometimes the painting was transportable, but it could never be seen in two places at the same time'. When the camera reproduces a painting, it destroys the uniqueness of its image. As a result it's meaning changes. Or, more exactly, Berger says, 'its meaning multiplies and fragments into many meanings' [Berger, p. 19]. The painting now travels to the spectator rather than the spectator to the painting; just as the picture now unfolds on the computer screen, or on many computer screens at the same time in many different places. 'In its travels, the pictures meaning is diversified'. One of the hallmarks of modernity, the centrality of the author/artist, is then gone. The original and authentic voice of the artist as author is silenced. Postmodernists, by adopting techniques of collage, pastiche and sampling, draw attention to the variety of subject positions from which the world can be viewed. Postmodernism (Roland Barthes) even proclaims the death of the author, shamelessly borrowing or reassembling images, sounds and text. Some would instead call it piracy and others sharing. Postmodernism thus seems to capture current copyright practices quite well.

After having seen the copy of the painting on the computer screen, we can still go to the museum and view the original. Berger, drawing from Walter Benjamin, says that the uniqueness of the original now lies in it being the original of a reproduction. 'The meaning of the original work no longer lies in what it uniquely says but in what it uniquely is' (John Berger). The question is how this unique existence is defined and evaluated in our culture.

The idea has travelled yet further towards the notion of 'a copy without an original' (Jean Baudrillard). And since the author is dead, the artist is no longer of any interest. Everything is (again) in the public domain. Or in hyperreality? Focus transfers from producer to consumer and the consumer becomes producer. So, while we might be standing on the shoulders of giants, we do not necessarily see the same things as the Giant. In fact, Orion was blinded by King Oinopion of Khios after trying to rape the King's daughter Merope. Orion's sight was, however, later recovered by the rising sun. In the end Orion turned into a star. After being killed by Artemis he was placed among the stars as the constellation of Orion. All this is, of course, just a story, or a myth. But since it is just a story, or a myth, it can be used for other, more serious purposes. 'The art of the past no longer exists as it once did. Its authority is lost. In its place there is a language of images' (John Berger). Berger tells us that what matters now is who uses that language for what purpose (Peter Gottschalk[3]).

3 Peter Gottschalk, PhD, Faculty of Law, University of Lund, Sweden, Peter.Gottschalk@jur.lu.se.

The story of Orion and Cedalion, to me, represents how we face challenges in the world which can be overcome if we help each other and work together. Orion was blind and a man of massive proportions. You would automatically think that he would not be able to accomplish anything. However, with the help of Cedalion – Cedalion supplying the eye and Orion the legs – they were able to move forward quickly. They journeyed to the East, where the rising sun restored Orion's sight.

Access to knowledge is a complex issue. It can be viewed and discussed from many angles, e.g. from a social, political or legal point of view. In my view, however, access to knowledge should not only be a matter of equality between the rich and the poor, the industrialized countries and the developing countries, and how to give the developing countries access to intellectual property rights and other knowledge that has been developed in the industrialized world. It should not just be a matter of how to divide a 'pie'. One important aspect should be to recognize that the sharing of knowledge, such as modern technology, in addition to serving human rights, can actually lead to greater development in the world and thus make the whole 'pie' larger.

In this connection, I think the story of Orion and Cedalion is a great metaphor. At risk of extending the story beyond its original meaning and overexploiting it as representation for access to knowledge, I think it can be used as an image of how the large developing world, with a little help to get access to knowledge, research and education, would be able to develop and move forward towards a point where it does not need to be helped anymore, where it can participate in and contribute to global development, both economic and social. That would be to the benefit of everyone (Katarina Granehult[4]).

As to the painting. I'm not fond of giants, whereas 'standing on their shoulders' seems to be a boring exercise. A giant (if it were for real) is, as goes with the name, giant. It obstructs the view, not to mention all the damage they cause with their clumsy uncontrolled feet. No, I wouldn't choose a giant as my companion. I do prefer the eyes of children. The small creatures, undisturbed by external impressions, open minded and curious. Ready to embrace the world and its thrilling adventures. That is my companion and that would be my initial starting point when approaching the task of modelling and balancing intellectual property and human rights. If we consider the option, standing on one of those clumsy giants, I do think that we may lose important perspectives. Of course we need to be aware of history and previous knowledge, but I do think that it might be an advantage if we start from scratch, comparing our findings with those of the giants afterwards, instead of beforehand. Giants mean large scale advantages, mass production and rational decisions and that is not the soil in which new ideas tend to grow!

4 Katarina Granehult, economist.

Putting on the glasses of the child I think we are in a better position to look upon our project. By having the aim of finding a reasonable protection for intellectual property it is possible to consider opposite interests (having human rights in mind). That might of course be regarded as obvious, but let me develop this line of thinking with an example. One much debated issue is the extension of protection in time. Do we really need protection for 70 years (post mortem actor) in the field of copyright? Of course not. Realizing that it might be an impossible task to change this situation, considering the fact that it is much harder to decrease protection than it is to increase it, it is still interesting to reflect upon the argument and ideas that justify the extension of rights. And the child, by the way, would look upon this problem in a more practical way, starting out from some kind of common ground for justification. Imagine that the child draws a painting – a princess or a racing car, it doesn't matter. This painting is protected by copyright (the child is skilled in the arts and the drawing is individual), but to what extent does the child enforce this right? To begin with it is likely that the child would want credit. This includes the right to show the painting for the first time and the right to be mentioned as the creator. If someone steals the painting, copies it and states that it is the work of the thief who stole it in the beginning, we may expect that the child feels their rights have been infringed. But what if it is borrowed and posted in the corridor outside the canteen, where the impressive drawings emanating from the children of the school in question are posted, if qualified enough. Would that be an infringement? From the child's perspective the answer would be obvious – No – this is not infringing but rather a homage to the creator, something that you would gladly accept without consent. There might be exceptions to this rule. One shy child may want to oppose the showing of the painting. It is likely though that the need to control the use of the copyrighted work is fulfilled if this need of the creator is satisfied upon request. But the school has to respect that the creator may choose not to show the drawing in public.

In this context we may find one important starting point in the discussion as to copyright and its content. Is the right supposed to be fixed and general or would it be possible to make the right dependent on the creator's factual actions. In today's world it is possible to opt out of copyright (e.g. in relation to Creative Commons agreements), but in the child's perception of a fair and balanced situation, I do think that it is natural to give the creator the possibility of opting into copyright, having Open Access as the principal rule.

Speaking of extension of copyright and the time issue, it is of course impossible for a child to think of a potential need for a +70-year period of protection. This alone does not provide us with convincing arguments in the struggle to find the proper and balanced timeframe for copyright protection, but it may provide us with an opening leading to a possible solution. In reality it is not only the child who may have problems foreseeing the future of copyright over +70 years and if that is the situation why should we, as a principle rule, state that every single (individual and creative) work should be protected for that period as a starting point. Wouldn't it be more appropriate if the creator, the one who gains from protection, is burdened with the task of claiming copyright in situations where a potentially copyrighted work is used. In such a situation the principle rule would be that you are allowed to use works of others, but you should be prepared to pay a reasonable fee if the creator claims that copyright exists in the work that you are using. In such an environment copyright would be dependent on the will of the creator and the creator's actions in preserving and protecting the work. It might seem like an uncontrolled situation with divergent protection, depending on the will of creators instead of one common system of rights afforded by the legislator. It would be more fair though and actually easier to justify. Furthermore, property rights in general are dependent on the will of the owners. One example illustrating this is the child creating one imaginative snowman during winter (or, making the example more vivid, an artist performing at the World Ice Art Championships in Alaska). Are there property rights in the sculptures? It can be questioned but from the child's perspective the answer would be a definitive: Yes. This property right, however, is dependent on preservation. The property will melt if the sun is shining. If you claim your right to the snowman you will have to preserve it, putting the sculpture in the fridge or moving to a country with an arctic climate. You have to be active to preserve your right and nobody questions the fact that it is fair and justifiable. Why should intellectual property be different?

I do think that we ought to look upon intellectual property right through the eyes of our children, trying to find reasonable and justifiable common principles that can be derived into something that we may regard as 'core rights' within the field of intellectual property. This is, of course, not a new idea (there are giants in this field as well – e.g. it may be stated that this line of thinking relates to the veil of ignorance using Rawls terminology), but I do think that it can be a creative and challenging experience to reflect upon this question starting with a blank paper and I do think that this experience could contribute to a better understanding of the balancing issue (Ulf Maunsbach[5]).

5 Ulf Maunsbach, Professor, Faculty of Law, Lund University, Sweden, Ulf.Maunsbach@jur.lu.se.

Bibliography

Albritton, R., 'A Practical Utopia for the Twenty-First Century', in: P. Vieira and M. Marder (eds), *Existential Utopia. New Perspectives on Utopian Thought* (Continuum International Publishing Group, London 2012).

Alexy, R., *A Theory of Constitutional Rights* (Oxford University Press, Oxford 2004).

Alfredsson, G., 'UNESCO and a Common Framework for Ethics. Human Rights Concerns', in: Bexell, G. and D.E. Andersson (eds), *Universal Ethics. Perspectives and Proposals from Scandinavian Scholars* (Martinus Nijhoff Publishers, Kluwer Law International, The Hague/London/New York 2002).

Alfredsson, G. and Eide, A. (eds), *The Universal Declaration of Human Rights. A Common Standard of Achievement* (Kluwer Law International, The Hague 1999).

Andersen, S. and Niekerk, K. (eds), *Concern for the Other: Perspectives on the Ethics of K.E. Løgstrup* (Notre Dame, University of Notre Dame Press 2007).

Arieli, Y., 'On the Necessary and Sufficient Conditions for the Emergence of the Doctrine of Man and His Rights', in: D. Kretzmer and E. Klein (eds), *The Concept of Human Dignity in Human Rights Discourse* (Kluwer Law International, The Hague, London, New York 2002).

Arnason, V. 'Universalism in Ethics and Cultural Diversity', in: Bexell, G. and D.E. Andersson (eds), *Universal Ethics. Perspectives and Proposals from Scandinavian Scholars* (Martinus Nijhoff Publishers, Kluwer Law International, The Hague/London/New York 2002).

Ayoubi, L., 'Human Rights Perspectives on Access of Blind, Visually Impaired and Other Reading Disabled Persons to Copyrighted Material', Master's Thesis (Master's Programme in International Human Rights Law and Intellectual Property Law, Faculty of Law, Lund University, supervisor: Anna Maria Andersen Nawrot).

Bader, R.M., 'The Framework for Utopia', in: R.M. Bader and J. Meadowcroft (eds), *Nozick's Anarchy, State and Utopia* (Cambridge University Press, Cambridge 2011).

Bainbridge, D., *Intellectual Property* (Pitman Publishing, Harlow 1999).

Barbosa Da Silva, A., 'Human Rights, Dignity and Autonomy' in *Health Care and Social Services: Nordic Perspectives* (Intersentia, Antwerp, Oxford, Portland 2009).

Bardziej, J. and Gockowski, J., *Rozmyślania o cywilizacji* [*Reflections on Civilization*] (Wydawnictwo Baran i Suszynski, Krakow 1997).

Bauman, Z. *Modernity and Ambivalence* (Cornell University Press, Ithaca, NY 1991).

Bauman, Z., *Postmodern Ethics* (Blackwell, Oxford 1993).

Bauman, Z. 'Wywiad z Baumanem' [An interview with Bauman] which is a transcript of conversations held in Leeds, England between 15–17 July. Published in: *1 Odra* (1995).

Bauman, Z., *Liquid Times: Living in an Age of Uncertainty* (Polity Press, Cambridge 2007).

Bauman, Z., *Culture in a Liquid Modern World* (Polity Press, Cambridge 2011).

Bauman, Z., *Etyka ponowoczesna* [*Postmodern Ethics*] (Wydawnictwo Aletheia, Warszawa 2012).

Bauman, Z. *Liquid Modernity* (Polity Press, Cambridge 2012).

Benczek, A., 'EU: Intellectual property – recent initiatives at EU level against counterfeiting and piracy', 25:8 *EIPR* (2003).

Bernesconi, R. and Wood, D. (eds), *The Provocation of Levinas: Rethinking the Other* (Routledge, London 1988).

Bexell, G., 'Universalism in Ethics and Cultural Diversity', in: Bexell, G. and D.E. Andersson (eds), *Universal Ethics. Perspectives and Proposals from Scandinavian Scholars* (Martinus Nijhoff Publishers, Kluwer Law International, The Hague/London/New York 2002).

Bexell, G. and D.E. Andersson (eds), *Universal Ethics. Perspectives and Proposals from Scandinavian Scholars* (Martinus Nijhoff Publishers, Kluwer Law International, The Hague/London/New York 2002).

Bolestuta-Kukulka, K., *Sociologia ogólna* [*General Sociology*] (Oficyna Wydawnicza ASPRA-JR, Warszawa, 2003).

Bollier, D., 'The power of openness; why citizens, education, government and business should care about the coming revolution in open source code software', The Berkman Centre for Internet & Society at Harvard Law School, research publication Nos. 1999–02 (1999).

Bollier, D., 'The Growth of the Commons Paradigm', in: C. Hess and E. Ostrom (eds), *Understanding Knowledge as a Commons. From Theory to Practice* (The MIT Press, Cambridge 2007).

Bouchetoux, F. and Jones, C., 'Sociality and Money, Business Ethics', 16(3) *A European Review* (2007).

Boyle, J., *The Public Domain. Enclosing the Commons of the Mind* (Yale University Press, New Haven, London, 2008).

Boyle, J., 'A Manifesto on WIPO and the Future of Intellectual Property', 0009 *Duke Law and Technology Review* (2009).

Brodecki, Z., 'Art the Comparison', in: Brodecki, Z., Konopacka, M. and Brodecka-Chamera, A., *Komparatystyka kultur prawnych* [*Art de comparison of the legal cultures*] (Wydawnictwo Wolters Kluwer, Warszawa 2010).

Brodecki, Z., Konopacka, M. and Brodecka-Chamera, A., *Komparatystyka kultur prawnych* [*Art de comparison of the legal culture*] (Wydawnictwo Wolters Kluwer, Warszawa 2010).

Brodecki, Z. and Nawrot, A.M., 'Świątynia w cyberkulturze. Technologie cyfrowe i prawo w społeczeństwie wiedzy' [*Temple in Cyberculture. Digital Technologies and Law in Information Society*] (Wydawnictwo Uniwersytetu Gdanskiego 2007).

Brodecki, Z. and Nawrot, A.M., 'In Search for Common Sense in Cyberspace', *Masaryk University Journal of Law and Technology*, 2/2008.

Burghardt, W.J., *Sprawiedliwość* [*Justice*] (Wydawnictwo WAM, Kraków 2006).

Cern, K. and Wojciechowski, B., 'O koniecznych zwiazkach miedzy dyskursem prawnym a moralnym' [About required connections between legal and moral discourse], in: J. Zajadlo (ed.), *Dziedzictwo i przyszlosc. Problemy wspolczesnej niemieckiej filozofii prawa* (Arche, Gdansk 2010).

Chekola, M., 'Book Review: Plurality of Aims and Desires versus Overall Judgments', 8 *Journal of Happiness Studies* (2007).

Chon, M., 'A Rough Guide to Global Intellectual Property Pluralism', in: R.C. Dreyfuss, H. First and D.L. Zimmerman, *Working within the Boundaries of Intellectual Property. Innovation Policy for the Knowledge Society* (Oxford University Press, Oxford 2010).

de Cock Buning, M., 'Expansion and Convergence in Copyright Law', in: W. Grosheide (ed.), *Intellectual Property and Human Rights: A Paradox* (Edward Elgar, Cheltenham, UK 2010).

Cohen, W.M. and Walsh, J.P., 'Access – or Not – in Academic Biomedical Research Pluralism', in: R.C. Dreyfuss, H. First and D.L. Zimmerman, *Working Within the Boundaries of Intellectual Property. Innovation Policy for the Knowledge Society* (Oxford University Press, Oxford 2010).

Colston, C. and Middleton, K., *Modern Intellectual Property* (Cavendish Publishing, London, Sydney, Portland, Oregon 2005).

Coomans, F., 'Content and Scope of the Right to Education as a Human Right and Obstacles to Its Realization', in: Y. Donders and V. Volodin (eds), *Human Rights in Education, Science and Culture. Legal Developments and Challenges* (Ashgate, UNESCO 2007).

Crane D.A., 'Patent Pools, RAND Commitments and the Problematics of Price Discrimination', in: R.C. Dreyfuss, H. First and D.L. Zimmerman, *Working Within the Boundaries of Intellectual Property. Innovation Policy for the Knowledge Society* (Oxford University Press, Oxford 2010).

Davidow, J., 'Liberalization of antitrust rules for IP licensing. Global trends and unresolved issues', 5(7) *JWIP* (2004).

Davies, G., *Copyright and the Public Interest* (Thomson Sweet & Maxwell, London 2002).

Deazley, R., *Rethinking Copyright. History, Theory, Language* (Edward Edgar Publishing, Northampton 2006).

Dehnel, P. and Sierocka, B., 'Rozmowa którą jesteśmy' [Conversation which we are], in: Gadamer, H.G., *Język i Rozumienie* [*Language and Understanding*] (Fundacja Aletheia, Warszawa 2003).

Derrida, J., *Adieu to Emmanuel Levinas* [*Meridian: Crossing Aesthetics*] (Stanford University Press, Stanford 1999).

Dicke, K., 'The Founding Function of Human Dignity in The Universal Declaration of Human Rights', in: D. Kretzmer and E. Klein (eds), *The Concept of Human Dignity in Human Rights Discourse* (Kluwer Law International, The Hague, London, New York 2002).

Donders, Y., 'The Legal Framework of the Right to Take Part in Cultural Life', in: Y. Donders and Y. Volodin (eds), *Human Rights in Education, Science and Culture. Legal Developments and Challenges* (Ashgate, Unesco Publishing 2007).

Donders, Y. and Volodin, V. (eds), *Human Rights in Education Science and Culture. Legal Developments and Challenges* (Ashgate, UNESCO 2007).

Douzinas, C., *The End of Human Rights* (Hart Publishing, Oxford, Portland, Oregon 2000).

Dreyfuss, R., Zimmerman, D.L. and First, H. (eds), *Expanding the Boundaries of Intellectual Property. Innovation Policy for the Knowledge Society* (Oxford University Press, Oxford 2001).

Drucker, P., *Post-Capitalist Society* (Harper, New York 1993).

Dumont, L., *Essays on Individualism: Modern Theory in Anthropological Perspective* (University of Chicago Press, Chicago 1986).

Dupre, C., 'Unlocking Human Dignity: Towards a Theory for the 21st Century', 2 *European Human Rights Law Review* (2009).

Dybel, P., *Granice rozumienia i interpretacji. O hermeneutyce H.-G. Gadamera* [*The Limits of Understanding and Interpretation. On H.-G. Gadamer's Hermeneutics*] (Towarzystwo Autorów i Wydawców Prac Naukowych, UNIVERSITAS, Krakow 2004).

Eide, A., 'Interdependence and Indivisibility of Human Rights', in: Y. Donders and V. Volodin (eds), *Human Rights in Education, Science and Culture. Legal Developments and Challenges* (Ashgate, Unesco Publishing 2007).

Endeshaw, A., 'Reconfiguring intellectual property for the information age – towards information property?', 5(2) *JWIP* (2004).

Fouad Makeen, M., *Copyright in a Global Information Society. The Scope of Copyright Protection Under International US, UK and French Law* (Kluwer Law International, the Hague, 2000).

Franz, V., 'Back to Balance: Limitations and Exceptions to Copyright', in: G. Krikorian and A. Kapczyński (eds), *Access to Knowledge in the Age of Intellectual Property* (Zone Books, New York 2010).

Gadamer, H.G., *Prawda i Metoda* [*Truth and Method*]. *Zarys hermeneutyki filozoficznej* [*An Outline of Philosophical Hermeneutics*] (Wydawnictwo Inter Esse, Krakow 1993).

Gadamer, H.G., 'Granice Języka' [The Limits of Language], in: *Język i rozumienie* [*Language and Understanding*] (Fundacja Aletheia, Warszawa 2003).

Gadamer, H.G., *Język i rozumienie* [*Language and Understanding*] (Fundacja Aletheia, Warszawa 2003).

Gadamer, H.G., 'Retoryka, Hermeneutyka i krytyka ideologii' [Rhetoric, Hermeneutics and Ideology Critique], in: *Język i rozumienie* [*Language and Understanding*] (Fundacja Aletheia, Warszawa 2003).

Gadamer, H.G., 'Romantyzm, Hermeneutyka, Dekonstrukcja' [Romanticism, Hermeneutics, Deconstruction], in: *Język i rozumienie* [*Language and Understanding*] (Fundacja Aletheia, Warszawa 2003).

Gay, J. (ed.), *Free Software, Free Society: Selected Essays of Richard M. Stallman* (Free Software Foundation, GNU Press Boston 2002).

Gerle, E. 'Features of Contemporary Globalization and Ethical Challenges they Pose to Universal Ethics. Globalization with Many Faces', in: Bexell, G. and D.-E. Andersson (eds), *Universal Ethics. Perspectives and Proposals from Scandinavian Scholars* (Martinus Nijhoff Publishers, Kluwer Law International, The Hague/London/New York 2002).

Giddens, A., *Stanowienie Społeczeństwa* [*The Constitution of Society*] (Wydawnictwo Zysk i S-ka, Poznan 2003).

Glatzer, W., 'Quality of Life in the European Union and the United States of America: Evidence from Comprehensive Indices', 1:169–188 *Applied Research in Quality of Life* (2006).

Görman, U. 'Universal Ethics – A Futile Effort?. A Contractual Analysis of the Search for Universal Ethics', in: Bexell, G. and D.-E. Andersson (eds), *Universal Ethics. Perspectives and Proposals from Scandinavian Scholars* (Martinus Nijhoff Publishers, Kluwer Law International, The Hague/London/New York 2002).

Gostin, L.O. and Lazzarini, Z., *Human Rights and Public Health in the AIDS Pandemic* (Oxford University Press, Oxford 1997).

Grondin, J. 'Unterwegs zur Rhetorik'. Gadamers Schritt von Platon zu Augustin in 'Wahrheit und Methode', in: G. Figal, J. Grindin and D. Schmidt (eds), *Hermeneutische Wege* (Tubingen 2000).

Grondin, J., *Wprowadzenie do hermeneutyki filozoficznej: Myśl Filozoficzna* [*An Introduction to Philosophical Hermeneutics: Philosophical Thought*] (Wydawnictwo WAM, Krakow 2007).

Groni, Ch., 'The right to take part in cultural life', paper submitted for Day of General Discussion on Right to take part in cultural life (article 15(1)(a) of the Covenant), Friday, 9 May 2008, UN Economic and Social Council, Distr. General, E/C.12/40/15, Committee on Economic, Social and Cultural Rights, 40th session, Geneva, 28 April–16 May 2008.

Grosheide, W. (ed.), *Intellectual Property and Human Rights A Paradox* (Edward Elgar, Northampton 2010).

Guadamuz, A., 'Free and Open-Source Software', in: L. Edwards and Ch. Waelde (eds), *Law and the Internet* (Hart Publishing, Oxford and Portland, Oregon 2009).

Guibault, L., 'The Limit of Balancing Interests Through Copyright Levies', in: Ch. Lenk, N. Hoppe and R. Andorno (eds), *Ethics and Law of Intellectual Property* (Ashgate, Hampshire 2007).

Habermas, J. *Between Facts and Norms* (The MIT Press, Cambridge, MA 1996).

Habermas, J., *The Concept of Human Dignity and the Realistic Utopia of Human Rights* (Metaphilosophy LLC and Blackwell Publishing Ltd. 2010).

Hahn, L.E. (ed.), 'The Philosophy of Hans-Georg Gadamer', *The Library of Living Philosophers, vol. XXIV* (Chicago, Illinois 1997).

Haybron, D.M., *The Pursuit of Unhappiness: The Elusive Psychology of Well-Being* (Oxford University Press, Oxford, 2008).

Helfer, L.R., 'Human Rights and Intellectual Property: Conflict or Coexistence?', 5 *Minn. Intell. Prop. Rev.* (2003).

Helfer, L.R., 'Toward a Human Rights Framework for Intellectual Property', 40 *U.C. Davis Law Review* (2007).

Helfer, L.R. and Austin, G., *Human Rights and Intellectual Property. Mapping the Global Interface* (Cambridge University Press, Cambridge 2011).

Hess, C. and Ostrom, E. (eds), 'Introduction: An Overview of the Knowledge Commons', in: *Understanding Knowledge as a Commons. From Theory to Practice* (The MIT Press, Cambridge 2007).

Hestermeyer, H., *Human Rights and the WTO. The Case of Patents and Access to Medicines* (Oxford University Press, Oxford 2007).

Hietanen, H. and Valimaki, M., 'Challenges of open content licensing in Europe', an article presented at the conference: Intellectual Property beyond Rights, 25–26 October 2004, Hanasaari, the Swedish-Finnish Cultural Centre, Espoo, Finland.

Hodgson, D., *The Human Right to Education* (Ashgate, Dartmouth 1998).

Hornborg, A., *Global Inequalities of Economy, Technology and Environment* (AltaMira Press, US 2001).

Hornborg, A., 'Challenges in Conceptualizing Environmental Load Displacement and Ecologically Unequal Exchange in the World-System', International Journal of Comparative Sociology (2009).

Hurka, T., *Perfectionism* (Oxford University Press, Oxford 1993).

Ingarden, R., *Książeczka o człowieku* [*Little Book About Man*] (Wydawnictwo Literackie, Krakow 2003).

Inglehart, R., *Modernization and Postmodernization. Cultural, Economic and Political Change in 43 Societies* (Princeton University Press, Princeton 1997).

Jonas, H., *Philosophical Essays: from Ancient Creed to Technological Man* (Prentice Hall, Englewood Cliffs 1974).

Jones, L., 'An Artist's Entry Into Cyberspace: Intellectual Property On The Internet', 22(2) *EIPR* (2000).

Kacperczyk, A., 'Zastosowanie koncepcji społecznych światów w badaniach empirycznych' [Application of the Social Worlds Concept in Empirical Research], in: E. Hałas and E. Konecki (eds), *Konstruowanie jaźni i społeczeństwa: Europejskie warianty interakcjonizmu symbolicznego* [*Construction of the Self and Society: European Variants of Symbolic Interactionism*] (Wydawnictwo Naukowe Scholar, Warszawa 2005).

Kapczyński, A., 'Access to Knowledge: A Conceptual Genealogy', in: G. Krikorian and A. Kapczyński (eds), *Access to Knowledge in the Age of Intellectual Property* (Zone Books, New York 2010).

Karpińska-Musiał, B., 'Czy można przezwyciężyć sokratejską aporię w postmodernistycznej wizji dialogu kulturowego?' [Can Socratean aporia be overcome in the postmodern vision of a cultural dialogue?] in: S. Kruszyńska, K. Bembennek and I. Krupecka (eds), *Dialog. Idea i Doświadczenie* [*Dialogue. Idea and Experience*] (Wydawnictwo Uniwersytetu Gdanskiego, Gdansk 2011).

Kępiński, *Rytm życia* [*The Rhythm of Life*] (Wydawnictwo Literackie, Krakow 1972).

Knutsson, K.E., 'Globalization and the Dimension of Culture and Values', in: Bexell, G. and D.-E. Andersson (eds), *Universal Ethics. Perspectives and Proposals from Scandinavian Scholars* (Martinus Nijhoff Publishers, Kluwer Law International, The Hague/London/New York 2002).

Kołakowski, L., *Mini wyklady o maxi sprawach* [*Mini-lectures on maxi-issues*] (Wydawnictwo Znak, Krakow 2006).

Korzeniewski, B., 'Levinasa podróż po krainie wrażliwości' [A Journey of Levinas through the Land of Sensitivity], in: P. Orlik (ed.), *Rozdroża i* ścieżki *wrażliwości* [*Crossroads and Paths of Sensitivity*] (Poznan 2000).

Koskenniemi, M., *From Apology to Utopia. The Structure of International Legal Argument* (Cambridge University Press, Cambridge 2007).

Kozak, M., 'Dlaczego Levinas nie jest filozofem dialogu' [Why Levinas is not a philosopher of a dialogue], in: S. Kruszyńska, K. Bembennek, I. Krupecka, (eds), *Dialog. Idea i Doświadczenie* [*Dialogue. Idea and Experience*] (Wydawnictwo Uniwersytetu Gdanskiego, Gdansk 2011).

Kraenzel, F., 'Nicolai Hartmann's Doctrine of Ideal Values: An Examination', 18 *Journal of Value Inquiry* (1984).

Kreft, D., 'Dialog podstawa więzi międzyludzkiej w filozofii Bubera i Bartha' [Dialogue as a foundation of an interpersonal bond in the philosophy of Buber and Barth], in: S. Kruszyńska, K. Bembennek, I. Krupecka (eds), *Dialog. Idea i Doświadczenie* [*Dialogue. Idea and Experience*] (Wydawnictwo Uniwersytetu Gdanskiego, Gdansk 2011).

Krikorian, G., 'Access to Knowledge as a Field of Activism', in: G. Krikorian and A. Kapczynski (eds), *Access to Knowledge in the Age of Intellectual Property* (Zone Books, New York 2010).

Kubiak, A., *Emmanuel Levinas – prologomena do instrukcji obslugi* [*Emmanuel Levinas – Prologue to a User Manual*] (Polska Siec Filozoficzna, 2001).

Kuhlen, R., 'Knowledge and Information – Private Property or Common Good? A Global Perspective' (in:) Ch. Lenk, N. Hoppe and R. Andorno (eds), *Ethics and Law of Intellectual Property* (Ashgate, Hampshire 2007).

Kymlicka, W., *Contemporary Political Philosophy. An Introduction* (Clarendon Press, Oxford 1990).

Lambert, P., 'Copyleft, copyright and software IPRS: is contract still king', 23(4) *EIPR* (2001).

Land, M.B., 'Intellectual Property Rights and the Right to Participate in Cultural Life', paper submitted for Day of General Discussion on Right to take part in cultural life (article 15(1)(a) of the Covenant), Friday, 9 May 2008, UN Economic and Social Council, Distr. General, E/C.12/40/15, Committee on Economic, Social and Cultural Rights, 40th session, Geneva, 28 April–16 May 2008.

Laurent, A.M. St., *Understanding Open Source & Free Software Licensing* (O'Reilly Media, Sebastopol 2004).

Lessig, L., *The Future of Ideas. The Fate of the Commons in a Connected World* (Vintage Books, New York 2001).

Lessig, L., *Free Culture. The Nature and Future of Creativity* (Penguin Books, London 2004).

Lessig, L., *Wolna Kultura* [*Free Culture*] (Wydawnictwa Szkolne i Pedagogiczne, 2005).

Lessig, L., *Code version 2.0* (Basic Books, New York 2006).

Levinas, E., *Ethics and Infinity: Conversations with Philippe Nemo* (Duquesne University Press, Pittsburgh 1985).

Levinas, E., 'The Paradox of Morality', an interview with Emmanuel Levinas conducted by Tamara Wright, Peter Hayes and Alison Ainley, translated by Andrew Benjamin and Tamara Wright, in: Robert Bernesconi and David Wood (eds), *The Provocation of Levinas: Rethinking the Other* (Routledge, London 1988).

Levinas, E., *Time and the Other* (Duguesue University Press 1990).

Levinas, E., *O Bogu, który nawiedza myśl* [*Of God who Comes to Mind*] (Wydawnictwo Homini, Krakow 1994).

Levinas, E., *Inaczej niż być lub ponad istotą* [*Otherwise than Being or Beyond Essence*] (Fundacja Aletheia, Warszawa 2000).

Levinas, E., *Unforseen History* (University of Illinois Press 2004).

Levinas, E., *Humanism of the Other* (Fata Morgana, University of Illinois 2006).

Levinas, E., *O Uciekaniu* [*On Escape*] (Wydawnictwo Instytutu Filozofii i Socjologii PAN, Warszawa 2007).

Levinas, E., *Całość i nieskończoność. Esej o zewnętrzności* [*Totality and Infinity. An Essay on Exteriority*] (Wydawnictwo Naukowe PWN, Warszawa 2012).

Li, X. and Correa, C.M. (eds), *Intellectual Property Enforcement* (Edward Elgar, Cheltenham, UK 2009).

Lindholm, T., 'Ethical Justification of Universal Rights Across Normative Divices', in: Bexell, G. and D.-E. Andersson (eds), *Universal Ethics. Perspectives and Proposals from Scandinavian Scholars* (Martinus Nijhoff Publishers, Kluwer Law International, The Hague/London/New York 2002).

Løgstrup, K.E., *The Ethical Demand.* Introduction by Hans Fink and Alasdair MacIntyre (University of Notre Dame Press, Notre Dame and London 1997).

Løgstrup, K.E, *Beyond the Ethical Demand* (University of Notre Dame Press, Notre Dame, 2007).

Luban, D, *Legal Ethics and Human Dignity* (Cambridge University Press, Cambridge 2008).

Lukoseviciene, A., 'Beyond the Creative Commons Framework for production and dissemination of information'. Master's thesis, Faculty of Law, Lund University, Sweden (Master's Programme in International Human Rights Law and Intellectual Property 2011, supervisor: Anna Maria Andersen Nawrot).

McGillivray, M. and Clarke, M. (eds), *Understanding Human Well-Being* (United Nations University Press, Tokyo, New York, Paris, 2006).

Macqueen, H. L, 'Appropriate for the Digital Age? Copyright and the Internet: 1. Scope of Copyright', in: L. Edwards and Ch. Waelde (eds), *Law and the Internet* (Hart Publishing, Oxford and Portland, Oregon, 2009).

Manderson, D., 'Emanuel Levinas and the Philosophy of Negligence', 14 *Tort Law Review* (2006).

Marder, M. and Vieira, P., 'Existential Utopia: Of the World, the Possible, the Finite', in: P. Vieira and M. Marder (eds), *Existential Utopia. New Perspectives on Utopian Thought* (Continuum International Publishing Group, New York, London, 2012).

Matthews, D., *Intellectual Property, Human Rights and Development. The Role of NGO's and Social Movements* (Edward Elgar, Cheltenham, UK 2011).

Meyer, M.J., 'Dignity as a (Modern) Virtue', in: D. Kretzmer and E. Klein (eds), *The Concept of Human Dignity in Human Rights Discourse* (Kluwer Law International, The Hague, London, New York 2002).

Migasiński, J., Posłowie [Afterword], in: E. Levinas, *O Uciekaniu* [*On Escape*] (Wydawnictwo Instytutu Filozofii i Socjologii PAN, Warszawa 2007).

Morawski, L., *Główne Problemy Współczesnej Filozofii Prawa* [*Central Problems of Modern Philosophy of Law*] (LexisNexis, Warszawa 2003).

Murphy, T., 'Repetition, Revolution and Resonance: An Introduction to New Technologies and Human Rights', in: *New Technologies and Human Rights* (Oxford University Press, Oxford 2009).

Muzaka, V., *The Politics of Intellectual Property Rights and Access to Medicines, International Political Economy Series* (Palgrave Macmillan, New York 2011).

Nawrot, A.M., 'The Meaning of Intellectual Property Rights in the Knowledge Society – EU Perspective', in: S.M. Mercado Kierkegaard (ed.), *Legal, Privacy and Security Issues in Information Technology. Vol. 2*. The First International Conference on Legal, Privacy and Security Issues in IT, Hamburg, Germany, 30 April–2 May 2006, COMPLEX 4/06 (Institutt for rettsinformatikk, Oslo).

Nawrot, A.M., 'Why Do We Need Social Worlds While Talking about D-Knowledge Commons Ecosystem in Cyberspace?' 2 *Masaryk University Journal of Law* (2008).

Nawrot, A.M., 'The Involvement of Human Rights in Limiting the Adverse Effects on Access to Digital Knowledge – as One Step Towards a Multicentric Principle of Access to Digital Knowledge', in: M. Zirk-Sadowski, M. Golecki and B. Wojciechowski (eds), *Multicentrism as an Emerging Paradigm in Legal Theory* (Peter Lang, Frankfurt am Main 2009).

Nawrot, O., 'Na kretych sciezkach bioetyki – 'etyka gatunku' Jurgena Habermasa' [On the bizzar paths of bioethics] in: J. Zajadlo (ed.), *Dziedzictwo i przyszlosc. Problemy wspolczesnej niemieckiej filozofii prawa* (Arche, Gdansk 2010).

Nicoletti Mizukami, P. and Lemos, R., 'From Free Software to Free Culture: The Emergence of Open Business', in: L. Shaver (ed.), *Access to Knowledge in Brazil* (Bloomsbury Academic, London, New York 2010).

Nowak, E. and Cern, K.M., *Ethos w zyciu publicznym* [*Ethos in the public life*], (PWN, Warszawa 2008).

Ohana, G., Hansen, M. and Shah, O., 'Disclosure and negotiations of licensing terms prior to adoption of industry standards: preventing another patent ambush', 24(12) *ECLR* (2003).

Pedley, P., *Digital Copyright* (Facet Publishing, London 2007).

Peperzak, A., *To The Other: An Introduction to the Philosophy of Emmanuel Levinas* (Purde University Press, West Lafayette Indiana 1993).

Põder, J.-Ch., *Evidenz des Ethischen. Die Fundamentalethik Knud E. Løgstrups* (Tübingen, Mohr Siebeck, 2011).

Pogge, T., Rimmer, M. and Rubenstein, K. (eds), *Incentives for Global Public Health. Patent Law and Access to Essential Medicines* (Cambridge University Press, Cambridge 2010).

Pollaud-Dulian, F. (eds), *Perspectives on Intellectual Property. The Internet and Authors' Rights* (Sweet & Maxwell, London 1999).

Posey, D.A. and Dutfield, G., *Beyond Intellectual Property. Toward Traditional Resource Rights for Indigenous Peoples and Local Communities* (International Development Research Centre, Ottawa 1996).

Post, D.G., *In Search of Jefferson's Moose. Notes on the State of Cyberspace* (Oxford University Press, Oxford 2009).

Prescott-Allen, R., *The Wellbeing of Nations. A country by Country-by-Country Index of Quality of Life and the Environment* (International Development Research Centre and Island Press, Washington, Covelo, London 2001).

Pulido, C.B., 'The Rationality of Balancing', 92 ARSP (2007).

Raymond, E.S., *The Cathedral and the Bazaar: Musings on Linux and Open Source by an Accidental Revolutionary* (O'Reilly Media, Sebastopol 2001).

Ress, M.A. 'Open-Access Publishing: From Principles to Practice', in: G. Krikorian and A. Kapczyński (eds), *Access to Knowledge in the Age of Intellectual Property* (Zone Books, New York 2010).

Robertson, R., 'Globality, Global Culture and Images of World Order', in H. Haferkamp and N.J. Smelser (eds), *Social Change and Modernity* (California University Press, Berkeley 1992).

Rosen, L., *Open Source Licensing. Software Freedom and Intellectual Property Law* (Prentice Hall Books, New Jersey 2004).

Rosner, K., 'Dialog jako temat filozofii współczesnej: Buber, Gadamer, Habermas' [Dialogue as a Subject of Modern Philosophy: Buber, Gadamer, Habermas] in: S. Kruszyńska, K. Bembennek and I. Krupecka (eds), *Dialog.*

Idea i Doświadczenie [*Dialogue. Idea and Experience*] (Wydawnictwo Uniwersytetu Gdanskiego, Gdansk 2011).

Rowland, D., Kohl, U. and Charlesworth, A., *Information Technology Law* (Fourth Edition, Routlege, London, New York 2011).

Santiago, Nino C., *The Ethics of Human Rights* (Clarendon Press, Oxford 1994).

Schabas, W.A., 'Study of the Right to Enjoy the Benefits of Scientific and Technological progess and Its Applications', in: Y. Donders and V. Volodin (eds), *Human Rights in Education, Science and Culture. Legal Developments and Challenges* (Ashgate, Unesco Publishing 2007).

Sen, A., *The Idea of Justice* (Allen Lane *an imprint of* Penguin Books, London 2009).

Shaver, L., 'Intellectual Property, Innovation and Development: The Access to Knolwedge Approach', in: L. Shaver (ed.), *Access to Knowledge in Brazil* (Bloomsbury Academic, London, New York 2010).

Shaver, L., 'The Right to Science and Culture', 2010 *Wisconsin Law Review* (2010), pp. 121–185.

Sinjela, M. (ed.), *Human Rights and Intellectual Property Rights, Tensions and Convergences* (Martinus Nijhoff Publishers, Leiden, Boston 2007).

Skarga, B., Wstęp do (Introduction to): E. Levinas, *Całość i nieskończoność Esej o zewnętrzności* [*Totality and Infinity. An Essay on Exteriority*] (Wydawnictwo Naukowe PWN, Warszawa 2012).

Smiers, J., 'No copyright and no domination of cultural markets – two conditions for realizing active participation in cultural life', paper submitted for Day of General Discussion on Right to take part in cultural life (article 15(1)(a) of the Covenant), Friday, 9 May 2008, UN Economic and Social Council, Distr. General, E/C.12/40/6, Committee on Economic, Social and Cultural Rights, 40th session, Geneva, 28 April–16 May 2008.

Smiers, J., 'Is Copyright fit for the 21st century? No!', in: W. Grosheide (ed.), *Intellectual Property and Human Rights. A Paradox* (Edward Elgar, Cheltenham, UK 2010).

Smith, M.B., *Toward the Outside. Concepts and Themes in Emmanuel Levinas* (Duquesne University Press 2005).

Sterckx, S., 'Lack of Access to Essential Drugs: A Story of Continuing Global Failure, with Particular Attention to the Role of Patents', in: Ch. Lenk, N. Hoppe and R. Andorno (eds), *Ethics and Law of Intellectual Property* (Ashgate, Hampshire 2007).

Stokes, S., *Digital Copyright. Law and Practice* (Hart Publishing, Oxford and Portland 2009).

Sztompka, P., *Encyklopedia Socjologii* [*Encyclopedia of Sociology*] (Oficyna Naukowa, Warszawa 1998).

Sztompka, P., *Socjologia. Analiza Społeczeństwa* [*Sociology. An Analysis of Society*] (Wydawnictwo Znak, Krakow 2004).

Tatarkiewicz, W., *O Szczęściu* [*On Happiness*] (Państwowe Wydawnictwo Naukowe, Warszawa 1979).

Taubman, A.S., 'TRIPS Jurisprudence in the Balance: Between the Realist Defence of Policy Space and a Shared Utilitarian Ethic', in: Ch. Lenk, N. Hoppe and R. Andorno (eds), *Ethics and Law of Intellectual Property*, (Ashgate, Hampshire 2007).

Thornberry, P., 'Cultural rights and universality of human rights', paper submitted for Day of General Discussion on Right to take part in cultural life (article 15(1)(a) of the Covenant), Friday, 9 May 2008, UN Economic and Social Council, Distr. General, E/C.12/40/15, Committee on Economic, Social and Cultural Rights, 40th session, Geneva, 28 April–16 May 2008.

Tischner, J., *Myślenie według wartości* [*Thinking in Values*] (Wydawnictwo Znak, Krakow 2011).

Tischner, J., *Filozofia Dramatu* [*Philosophy of Drama*] (Wydawnictwo Znak, Krakow 2012).

Tokarczyk, R., *Polska myśl utopijna. Trzy eseje z dziejów* [*Polish Utopian Thought – Three Essays from the Times*] (Wydawnictwo UMCS, Lublin 1995).

Tokarczyk, R., *Współczesne doktryny polityczne* [*Contemporary Political Doctrines*] (Wolters Kluwer Polska, Warszawa 2006).

Towse, R., *Creativity, Incentive and Reward* (Edward Elgar, Cheltenham, UK 2001).

Vaidhyanathan, S., *Copyrights and Copywrongs: The Rise of Intellectual Property and How it Threatens Creativity* (New York University Press, New York 2001).

Valimaki, M. and Oksanen, V., 'How to manage IPR infringement risks in open source development?', an article presented at the conference 'Intellectual Property beyond Rights', 25–26 October 2004, Hanasaari, the Swedish-Finnish Cultural Centre, Espoo, Finland.

White, N., *A Brief History of Happiness* (Blackwell Publishing, UK/USA 2006), pp. 41–75.

Wojciechowski, B., *Interkulturowe prawo karne. Filozoficzne podstawy karania w wielokulturowych społeczeństwach demokratycznych* [*Intercultural Criminal Law. Philosophical Grounds for Penalization in Democratic Societies*] (Wydawnictwo Adam Marszalek, Torun 2009).

Wojciechowski, B., *Philosophical Approach to the Interculturality of Criminal Law* (Peter Lang. International Academic Publishers, Series: Studies in Philosophy and Social Science, Frankfurt am Main – Berlin – Bern – Bruxelles – New York – Oxford – Wien 2010).

Wojciechowski, B., Zirk-Sadowski, M. and Golecki, M.J. (eds), 'Between Complexity of Law and Lack of Order'. *Philosophy of Law in the Era of Globalization* (Wydawnictwo Adam Marszalek, Torun-Bejing 2009).

Wong, M.W.S., 'Toward an Alternative Normative Framework for Copyright. From Private Property to Human Rights', 26:775 *Cardozo Arts and Entertainment* (2009).

Yamane, H., *Interpreting TRIPS. Globalisation of Intellectual Property Rights and Access to Medicines* (Hart Publishing, Oxford, Portland, Oregon 2011).

Zajadlo, J. (ed.), *Leksykon wspolczesnej teorii i filozofii prawa* [*Lexicon on the contemporary theory and philosophy of law*] (Wydawnictwo C.H. Beck, Warszawa 2007).

Zemer, L., *The Idea of Authorship in Copyright, Applied Legal Philosophy* (Ashgate, Hampshire 2007).

Zirk-Sadowski, M., *Wprowadzenie do filozofii prawa* [*Introduction to Philosophy of Law*] (Wolters Kluwer Polska, Warszawa 2011).

Zirk-Sadowski, M., Golecki, M. and Wojciechowski, B. (eds), *Multicentrism as an Emerging Paradigm in Legal Theory* (Peter Lang, Frankfurt am Main 2009).

Index

For Product Safety Concerns and Information please contact our EU representative GPSR@taylorandfrancis.com
Taylor & Francis Verlag GmbH, Kaufingerstraße 24, 80331 München, Germany

www.ingramcontent.com/pod-product-compliance
Ingram Content Group UK Ltd.
Pitfield, Milton Keynes, MK11 3LW, UK
UKHW011007180926
475701UK00004B/604
* 9 7 8 0 3 6 7 6 0 0 8 1 5 *